Frontispiece. Interior of the Painted Chamber, looking west, before the discovery of its murals: view by William Capon, 1799

The Painted Chamber at Westminster

By Paul Binski, M.A., Ph.D.

Occasional Paper (New Series) IX

THE SOCIETY OF ANTIQUARIES
OF LONDON

Burlington House, Piccadilly, London W1V 0HS

Published with the assistance of the J. Paul Getty Trust
1986

Distributed by Thames and Hudson Ltd

Printed in Great Britain by
Adlard & Son Ltd, Dorking, Surrey

Contents

Editorial Note

The Society is deeply grateful to the J. Paul Getty Trust, without whose generous financial assistance this book could not have been published so promptly, and to the Master and Fellows of Gonville and Caius College, Cambridge, for a grant which permitted the work to be more liberally illustrated.

S.M.
F.H.T.

Illustrations

COLOUR PLATES
(following p. 84)

PLATES
(following p. 166)

Preface

It is a pleasure to be able to acknowledge the help that I have received from many people in the course of writing this book: to all of them I extend my warmest thanks. My greatest debt is to the supervisor of my research, Dr George Henderson, F.S.A., whose studies of thirteenth-century manuscript illumination first stimulated my interest in the Painted Chamber at Westminster, whose influence on my thought has been considerable, and whose friendly support has been endless. I am also much obliged to Professor Christopher Brooke, F.S.A., for his generous encouragement and guidance, and to Lady Wedgwood (Pamela Tudor-Craig), F.S.A., whose kindness and enthusiasm have been an inspiration. I also wish to thank the Master and Fellows of Gonville and Caius College, Cambridge, for electing me into a Research Fellowship, and so providing the leisure and resources with which to complete this work.

The text has benefited greatly at various stages from the helpful and authoritative criticism of Dr Jonathan Alexander, F.S.A., Christopher Brooke, Dr Thomas Cocke, F.S.A., George Henderson, Mr Nigel Morgan and Pamela Wedgwood. With their help it is now better ordered in thought, and freer of infelicities of expression and judgement. Every error in this work is, however, mine. For unstinting assistance in my research I would also like to thank Dr Adelaide Bennett, Professor Julian Brown, F.S.A., Mr Howard Colvin, F.S.A., Professor J. M. Crook, F.S.A., Dr Michael Franklin, Miss Margaret Freel, Dr James Golob, Dr Henry Mayr-Harting, the late Dr Ruth Morgan, the late Mr Howard Nixon, F.S.A., and Mrs Enid Nixon, Dr Christopher Norton, Dr Dorothy Owen, F.S.A., Mr David Park, F.S.A., Dr Nigel Ramsay, Professor Dr Gerhard Schmidt, and Dr Christopher Wilson. My debt to the many institutions that have helped me in my research and provided illustrations for this work is immense; special mention must be made of the staff of the University Library at Cambridge, the Ashmolean Museum, and the Society itself. I am grateful to Mrs Patricia McCullagh and Mrs Edna Pilmer for help in typing, and to Mr Bernard Thomason for his care and patience in drawing the figures illustrated here.

Finally, I should like to express my gratitude to Miss Sarah Macready and Mr Hugh Thompson for their tolerance and expertise in seeing the manuscript through to publication.

Gonville and Caius College   PAUL BINSKI
Cambridge
January 1986

Abbreviations

BAA   British Archaeological Association.

BAR   British Archaeological Reports.

Binski 1983   P. Binski, 'The Painted Chamber and Painting at Westminster *c.* 1250 to 1350', Ph.D. thesis, University of Cambridge, 1983.

BL   British Library.

Borenius 1943 T. Borenius, 'The cycle of images in the palaces and castles of Henry III', *JWCI*, iv (1943), 40.

BN   Bibliothèque Nationale.

Brieger 1968   P. Brieger, *English Art 1216–1307*, 2nd edn. (Oxford, 1968).

CCR   *Calendar of Close Rolls* (Public Record Office, Texts and Calendars).

CLR   *Calendar of Liberate Rolls* (Public Record Office, Texts and Calendars).

CPR   *Calendar of Patent Rolls* (Public Record Office, Texts and Calendars).

Capon 1835   W. Capon, 'Notes and remarks, by the late Mr William Capon, to accompany his plan of the ancient Palace of Westminster', *Vetusta Monumenta*, v (1835), pl. XLVII, 1–7 (read 23rd December 1824).

Colvin 1971   H. M. Colvin (ed.), *Building Accounts of King Henry III* (Oxford, 1971).

Esposito 1960 M. Esposito (ed.), *Itinerarium Symonis Semeonis Ab Hybernia Ad Terram Sanctam* (Scriptores Latini Hiberniae, iv) (Dublin, 1960).

Henderson   G. Henderson, 'Studies in English manuscript illumination',
1967, 1968   *JWCI*, xxx (1967), 71, and xxxi (1968), 103.

JBAA   *Journal of the British Archaeological Association.*

JWCI   *Journal of the Warburg and Courtauld Institutes.*

KW   H. M. Colvin (ed.), *The History of the King's Works*, i, ii (London, 1963), v (London, 1976), vi (London, 1973).

Lethaby 1905 W. R. Lethaby, 'English primitives—the Painted Chamber and the early masters of the Westminster School', *Burlington Magazine*, vii (1905), 257.

——— 1906   W. R. Lethaby, *Westminster Abbey and the King's Craftsmen* (London, 1906).

——— 1925   W. R. Lethaby, *Westminster Abbey Re-examined* (London, 1925).

——— 1927   W. R. Lethaby, 'Medieval paintings at Westminster', *Proceedings of the British Academy*, xiii (1927), 123.

PL   *Patrologiae cursus completus. Series Latina*, ed. J. P. Migne (Paris, 1844–55).

PRO	Public Record Office.
RCHM	Royal Commission on Historical Monuments (England).
Rokewode 1885	J. Gage Rokewode, 'A memoir on the Painted Chamber in the Palace of Westminster', *Vetusta Monumenta*, vi (1885), pls. XXVI–XXXIX (read 12th May 1842).
RS	*Rolls Series.*
Smith 1807	J. T. Smith, *Antiquities of Westminster* (London, 1807).
Stone 1972	L. Stone, *Sculpture in Britain: the Middle Ages*, 2nd edn. (Harmondsworth, 1972).
Stothard 1823	Mrs C. Stothard, *Memoirs . . . of the Late Charles Alfred Stothard* (London, 1823).
Tristram 1950	E. W. Tristram, *English Medieval Wall Painting: the Thirteenth Century*, 2 vols. (Oxford, 1950).
——— 1955	E. W. Tristram, *English Wall Painting of the Fourteenth Century* (London, 1955).
Tudor-Craig 1957	P. Tudor-Craig, 'The Painted Chamber at Westminster', *Archaeological Journal*, cxiv (1957), 92.
Wormald 1949	F. Wormald, 'Paintings in Westminster Abbey and contemporary paintings', *Proceedings of the British Academy*, xxxv (1949), 161.

INTRODUCTION

A fourteenth-century itinerary in Cambridge has preserved for us an intriguing account of the pilgrimage made by two Irish friars to Palestine in the 1320s.[1] The friars, Symon Semeonis and Hugo Illuminator, saw many remarkable sights as they passed, 'inflamed with seraphic ardour', across Europe to the Holy Land: Notre-Dame and the Sainte-Chapelle in Paris, St Mark's in Venice, the beautifully decorated houses of the Saracens, the citadel of the Sultan at Cairo, and the Pyramids, 'the barns of Joseph', of 'such size and height that at a distance they look more like the summits of mountains than repositories of corn'.[2]

The journey of Symon and Hugo 'to meditate with Isaac in the field' took them first, in the spring of 1323, across the Irish Sea, past the Welsh castles built by Edward I and the towns of Chester and Lichfield, to London. Their panoramic description of the city is mostly recognizable to us today. The outstanding sights were London Bridge, St Paul's, where at mass were chanted sweet and joyous melodies 'quite unlike the shouting of Lombards and the howling of Germans', the Tower, and Westminster Abbey, the burial place of the English kings.[3] The next item on their agenda is less familiar, however. The *Itinerarium* goes on to observe that by the abbey stood

> the celebrated palace of the kings of England, in which is that famous chamber on whose walls all the warlike stories of the whole Bible are painted with wonderful skill, and explained by a complete series of texts accurately written in French to the great admiration of the beholder and with the greatest royal magnificence.

The famous chamber at Westminster is one of several interiors mentioned in the *Itinerarium* as being decorated with Bible stories; the friars also admired those in the Lady Chapel at St Paul's, the Sainte-Chapelle in Paris, and St Mark's in Venice. But the unusual nature and context of the Westminster paintings seems particularly to have stirred their imagination. Their relatively detailed account of the stories suggests that they possessed an especially memorable character, worthy of mention amongst the great monuments of London.

Many of the attractions described in the itinerary of Symon and Hugo have, inevitably, either changed beyond recognition or vanished completely since their day. Fortune has been particularly unkind to the royal residences of medieval England, and it is well known that the 'celebrated palace of the kings of England' at Westminster largely perished, along with its famous chamber, in the terrible fire of October 1834. Yet, as chance would have it, we have been left with more information about this chamber than the tantalizing verbal residue in the account in the *Itinerarium*. The story of the medieval decorations of the old Palace of Westminster began anew and unexpectedly over thirty years before its destruction, when it was found that the large room called anciently the Painted Chamber (frontispiece) still retained evidence of its original splendour. The Painted Chamber proved to be one and the same as the famous chamber described by Symon and Hugo. It indeed contained warlike scenes from the Bible explained by inscriptions in French, and more besides, fully justifying the enthusiastic reception given to it by those who saw it when new. This book is devoted to a study of the extraordinary medieval decorations discovered, and recorded, in the Painted Chamber at Westminster in the early nineteenth century.

Although the Painted Chamber was lost just over 150 years ago, we know a considerable amount about the history of its fabric and decorations. From the late eighteenth century it, and the Palace of Westminster as a whole, became the subject of intense interest and, at times, acrimonious debate. The room was known to be physically vulnerable, and was duly measured, surveyed and drawn; eventually, what remained of its mural decorations was copied. More and more of the medieval documentation for work in the Painted Chamber became known. Cumulatively, the evidence shows that by the time it was admired by the Irish friars, the Painted Chamber had already had a long history. The Painted Chamber was an important element in the complex of buildings that lay between Westminster Abbey and the River Thames. In the thirteenth century, the apartment was known as the king's chamber, the room next in importance after the two halls in the palace, the Great Hall constructed by William Rufus, and the Lesser Hall, to which the king's chamber was joined from the twelfth century. Its actual function in the thirteenth century is hard to define with precision, as the routine use of great chambers of this type was only formalized in the later Middle Ages. Although it was decorated formally, the use of the room had to be flexible. Among its more permanent features was the royal bed, which, although lost, appears from contemporary records to have been a substantial and ornate piece of furniture, truly a state bed, a focus of importance in a room of considerable size. Even though it was the royal bedroom, the king's chamber was by no means private, for this was an age when physical proximity to the monarch mattered. The room also served for a variety of public and state functions, a consideration of significance for the meaning of its wall paintings. Much of the interest of the Painted Chamber also arises from its having been one of the first meeting-places of Parliament, and from its increasing adoption, in the fourteenth century, for more public than private activities.

The development of its murals can be traced with certainty from the reign of Henry III (1216–72) to the time of the coronation of Edward II in 1308, from whose reign onwards the room became generally known as the Painted Chamber. Its history in these years was not straightforward, for it was badly damaged by a fire in the last years of Henry's reign. The paintings described by Symon and Hugo were, in fact, creations of the late thirteenth century, and products of the art patronage of both Henry III and his son, Edward I. Together, these kings ensured that the room was the most spectacular of the truly accessible royal apartments in the palace throughout the fourteenth century.

The discovery that the Painted Chamber still retained evidence of its medieval magnificence occurred in 1799. Late in that year, the Westminster antiquarian William Capon (1757–1827) was contemplating its walls when he noticed (pl. XXVI) 'several projections where the paint, or what he supposed to be paint, advanced beyond the surface of the whitewashed walls'.[4] Shortly afterwards, in 1800, the Painted Chamber was the subject of some alterations which entailed the destruction of thirteenth-century tracery in its east windows and the removal of tapestry decorations.[5] Scaffolding was erected in order to hang wallpaper in what was to act as the Parliament chamber for a while, and from it large expanses of archaic-looking wall paintings became visible. Here and there, some curious workmen scrubbed at the paintings with brushes and water, but before more investigation or damage could take place, the walls had to be papered over, so, inadvertently, preserving the murals beneath.[6]

They remained hidden for nearly twenty years. This was without doubt to their advantage, because at the time of their first discovery a storm had broken over the current treatment of the other medieval building in the palace with significant wall paintings, St Stephen's Chapel, the home of the Commons.[7] In 1800, the Act of Union with Ireland increased the number of members of the Commons, and the controversial James Wyatt (1746–1813) started to expand the amount of seating-space in the chamber within the shell of the medieval chapel. Seats and panels were ripped out, and in the process mural paintings were found.[8] By August 1800, as the walls of the Painted Chamber were being stripped, painted figures of soldiers were found in the chapel, and the antiquarian J. T. Smith (1766–1833) moved in quickly to take copies of what were proving to be significant discoveries. But Smith later complained that

> The workmen very often followed him so close in their operations, as to remove, in the course of the same day on which he had made his drawing, the painting which he had been employed in copying that very morning.[9]

The official artist to the Society of Antiquaries in London, Richard Smirke (1778–1815), arrived on site to find that he had to copy medieval paintings that had been removed from the chapel with a minimum of ceremony by Wyatt's men (pl. XXXIV).[10] John Carter (1748–1817), that most indefatigable of early conservationists, arrived at the palace and was promptly refused admission by Wyatt, an insult which compounded Carter's chagrin at having been replaced as official artist to the Society of Antiquaries by Smirke.[11] The ensuing discord spread across the pages of the *Gentleman's Magazine*.[12]

The years around 1800, which also saw the discovery of paintings in the chapter house of Westminster Abbey,[13] were therefore unhappy ones in the history of the medieval antiquities of Westminster. It had long been understood that the ancient palace was no longer able to cope with the growing volume of parliamentary business, and that in its decayed state it presented a fire risk.[14] The event of 1834 cannot have come as a surprise. As early as the 1790s the more astute members of the Society of Antiquaries realized that time was not in their favour, and it was proposed that Carter should execute drawings of the known antiquities in the palace.[15] In 1793 Carter was at work on the fabric of the Painted Chamber (pl. XXX), and by 1795 Capon was surveying the palace as a whole.[16] The St Stephen's Chapel fiasco then added ominous substance to the fears of the conservationists. Thereafter, Carter devoted himself to polemical writing on the subject in the *Gentleman's Magazine*, and Smith observed that the Painted Chamber should be investigated and copied.[17]

By the time of the rediscovery of the Painted Chamber murals in 1818–19, Carter's sentiments prevailed. Once again, William Capon was one of the first on site as yet more alterations to the room took place. In 1818, he washed off dense coats of whitewash and uncovered splendid paintings of armed female figures on the window splays of the room, which constituted part of a series of Triumphant Virtues (col. pl. II).[18] By the summer of 1819 the true extent of the paintings became known as work on the room proceeded under the supervision of Edward Crocker (*c.* 1757–1836).[19] Once again, scaffolding was erected, this time in order to open a new window high up on the south wall. Areas of painted plaster were prized off the walls revealing older, blocked windows on the south side of the room; here further figures were found painted on the splays. All round the room were uncovered bands of narrative paintings and inscriptions, all brilliantly coloured (col. pls. III–V), while a large representation of the Coronation of St Edward was uncovered at the east end of the north wall (col. pl. I) (see the Catalogue).

The discoveries were met with appreciative excitement. The October issue of the *Gentleman's Magazine* for 1819 praised the 'exquisite beauty and freshness of the numerous paintings' and the 'well proportioned, and . . . admirably disposed' figures.[20] The official artist to the Society of Antiquaries, Charles Stothard, heard of the findings while travelling in Norfolk. He promptly returned to London to start work on copies of the murals.[21] Edward Crocker was completing a set of copies as well as a scaled plan and elevation of the room (pl. XXXII), with half-scale copies of the inscriptions where reasonably legible.[22] John Buckler (1770–1851) also took the opportunity to make sketches in the room in October 1819.[23] By 1820 the copyists had completed their work and the walls were repaired and plastered, covering over the decaying narrative scenes on the walls. Parts of the fabric were soon being discreetly removed from the site by enthusiasts; one of the ornamental *paterae* from the thirteenth-century wooden ceiling (pl. XXXIII) passed into the collection of Sir John Soane.[24] Sadly, no fragments of the paintings were preserved. By 1823 the nearby medieval fabrics of the original queen's apartments, then serving as the House of Lords, and the Prince's Chamber, to the south of the Painted Chamber, were demolished.[25] The Painted Chamber of the 1820s was used by the Court of Claims, and is shown in this period with only the paintings on the window splays of the south side intact (pl. XXVIII).[26] It was in this state that the room was gutted by fire in 1834. All that remained of the medieval building was its shell (pl. XXIX), together with its undercroft, and these were duly surveyed by Blore, Rokewode and Mackenzie.[27]

The discovery of the murals in the Painted Chamber was one of the most significant of its kind in the nineteenth century. Had the paintings of the Old Testament stories, the Virtues and the Coronation of St Edward survived, they would have provided us with much food for art-historical thought; no amount of documentary evidence can provide a substitute for the real thing.[28] Yet the evidence that we have is still sufficiently plentiful to provide the basis for a more detailed study. It allows us to approach the murals from several standpoints. We have, in the first place, unusually plentiful administrative records of contemporary work on the fabric and paintings of the room which provide us, in principle, with an almost year-by-year report from the 1230s through to the early fourteenth century. And we have a substantial antiquarian legacy of written accounts, drawings, surveys and copies providing a reasonably coherent picture of what remained in the early nineteenth century. The sources, being indirect, inevitably need to be treated with caution. The medieval records change in nature and emphasis as we work through the reigns of Henry III and Edward I, and our view of the Painted Chamber has to adapt accordingly. The copies of the murals by Charles Stothard in the Society of Antiquaries in London, and Edward Crocker in the Ashmolean Museum, Oxford, need close scrutiny. We are fortunate in having two independent sets of copies which, while differing somewhat in skill and in some matters of detail, still present an impressive agreement as to the basic appearance of the murals. The copies cannot be taken too literally, however. The Painted Chamber was discovered at a relatively early stage in the history of the appreciation and appraisal of medieval antiquities. The first written accounts of its contents are marked by misunderstandings typical of their time; for example, the belief that only Italian artists could have been capable of executing such fine works. The outstanding copyist, Charles Stothard, shared these prejudices. His drawings of medieval tombs, the Bayeux Tapestry, and the Painted Chamber look like products of their age in their classical restraint and slightly sentimental respect for the remnants of the chivalric past. There is no doubt that Stothard was a draughtsman of very considerable skill; it is hard to think of anyone else better fitted at that time to take a reliable record of what he saw. But the limiting factors in his, and Crocker's, work have to be taken into account; thus, the copies show that architectural forms proved easier to reproduce than the subtleties of facial types that matter so much to art historians. We cannot use all the material preserved in the copies; but much of it is extremely valuable, and makes sense in the light of what is generally known about thirteenth-century English painting.

The importance of the Painted Chamber has often been acknowledged in previous studies.[29] Yet at the time of writing there is still available no single investigation of English court painting of the thirteenth and early fourteenth centuries. This book does not pretend to be a full survey of all the aspects of the patronage of Henry III and Edward I. Its intention is, first, to set out fresh evidence for a study of the Painted Chamber and, second, to consider in more depth the complex stylistic and iconographic features of court painting in this period. The conclusions of this study inevitably extend beyond the Painted Chamber itself. Some of them are of more general historical interest. The Painted Chamber is intrinsically important because it is a unique representative of an entire genre of court art, allowing us to establish what impact was made on the Palace of Westminster by the two kings who dominated the thirteenth century. Its decorations lay at the heart of a palace which, in turn, lay at the heart of the realm. Earlier studies have provided no commentary on the rich and unusual iconography of the room.[30] This is surprising, for we would expect the images of so major an apartment to reflect the aspirations of the monarchs who lived there. Henry III and Edward I decorated the room in very different ways, but ways that are perfectly consonant with our understanding of them as kings. The evidence shows that Henry executed the paintings of the Coronation of St Edward and the Triumphant Virtues, and that Edward added the immense cycle of Old Testament scenes. The Painted Chamber in effect illustrates two prevailing notions of kingship: one pious, the other heroic; the first that of Henry III, the second that of Edward I.

Of the two kings, we know more about the preferences of Henry, because many of his instructions were recorded in the Close and Liberate Rolls, whereas Edward's were not. Henry was evidently sensitive to the relationship between images and the contexts in which they were seen. He was aware not only of their historical and allegorical levels of meaning, but also of their tropological significance: their reference to the moral nature of the king and his court. Thus the images Henry chose to surround the royal bed in the king's chamber, drawn from the life of St Edward, focused the substance of the royal cult directly on the person of the monarch in a specific context, for the bed was the highest point of status in the room. The same is true of a number of Henry's more moralizing themes, such as the Wise and Foolish Virgins, the story of Dives and Lazarus, and the legend of the King of the Garamantes, which took on a didactic quality precisely through their locations at meaningful points in his residences. In interpreting such images, we have to consider not only their history as images, but also their programmatic relationship to each other and to their spectators, the 'invisible complement' of the works of art.[31] Edward's choice of biblical narratives for a secular room, drawn moreover from areas of the Old Testament that were infrequently illustrated, presents further problems of interpretation. Although these scenes dominated the room visually, they were incomplete on discovery, and so confront us with the task of reconstructing their original text, as well as uncovering something of their meaning. The biblical narratives need closer study than they have hitherto received because they were evidently chosen to meet quite specialized narrative needs, needs which have to be understood more generally in the light of views of kingship at the court of Edward I.

Aside from its undoubted historical importance, a study of the Painted Chamber can also contribute something to our understanding of stylistic developments in the visual arts in the late thirteenth century. Because the copies are by their nature a source of contingent value, date attributions in this work have been established only by a combination of stylistic and iconographic analysis. But some broad patterns of value can be discerned. The murals in the Painted Chamber are datable with an unusual degree of precision by the plentiful documentary evidence, which provides us with certain quite clear-cut alternative periods when the murals must have been painted. The chronology of work proposed here reflects the considerable quantity of new evidence that has been brought forward since previous studies of the question, by the authors of *The History of the King's Works*.[32] We now understand much better the respective roles of Henry III and Edward I as patrons at Westminster as a result, and it is possible to offer a re-evaluation of Edward's activity at a time when court painting has always been regarded as something of an unknown quantity. The Painted Chamber enables us to clarify for the first time what may have been happening in the visual arts at court at Westminster in the 1260s and 1290s, periods of critical, but still unexplored, importance in the relationship between English and French figurative art. The works in the Painted Chamber were not stylistically isolated, but exhibited, so far as we can tell, close contacts with other major instances of court painting such as the Douce Apocalypse and the Westminster Retable. The detailed dating evidence for the Painted Chamber can enable us to reassess the complicated dating problems posed by these, and other, famous works, and to come up with some wider-ranging conclusions as to the transformations that took place in English figurative art from the 1260s to the end of the century.

The Painted Chamber has been described as the central problem of English thirteenth-century painting.[33] There may be some truth in this, because it is hard to think of a scheme of this period that can have had comparable authority and interest, or indeed such a long period of development. But it must be remembered at all times that the study of a lost work of art is as much an exercise of the imagination as of reason. The reader must now decide whether fact or fiction has prevailed in this work.

I. THE PAINTED CHAMBER: THE EVIDENCE

The fabric of the Painted Chamber

The Painted Chamber was one of the rambling collection of structures that constituted the Palace of Westminster from the twelfth century, and was the third major building in order of importance after the Great and Lesser Halls.[1] It may well have been the king's principal apartment from the twelfth century.[2] On plan (fig. 1), it was disposed on an east–west axis directly south of the twelfth-century foundation of St Stephen's Chapel, to which it was eventually joined, in the fourteenth century, by an *alura* running parallel to the Thames.[3] Its east end ran close up to the river, and its west end joined the Lesser Hall, lying north–south, itself linked to the immense Great Hall at its north end. The Chapel, the Lesser Hall and the Painted Chamber (pl. XXVII) were from the start two-storeyed fabrics, in accordance with the standard arrangement for important palace buildings, as well as for many more humble domestic structures in England and on the Continent.[4] The painted first floor of the king's apartment, which must have commanded a fine view across the Thames, measured internally 24·5 by 7·9 m., with a height of 9·7 m. (pl. XXVI); for its width, the room was on the long side, and these proportions were uncommon in thirteenth-century domestic structures.[5] The thirteenth-century chamber (fig. 3, p. 37) was lit by large windows in the lateral walls, three on the north and two on the south, standing 4·6 m. tall and over 3 m. wide, with deep embrasures 1·2 m. wide cut into walls some 1·8 m. thick. Some of the window soffits were rounded, some were pointed; in some cases the springers consisted of simple rolled mouldings, in others of clumps of foliage. Two elegant thirteenth-century windows in the east wall overlooked the river. The flat, wooden ceiling of the room was studded with a pattern of lobed *paterae*, a decorative idea later taken up and developed on the ceiling of the celebrated Star Chamber at Westminster.[6] The chamber was entered at its west end by a large doorway in the south wall; smaller doors at the east end of the north and south walls led to a small attached chapel and the queen's apartments respectively.

The basic shape of the Painted Chamber was determined in the twelfth century, and in many ways it was suited to the reception of wall paintings, the definitive Romanesque form of interior decoration.[7] Internally it was architecturally plain, with comparatively few articulations to its large expanses of wall space, apart from bold door and window openings. It was relatively well illuminated by a total of seven windows. There is, however, no reason to suppose that the room was specifically designed as a vehicle for the type of mural display that characterized it by the end of the thirteenth century. Although a distinct class of painted chambers existed by the time of Henry III's accession to the throne, most notably that at Winchester Castle by the 1230s,[8]

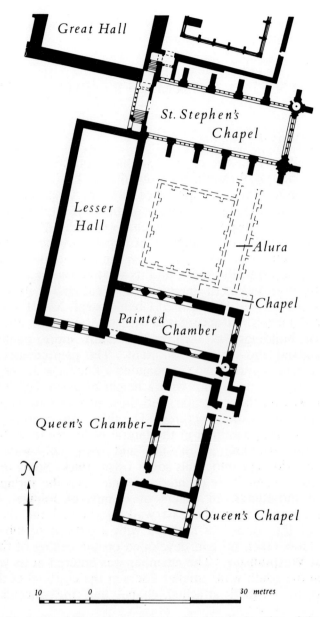

FIG. 1. The southern part of Westminster Palace, showing the location of the Painted Chamber

there is no evidence that such a chamber existed at Westminster in the early thirteenth century. Traces of decorative painting found on the splays of blocked twelfth-century windows in the Painted Chamber (pl. XXV*b*) prove that it once had an earlier form of decoration.[9] But nothing positive is known about the nature or extent of the adornments of the twelfth-century room. It did not have the sculptural enrichments of the Romanesque Great Hall, with its carved and historiated capitals;[10] but the absence of decorative sculpture is at best indirect evidence for the existence of painted surfaces of any importance in the room. As Henry II had paintings executed at Winchester Castle in the 1180s, it is by no means inconceivable that he also had some rooms painted at Westminster, perhaps during works at the palace recorded in the 1160s.[11] It is therefore possible that Henry III inherited older paintings at Westminster, paintings which may, to some extent, have conditioned the type of decoration he himself wished to introduce.

The salient point about the Painted Chamber at Westminster appears to be that, however formally decorated it became in the course of the thirteenth century—it was only known as the *camera depicta* from the fourteenth century—it probably started life with paintings of a routine, even informal, order. This is very much what we would expect of domestic interior decorations. The history of the Painted Chamber illustrates well the endless capacity of kings to rethink, revise, and sometimes radically extend, the decorations of their residences. The flexible and disposable nature of domestic wall painting reflects the fact that residential apartments like the king's chamber did not have precisely formalized uses of the sort that arose, gradually, in the later Middle Ages. They also, inevitably, had to accommodate the changing tastes of kings. One of the most important questions posed by the Painted Chamber is therefore why it was that its decorations became not only more extensive, but also more formalized, as the thirteenth century progressed.

The alterations made to the fabric of the twelfth-century king's chamber in the early part of the reign of Henry III mirror the decisive role as a patron he took on from the late 1220s. Henry's work on the palace in the 1220s and '30s included the last important contributions to the fabric of the room—with the exception of repairs to it after a fire in 1263—before the later Middle Ages. Henry inherited a room with all its twelfth-century features. As first conceived, it appears to have had four regularly disposed windows with rounded soffits in the south wall, and three of similar form in the north wall.[12] The twelfth-century painting on their embrasures (pl. XXV*b*) was uncovered along with the rest of the scheme in the early nineteenth century. In the years up to *c.* 1235, which saw considerable financial outlay on the Palace of Westminster as a whole, Henry effected a number of changes to the twelfth-century arrangements.[13] He decided to block two of the four windows in the south wall, those towards the west end of the room, and introduced two shapely windows in the east wall instead. Through the blocking fabric of one of the newly closed windows was inserted a fine entrance to the chamber, at the far west end of the south wall (pl. XXVI). Three of the remaining five windows in the lateral walls were given pointed arches, and all five were given new tracery consisting of two lights capped by an oculus. A newel staircase and vestibule were constructed within a few years at the south-east angle of the chamber, allowing access both to the ground floor and to the queen's chamber, constructed in the later 1230s.[14]

The implications of these changes for any mural decorations that might have survived in the room are unclear. In closing at least one big window Henry was in effect increasing the amount of wall space in the room on the south side, which could in turn suggest that he was planning more extensive wall paintings. The point is obviously uncertain, as the closure of the windows could have arisen from more functional considerations such as the construction of oriels on the outside of the south wall, one of which must have led to the new south wall entrance. One piece of evidence suggests that Henry was sometimes moved by a certain respect for decorations he had inherited. In 1233 he ordered that the painted chamber at Winchester Castle, the home of his minority, should be provided with new windows to the specification of Elias de Dereham, in such a way as to admit more light to the paintings, which were to be restored as they were before.[15] This is certainly an instance of Henry preserving murals—or at least their general subject-matter—while altering their architectural context, presumably by the introduction of more translucent window tracery. Henry's action here appears to parallel the way the twelfth-century murals in the nearby Holy Sepulchre Chapel of Winchester Cathedral were reproduced, in thirteenth-century form at around the same date, after the construction of a vault in the chapel damaged the earlier set of paintings.[16] But the analogy between Winchester and Westminster in the 1230s may well be a false one precisely because Winchester had a formal, and arguably familiar, painted chamber whereas Westminster did not. Henry's work at Westminster may accordingly have been more forward-looking.[17]

Henry's work at Winchester is relevant, however, in considering the type of architectural detailing employed by Henry at Westminster in the 1230s. The early years of Henry's majority saw documented work at a number of royal residences, and there is some evidence that in this period the king was employing masons who worked in a specific range of designs at several centres. A pivotal figure is Elias de Dereham, whose influence, direct or indirect, extended across much of southern England.[18] In points of detail the work done at Westminster in the 1220s corresponds closely to that done during the campaign at Winchester Castle, which included revisions to the painted chamber and the reconstruction of the Great Hall in the early 1230s. At both Westminster and Winchester, wall painting followed hard upon the completion of building work, starting in the king's chamber at Westminster in 1236–7 and recommencing at Winchester in 1233.[19] A good instance of the new detailing of Henry's masons in this period is provided by the principal entrance to the west end of the king's chamber at Westminster, the appearance of which was recorded by Capon and Carter (pls. XXVI, XXX, XXXI).[20] It was the largest and richest door in the room; its arch rose from moulded capitals supported on marble shafts, the springers rising vertically for a short distance before sustaining a low, obtusely pointed arch of distinctive character. This arch type was in use elsewhere at Westminster in the second quarter of the century, most notably in the new Exchequer Chamber, the queen's chamber and chapel built by the Cistercian laybrother Thomas of Waverley *c.* 1237–8 (in the rere-arches of the east windows of the chapel, for example),[21] and only slightly later in the north transept of Westminster Abbey.[22] Further examples are widespread in the south of England, to be found, for instance, in the Winchester Great Hall and at Salisbury Cathedral.[23]

The use of elegant marble shafts and rather angular arch and tracery forms also marked the windows inserted by Henry in the east wall of the king's chamber at Westminster. Here (pl. XXX), two-lighters supported a lozenge opening, rather than an oculus of the sort in the lateral windows, or a quatrefoil.[24] The use of lozenge shapes in this position occurs elsewhere in this period, again not always within a court context.[25] It is a device generally compatible in taste with the angular arch forms of the Westminster Abbey chapter-house vestibule, or the stark triangular arches of court-related architecture at Hereford Cathedral of a few years later.[26] But in this position it seems also to have been a peculiarity of earlier Cistercian architecture, and could attest to the influence of Thomas of Waverley in the king's chamber as well as the queen's apartments in this period.[27]

While sculptural ornament in the king's chamber was generally trivial, what was copied in the early 1800s is sufficient to demonstrate a transition from stiff-leaf to naturalistic carving of leaf forms in the room.[28] Evidence for the type of foliage sculpture executed *c.* 1240 at the palace is provided by Capon's copies of the cheerfully coloured sculptures in the queen's chapel, decorated *c.* 1241–2.[29] These show that stiff-leaf forms prevailed at this point. The intervention of more naturalistic forms would not indeed be expected until the mid-1240s, the earliest court instances including the chapel at Windsor begun in 1240, and Westminster Abbey, begun in 1245.[30] The copies of the king's chamber murals show that the springers of the lateral windows had an odd mixture of rolled, presumably twelfth-century, mouldings, stiff-leaf and more obviously naturalistic carving (pls. IV–VIII). Thus, by the head of the painting of the Virtue *Largesce* on one of the south window splays was a clump of gilt ivy leaves; from the same window, *Debonereté* had next to her a plain rolled moulding. It seems, therefore, that the splays were recarved at least once in the thirteenth century, possibly in the years *c.* 1230 and again after *c.* 1240— possibly after the fire of 1263. The basic width of the splays was, however, retained.[31]

There is some invaluable evidence for the internal layout of the room (fig. 3, p. 37), of critical importance for understanding its mural decorations. That the large door at the west end of the south wall was the principal public entrance to the room is strongly suggested by Henry's ordering in the 1230s that an hortatory text should be painted next to it.[32] The focus of the chamber undoubtedly lay at the far, east end, for it was here that the king's bed was situated. The bed was on this site from at least the 1230s. It was located with its head by the north wall, between the fireplace and the small doorway leading to the attached private chapel. At the head of the bed, to its left-hand side, was a quatrefoil opening at a height of 1·5 m. which evidently looked through in some way to the chapel.[33] Capon notes that this opening slanted obliquely through the wall.[34] In 1236 this opening, the *rotunda fenestra Regis juxta lectum Regis*, was glazed.[35] The chapel was thought of in relation to the bed in the main chamber; thus in 1255 the paintings in the *parva capella Regis juxta lectum Regis* were repaired.[36] Nothing is known of the appearance or date of the chapel itself.

The bed was a piece of state furniture, and had appended to it a particularly rich iconographic and decorative programme. Above the head of the bed was painted a rectangular representation of the Coronation of Edward the Confessor, measuring 1·7 by 3·2 m., containing figures of just under life size, and incorporating the foiled window into its design in an organic and integrated fashion (col. pl. I). To the right of the Coronation was painted an armed guard at the same scale, with the same sort of cusped arcading as that shown over the Coronation (pl. III); the symmetrical nature of the Coronation itself implies that a corresponding guard was once to be found on the other side, although no trace of it was found in 1819. The exact appearance of the bed itself can only be a matter of conjecture, but some documentary references are helpful. That the bed was slept in (i.e. that it was not a symbolic *lit de parade*) is suggested by a mandate of 1244 referring to green painted columns around the bed, spangled with gilt stars, and supporting curtains that could be drawn for the king's privacy—something which might suggest an important daytime function too.[37] The Westminster bed appears to have been an early example of the type of posted bed owned by Mahaut, Comtesse d'Artois between 1302 and 1329.[38] It was panelled in 1253 and presumably had some architectural substance, as the most important object known to have been in the room.[39] The reference of 1244 indicates that the bed comprised an outer bed (the tester, *celour* or canopy, curtained enclosure, etc.) and an inner bed (the surface for lying on located within the enclosure) of the sort recorded much later in the *Boke of Curtasye* of c. 1460.[40] The implication of this is that, if these bed arrangements pertained after the 1263 fire—and there is no reason to believe that they did not—the canopied enclosure of the bed would have surrounded the Coronation painting within, while the guardian figures were, appropriately enough, placed outside (fig. 2). In theory the Coronation mural could have been viewed in both public and private capacities, depending on whether the surrounding curtains were drawn to form a cubicle.[41] Two references of the post-1263 years, to the *picturae circa lectum Regis* and a *tabernaculum depictum circa lectum Regis*, are of critical importance (see below) as they show that the bed retained

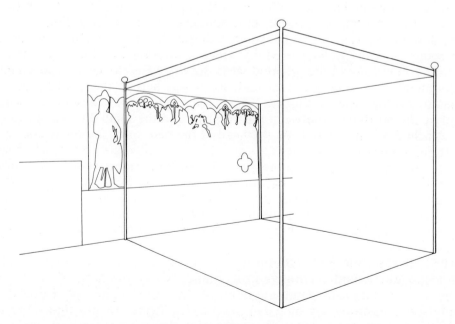

FIG. 2. Conjectural view of the bed enclosure in the king's chamber, showing the Coronation and Guardian murals in place, with fireplace to the left

its architectural status after the 1263 fire and survived as the dominant focus of wall painting in the room.[42] The *tabernaculum depictum* suggests that the bed structure itself was richly painted. Eames draws attention to the passage in Theophilus' *De Diversis Artibus* which describes how ornamental copper plating could be applied to painted chairs, stools, and beds, indicating that elaborately decorated beds of wood and metal, inlaid and painted, were in use among secular and ecclesiastical lords from the twelfth century.[43] It may be relevant that the painted canopy over the Coronation painting imitates the enamel and glass inlays associated with highly coloured woodwork objects like the Westminster Retable (col. pl. VI); was this painted canopy visually continuous with the actual canopy of the bed itself?[44] In any event, there is no doubt that the bed ensemble was of sufficient splendour and visual weight to form an obvious core of a scheme of wall paintings, lit from the south and east windows of the room.[45]

No significant work was undertaken in the room between the late 1230s and 1259. In that year, the chimney and fireplace were rebuilt and redecorated.[46] The work proved faulty, for in February 1263 a fire broke out in the room which, according to the *Dunstable Annals*, started in the chimney.[47] The fire damaged the king's chamber, its chapel, and related rooms such as the Lesser Hall. Repairs occurred in the period 1263–4, with the restoration of paintings to the room starting in late 1263.[48] It is reasonable to assume that the original roofing of the chamber was damaged in the fire. The appearance of the flat wooden ceiling which survived into the nineteenth century, with its pattern of lobed, metalwork-like *paterae* (pl. XXXIII), suggests that this was an introduction of the post-fire years.[49] There was evidently some uncertainty as to the final appearance of the ceiling, for it was found in the 1800s that the *paterae* had been laid over a half-complete set of painted heads.[50]

The 1263 fire provides us with a clear break in the continuity of the fabric and its decorations, and explains many features of the development of its wall paintings. The room retained all the features of its post-1263 repairs into the later thirteenth century. Minor additions were made in 1268–9 and 1274–9.[51] Repairs also took place from 1288, after a period of neglect of the palace by the court in the 1280s.[52] New paintings and repairs to older ones were undertaken in 1289–90 and again in the period 1292–7. This extended campaign was not prompted, as in the 1260s, by radical damage to existing paintings by fire. Similarly, there is no evidence that a further traumatic fire in the palace and its environs in 1298 damaged the room.[53] Thus, the recorded wall-painting activity in the chamber in 1307–8, the last of its sort there, can only have been needed because of routine wear and tear, or because of the existence of incomplete paintings in the room.[54]

The documentation of wall paintings

The architectural history of the Painted Chamber reveals two important phases in the development of its fabric: the first in the 1220s and '30s, and the second in the 1260s. Because, as we shall see, the fire of 1263 stimulated a major wall-painting campaign, its impact on Henry III's earliest decorations in the room must have been considerable. It is reasonable to assume from this that what was copied in 1819 is unlikely to have dated to before 1263. On to this basic chronological framework we can now superimpose the most valuable evidence for the history of the decorations of the Painted Chamber: first, the evidence of the remarkably thorough contemporary documentation for expenditure on wall paintings in the room; and, second, the invaluable evidence of the copies.

The documentation shows that four phases of work occurred in the room, and these will now be considered chronologically.

c. 1230 to 1263

From 1236, the year of the king's marriage, attention was turned to the construction and decoration of new chambers for the queen at Westminster. The first phase of expenditure on wall paintings therefore embraced both the king's and queen's apartments, and extended from 1236 to 1242. Painting at the palace had already begun in the Exchequer Chamber in 1228, and on images for the royal chapels in 1231–2.[55] In May 1236, the completion of the fabric of the king's chamber was marked by the glazing of the round window behind the king's bed; in the same month an order for painting required that the chamber was to be painted green in the manner of a curtain, and that a text was to be painted in the great gable of the room next to the entrance:[56]

> Mandatum est thesaurario Regis quod magnam cameram Regis apud Westmonasterium bono viridi colore depingi ad modum curtine, et in magno gabulo ejusdem camere juxta hostium depingi ludum illum 'Ke ne dune ke ne tine ne prent ke desire'; et etiam parvam garderobam Regis viridi colore ad modum curtine depingi faciat [etc.].

The formula *magna camera Regis* was retained with reference to the room until 1307–8. The scheme ordered by Henry was decorative rather than figurative, reminiscent of the earlier instruction of 1236 that the area around the royal seats in the Chapel of St Stephen should be painted green, and indeed resembling the considerable number of orders for purely decorative work involving green throughout Henry's residences.[57] In August 1237, £4. 11s. was given to the keeper of the works for painting in the king's chamber of unspecified type, but presumably relating to the 1236 writ.[58] Henry left Westminster shortly afterwards, but was informed that his instructions had not been followed:

> Mandatum est Odoni aurifabro quod picturam que incepta est depingi in magna camera Regis apud Westmonasterium subtus magnam historiam ejusdem camere, cum panellis continentibus species et figuras leonum, avium et aliarum bestiarum, sine dilatione deponi faciat et de viridi in modum curtine eam depingi faciat, ita quod illa magna historia conservetur illesa.[59]

Henry wanted his order of 1236 for decorative work in the room to be sustained; but it is evident from this record that not only had the painters started some description of bestiary or heraldic paintings, probably in the dado area, but also that there was already a figurative painting in the room, the *magna historia*, which Henry wished to retain unimpaired by the new additions. This instruction of 1237 therefore contains a cryptic reference to the decoration of the room as a whole in the 1230s, and will be the subject of further discussion.

In 1238 paintings were executed in the small chapel adjacent to the king's chamber.[60] The period 1238 to 1242 was occupied by work in the queen's chamber and chapel, including paintings of the Evangelists and the Lord and Angels, and the figure of Winter by the fireplace of the new chamber.[61] The first reference to figurative paintings in the king's chamber in the 1240s occurs in 1243; in April, lions were ordered to be painted in the gable at the west end of the chamber.[62] In October, Evangelists were to be added, in good and decent colours, one on each wall of the chamber.[63] At the same time the king's bed was redecorated with green posts spangled in gold, matching the prevailing colour scheme established in the chamber in the 1230s.[64] The decorations of 1243–4 in the king's chamber are the first to include figurative work that can with certainty be ascribed to Henry III there.

Further work occurred in the room after the introduction of these murals. In May and June 1249 the room was paved, presumably with tiles, and John of St Omer was ordered to paint the wardrobe in September.[65] In 1252 the keeper of the king's children supplied colours for the repair of paintings in the king's and queen's chambers;[66] in 1256, the garderobe where the king was wont to wash his head was painted with the story of the King of the Garamantes, by Master William.[67] In the previous year the paintings in the small chapel had been restored, and in 1259 the fireplace of the chamber was redecorated with a Tree of Jesse, while the other paintings were washed, work again done under Master William, the monk of Westminster.[68]

1263 to *c.* 1280

The extent of the work in the chamber carried out after 1263 suggests that the murals done in the preceding period were, at the very least, severely damaged by the 1263 fire. Repairs to the fabric of the room, conducted under Robert of Beverley, occupied the greater part of 1263, but by November Henry had ordered a series of paintings to be done in the chamber, its chapel and oriels, to be completed by Christmas of the same year.[69] Paintings were started, as a reference of September 1264 describes the chamber as *iam depicta*, but still in need of gilding; and in January 1265, £7. 10s. was provided for the scheme as outlined in 1263.[70] The accounts make it clear that from this point onwards the scheme was starting to grow in elaboration. In December 1266 the painter in charge of the new scheme is first mentioned by name: Master Walter, the king's painter of London, to whom £10 was sent to complete the work; at the same time a final account for the repairs to the fabric was drawn up.[71] Early in 1267, City debts to the king were diverted to Master Walter's work on the pictures in the king's chamber, to the tune of 20 marks.[72] A summary of very major work, indicating its extent and location, occurs by the end of 1267:

> Et pro auro in folio & aliis necessariis ad picturas circa lectum Regis in camera Regis ibidem. liij li. v sol. ij d. ob.[73]

Work was disrupted in the chamber by a riot in the palace in 1267, after which Master Walter received compensation:

> . . . Et Magistro Waltero pictori Regis pro dampnis & gravaminibus que sustinuit in servicio Regis tempore turbacionis habite in regno xl sol. per breve Regis.[74]

From September 1268 the accounts for works at Westminster fail increasingly to distinguish between painting in the palace and in the abbey, prior to the dedication of the church in 1269. How much was spent on the king's chamber in this period cannot therefore be calculated; but work is still specified. The Pipe Roll for September 1267 to December 1269 includes:

> Et in auro in folio. aimallis. diversis coloribus & aliis necessariis ad picturas voltarum ecclesie supradicte & magne camere Regis sicut continetur ibidem lxviij li. xviij sol. ix d. ob.[75]

The same type of account occurs in 1269–71 for £32. 16s. 1½d. including painting 'ad picturas capse in qua reponitur corpus beati Edwardi', and work on the king's chamber and in the abbey.[76] Comparable payments were made in 1271–2, totalling £17. 17s. 3½d.[77] An account for this period records earlier work by William the Painter:

> Et magistro Willielmo pictori monacho Westmonasterij pro tabernaculo depicto circa lectum Regis in camera sua apud Westmonasterium xx. marcas.[78]

Finally, an account of 1272 includes a payment of £7. 19s. 11d. for the king's chamber alone.[79]

The fall-off in outlay on the king's chamber by 1272 indicates that the post-fire campaign on the murals was substantially completed in the period 1263–72. On Henry's death in 1272 work at the palace effectively ceased until the return of Edward I for his coronation at Westminster in 1274, although preparations for this were under way in 1273.[80] Further work continued in the palace and king's chamber from 1274, but its exact nature is hard to ascertain. An account for 1274–7 includes the purchase of materials for wall paintings and notes also that a painting in the king's chamber was to be dried with hot coals: 'Roberto King pro j caretta carbonis ad picturam camera regis desiccandam iij s. viij d. [etc.]'.[81]

An account for 1274–8 mentions repairs to paintings in the king's and queen's chambers.[82] The accounts for this period show that Edward I was still supporting an *atelier* of wall painters in the palace, although it cannot be stated with absolute certainty whether the workforce was the same as that employed there under Henry III.[83] Edward's work seems to have been limited to adjusting the existing facilities of the palace to the needs of the new household, and there is no evidence that he had begun significant new wall-painting decorations there.[84] The refurbishment of the palace was completed by *c.* 1279, and in 1281 Edward ended his first phase of sustained residences there.[85]

1288 to 1297

The 1280s saw a period of neglect of the Palace of Westminster by the court, of a sort unknown under Henry III. For political reasons Edward was largely absent from Westminster and can have shown little interest in the decoration of its residential parts.[86] This situation changed in the late 1280s. In October 1289, Edward returned to Westminster, having last been there for a short time in 1286.[87] Work had started at the palace prior to his return, beginning with the fabrics of the halls;[88] during 1289 more extensive operations were under way on the construction of new chambers and the provision of wall paintings.[89] A stone chamber was erected and decorated with elaborate tiles and decorative painting by the *chef d'atelier* employed at Westminster in the 1260s, Master Walter of Durham;[90] repairs to the fabric and the glazing of the king's chamber occurred.[91] An account of 1289 refers to purchases of materials for painters, glaziers and image-makers, with work under Master Walter 'ad viridand' novam cameram de petra et ad emendaciones picture mangne [*sic*] camere Regis'.[92] A Majesty and the Evangelists were painted in the new green chamber; Walter was employed here for 13 weeks; repairs were also under way on the king's chamber.[93] For his work in the chambers in this period, Walter was paid for a total of 25 weeks and 5 days, receiving 4s. a week; his assistants received in total £14. 7s. 11d.[94]

This activity was stimulated by the neglect of the palace in the 1280s. Yet it is less easy to explain the renewal of wall painting that took place from 1292 in these terms. From April 1292 to April 1295, the phase covered by the first set of accounts for the reconstruction of St Stephen's Chapel, there occur forty-two accounts of particulars of wages and materials for wall painting in the palace under Master Walter.[95] Two accounts from this series mentioning the king's chamber were published by Rokewode.[96] A further eleven were published by Smith.[97] However, the extent, contents and importance of the remaining accounts have never been noted. The first roll of the first bundle of accounts for the reconstruction of the palace chapel is headed 'prima operacio picture', continuing

Rotulus de expensis et misis factis per manus Magistri Walteri pictoris circa emendacionem pictorie in magna camera Regis . . .[98]

Work started on 28th April 1292. Alder-wood scaffolding was obtained from Jak' Calnar,[99] and Walter was engaged with five assistants on the king's chamber. Thereafter, six campaigns of wall painting in the Palace of Westminster can be traced into the spring of 1295, occupying April–July 1292, November 1292 to January 1293, August–September 1293, March 1294, July–September 1294 and April 1295.[100] On only two occasions, in 1292 and in August 1294, when work 'ad magnam cameram . . . Regis . . . depingendam' is specified,[101] is the location of this work identified. The workforce was potentially large, drawing on up to twenty-seven individuals with Master Walter, and with his son Thomas ('filius magistri') employed from June 1292.[102] Also, considerable quantities of gold, silver, azure and sinopia were purchased and used steadily throughout the work recorded between 1292 and 1295.

Wall painting continued in the palace up to 1297, parallel to, but separate from, additional wall painting taking place in chambers reserved for the king's use at the house of the Archbishop of York at Westminster from the mid-1290s through to 1304–5.[103] Although the details of the subsequent campaigns at the Palace of Westminster cannot be followed in the period 1295–7, further significant references occur. In January 1296 a directive was sent to the deputy treasurer, chamberlains and barons of the Exchequer:

> Derechef de cesser de totes maneres de oueraignes sauve le oueraigne de Gales e les peintures des chaumbres de Wesmoster deuisees.[104]

That the painting of the king's chambers at Westminster was both important and urgent is suggested by the exclusive nature of the directive urging the continuation of all works in Wales and the paintings, but no others in the event of impending financial crisis. An account for the summer of 1297 shows that 'les peintures des chaumbres de Wesmoster' included the king's chamber; in August, payments were made to Walter:

> Magistro Waltero pictori lxxii s. iii d. pro operacionibus suis et servientium suorum in oratorio juxta magnam cameram Regis.[105]

On 28th August financial pressures brought the work to a close with payments of 54s. 7d., continuing [106]

> Et dictum est per dominum P. de Wylughby quod decetero non pingat in eadem quousque per dominum Regem vel prefatum P. specialiter ad hoc premuniatur.

This instruction to Walter occurred only a month after the halting of work on the first campaign on the fabric of the new chapel.[107] Activity on the chapel and on the palace wall paintings thus extended from 1292 to 1297. But it is clear from the well-understood chronology of the first phase of the building of the lower chapel at Westminster that the wall painting accounts, although included within the chapel particulars, cannot have referred to wall painting in the chapel. At the first mention of painting in 1292 work was barely complete on the foundations of the chapel, and its lower vaults were only nearing completion in 1294 or later.[108] The accounts for wall painting, as suggested by the 1296 directive, must apply to the secular rooms of the palace. As in 1289–90, and later in 1307–8, several rooms were probably decorated at once; but the only location of work specifically mentioned is the king's chamber, in 1292, 1294 and at the close of work in 1297. The implication of this is that much of, if not all, the work of the period 1292–7 was concerned with a very substantial campaign of wall painting in the king's chamber.

The workforce employed in the palace also worked on the funerary monuments required by the death of Eleanor of Castile in 1290, and on the completion of the tomb of Henry III.[109] The documentation of paintings in this context accords perfectly with the chronology of work in the palace viewed in detail. Master Walter was first engaged on paintings around the heart burial of Queen Eleanor at Blackfriars in the autumn of 1291 and in the spring of 1292.[110] In April 1292, after finishing at Blackfriars, Walter moved into the

Palace of Westminster and the king's chamber. He was employed there until January 1293; in the Hilary term of 1293 he appears at Westminster Abbey working on paintings around the tomb of Eleanor and on the wooden covers of the tombs of Eleanor and Henry III.[111] By August he was once more in the palace. Walter and his assistants were therefore employed more or less steadily at Blackfriars and Westminster from 1291 to 1297. There is a correlation between the king's residence at the palace and Walter's periods of employment there; thus, in the spring of 1293 Walter moved from the palace to the abbey when Edward returned into residence. This supports the theory that extensive work was taking place in domestic rooms in the palace such as the king's chamber when the king was absent.[112]

The cessation of work on St Stephen's Chapel and the king's chamber in 1297 marked the end of sustained work on the chapel for over 20 years and in the chamber for a decade; as work in the chamber was broken off, it may have been incomplete.[113] Edward urged the paintings ahead in 1296–7, possibly in order to have them completed by the time of his remarriage, which eventually occurred in 1299. However, funds ran out and, while the design of the upper chapel and the disposition of the murals executed in the palace were certainly settled by 1297, elements for the chapel had to be stored for subsequent assembly when the masons' lodge reformed under Edward II.[114] Work in the king's chamber was completed in 1307–8, however.

1307–8

Wall painting in the Palace of Westminster of this period is more thoroughly documented as regards its locale than in the 1290s.[115] Work began in September 1307 under a new master, Thomas of Westminster, probably the son of Master Walter recorded in the palace from 1292. Master Walter retired from active service between 1300 and 1304–5.[116] Thomas was employed as a guest painter, perhaps because he was familiar with the nature of the work undertaken between 1292 and 1297. His terms of employment are stated in the principal account surviving for the work of 1307–8:

> Magistro Thomae le Peyntur assignato et misso de Burgo per dominum Regem et thesaurium ad ordinandum reparandum et emendandum quosdam defectus existentes in diversis historiis in camera depicta et ad emendandum diversas depicturas et protracturas in diversis capellis cameris et domibus in palatio et ad essendum magistrum in officio pictorie et ordinandum de eodem etc.
>
> Per quod idem magister vadia septimanalia de Rege recipere noluit nisi tamen strictas expensas suas pro tempore quo eum morari circa idem officium contigerat eidem operanti et ordinanti ut patet in rotulis de pictoribus [etc.]. (Cancellatur que alibi)[117]

Thomas was sent for from Peterborough[118] to repair faults in the histories in the *camera depicta* and other palace rooms. As master of the *atelier* he chose not to receive a weekly wage, but instead received expenses for the period of his residence in the palace. The accounts state that in September 1307 scaffolding was erected for the painters in the Great Hall.[119] By early October the painters moved through the palace, first into the Lesser Hall and then into the Painted Chamber:

> Magistro Thomae de Westm' pictori operanti circa parvam Aulam depingendam et circa cameram Regis depictam emendandam . . .[120]

Thomas was employed with five assistants and was paid for transporting materials from London to Westminster. From October to December the painters were engaged in several rooms and on the king's ship, 'La Margarete de Westmonasterio', in which Edward II was to sail to France, presumably direct from the palace wharf, to collect his bride.[121] In December work continued in the Painted Chamber:

> Magistro Thomae de Westm' pictori operanti circa diversos defectus in camera depicta existentes tam in cumblea quam in muris et fenestris reperandis [*sic*] et emendandis [etc.].[122]

This entry reveals the extent of the work on the Painted Chamber, entailing repairs to the ceiling, windows,[123] and walls. The work was at its most intense in December 1307, when Thomas employed twelve men in the palace, and continued into the period before the coronation of Edward II in February 1308, thereafter declining in intensity.[124] Thomas appears to have left the palace at some point before 1309, as from that year a 'Hugo le peyntur depictor Regis' is found at Westminster.[125] A summary account notes that Thomas was employed for 264 days in the palace on the Painted Chamber and other rooms, including the 'camera Marculfi'.[126] Many of these repairs must have been entailed as a result of the fire of 1298, which occurred in the palace and the conventual buildings of Westminster Abbey.[127] However, there is no evidence that either the new chapel or the Painted Chamber were damaged, for neither is mentioned in accounts for repairs to rooms documented as damaged at the time of the accession of Edward II.[128] Cumulatively, the documentary evidence suggests that the work in the Painted Chamber was on paintings that were either left incomplete in 1297, or had simply been the subject of routine wear and tear.

From this account it can be seen that painting in the Painted Chamber, nominally speaking the king's chamber up to 1297, fell broadly into four phases.

1. The first, of 1236 to the mid-1240s, saw the execution of purely decorative painting, Evangelists, heraldic lions and the retention of a *magna historia* of unspecified and uncertain date and contents; a Jesse Tree was subsequently painted after the rebuilding of the fireplace and mantelpiece of the room in 1259. The additions that can safely be ascribed to Henry III in this period do not suggest the presence of extensive figural painting in the room, although the extent of the *magna historia* remains uncertain. These paintings were damaged in the fire of 1263.
2. Redecoration followed from late 1263 to 1272, by which time the series of paintings in the vicinity of the king's bed was completed. The documents do not clarify whether these paintings were restoring or revising the contents of

the murals as they stood before 1263. It is likely, however, that these paintings were the subject of repairs under Edward I in the mid-1270s; in other words, the second phase may be said to have extended at most from 1263 to *c*. 1279, but was at its most intensive from 1263 to 1272.

3. Restorations of the existing paintings were carried out in 1289–90. From 1292 a new period of wall paintings began at the same time as the start of work on the new palace chapel. That this was not conservative in nature is shown by the persistence of records of work in the king's chamber up to 1297. The third phase, of 1292–7, must have been in part concerned with either supplanting or extending the murals conserved in 1289–90.

4. The fourth phase, that of 1307–8, either repaired or completed the work of 1292–7. It also saw the emergence of the term *camera depicta* or *camera Regis depicta*, replacing the thirteenth-century formula *magna camera Regis* in use until 1297. This change in terminology at so late a date is striking, and invites two interpretations. It could, first, point to a change in the function of the room; it ceased to be the king's chamber in its thirteenth-century sense, and so was defined by its next most outstanding feature, its murals. Second, it could suggest that by 1307–8 the room had only recently acquired a sufficiently extensive series of murals to justify the change in terminology. If the work of the 1290s was demonstrably extensive, this interpretation may be likely, and does not rule out the possibility that the function of the room was also changing in some way in these years. The relatively late occurrence of the term *camera depicta* in association with the king's chamber in any event presents a serious difficulty for the accepted view that all the paintings discovered in the room in the early 1800s had been completed by 1272.[129]

The usual view of the chronology of work in the king's chamber originated in the antiquarian accounts of the paintings, together with the selection of documents collected by John Gage Rokewode, W. R. Lethaby and E. W. Tristram. The eye-witness descriptions of the paintings deserve close scrutiny, as they suggest that the murals had in some way seen a prolonged process of repair and revision. The later, art-historical discussion which followed was in effect concerned only with the first two phases that have been outlined here: of the mid-1230s through to 1263, and of 1263 to 1272. Inevitably, because of the 1263 fire, there remained doubt as to the relationship of the first to the second period. Tristram proposed that the first series was restored to its pre-fire form after 1263, and so considered the entire copied cycle to be a work of the early years of Henry III's reign.[130] Tudor-Craig, following Lethaby, suggested that the 1260s saw the inception of an entirely new cycle.[131] It was assumed that the later accounts for painting, of the 1290s and 1307–8, only recorded repairs to a pre-existing programme. The Painted Chamber was thus held to be a masterpiece of the art patronage of Henry III conserved by Edward I.

The principal consideration which sustained this view was a misunderstanding of the chronology of the rebuilding of St Stephen's Chapel. The order of work in the Painted Chamber is incomprehensible without the evidence for the chapel's construction brought forward by J. M. Hastings, J. H. Harvey and H. M. Colvin for the years 1292–7.[132] Tristram, who first noticed the extent of the work in the accounts of particulars for this period, believed that the chapel was reconstructed not by Edward I, but by Edward III, and so was able to attribute the evidence in the 1290s' accounts to work not in the king's chamber, but on murals in St Stephen's Chapel, except when they specifically mentioned the king's chamber.[133] This isolated the three accounts known from Rokewode, for work in the chamber in 1289, 1292 and 1294, from what can now be seen to have been a more extensive period of work in the chamber. These documents, taken alone, simply asserted that earlier work in the chamber was being repaired by Edward I.

The argument presented here differs from previous surveys in redefining the relationship of the work at the end of Henry's reign, after 1263, to that under Edward I from 1292. The documentation suggests that artistic activity in the king's chamber was closely related to the architectural history of the palace as a whole, and especially to the rebuilding of St Stephen's Chapel, as part of a more ambitious programme of patronage conducted by Edward at the end of his reign. Indeed, it may also cast more general doubt on the usual understanding of the relationship between the patronage of Henry III and his son. This question will be returned to at a later point. Quite clearly, however we interpret the evidence of the fabric and the documentation for the Painted Chamber, our conclusions cannot be radically at variance with the most direct and fascinating evidence for the appearance of the room itself, that provided by the copies and descriptions of the room by those who actually saw it in the early 1800s. This uniquely important, and oddly neglected, resource must now be considered, assessed, and reconciled with the evidence put before the reader so far.

The copies and descriptions

It is seldom the case in the study of English medieval art that we can have access to so rich and diverse a collection of sources for a lost work as we do for the Painted Chamber. But while the archaeological and documentary evidence for the room to some extent speaks for itself, the visual evidence has come down to us in an interpreted form, translated by the process of copying, and subjected to the normal prejudices of early nineteenth-century antiquarian thought. Before using the evidence of the copies and descriptions, we must place them in their immediate context, to see how much can be recuperated as the basis for an art-historical investigation, and how much is to be disregarded as a sign of its times.

The most well-known artist at work in the Painted Chamber in 1819 was Charles Stothard (1786–1821). Stothard obtained the post of historical draughts-man to the Society of Antiquaries in 1815, on the death of Richard Smirke.[134] His copies of the Painted Chamber were executed for the Society with the encouragement of its Secretary, Henry Ellis, an Anglo-Saxon scholar and a colleague of John Gage Rokewode (1786–1842).[135] Stothard's copies, superbly finished in watercolours, are preserved in the library of the Society. They show a number of affinities with the acclaimed drawings in his series *The Monumental Effigies of Great Britain*, undertaken in 1811 and published in 1817.[136] The copies were carefully measured with graduated lines, but employed neither tracings (which would have been impractical given the considerable size of some of the paintings), nor a consistent scale.[137] Nevertheless, Stothard's reputation as a pure draughtsman was, and remains, high. His *Memoirs*, assembled by his wife after his tragic death in 1821, demonstrate his concern for neutral observation and factual representation, criticizing Gough's *Sepulchral Monuments* for the inaccuracy of its drawing, and stressing the value of cleaning effigies before copying them.[138]

Stothard was certainly familiar with medieval idioms in several media; in 1816 he conducted an investigation of the painted details of the tombs at Fontevrault,[139] and while in France he studied the enamel plaque of Geoffrey of Anjou and prepared a distinguished series of drawings for the Society of Antiquaries of the Bayeux Tapestry, published in 1819.[140] His Bayeux Tapestry copies, finished shortly before his activity in the Painted Chamber at Westminster, unquestionably represent a considerable advance in fidelity to medieval style since the days of Montfaucon.[141] The difficulties raised by his copies for art-historical investigation do not relate so much to their sense of style (although this is inevitably a problem) as to their sense of archaeological enquiry. Stothard's principal experience of medieval painting was obtained through the study of tomb polychromy; but although he was familiar with medieval panel painting,[142] he had not by 1819 studied wall paintings, and in many respects his methods of presentation were not ideally suited to the special, yet historically important, difficulties posed by murals, such as the interpretation of decayed paint surfaces, and the suggestion of their subcutaneous qualities. His Painted Chamber series has the same factual and yet superficial nature as the copies made in St Stephen's Chapel by his predecessor Smirke (pl. XXXIV); it is hard to tell from it exactly what state of preservation the murals were in, when uncovered. This was partly a matter of Stothard's technique and the relatively small scale of his copies (the largest, that of the Coronation of St Edward, being 33 cm. wide). Also, his work in the *Monumental Effigies*, because (unlike the Painted Chamber) it can be compared with the surviving evidence, has a demonstrable element of politeness and compromise. Here, Stothard published two types of drawing, one of large scale and uncoloured, sensitively executed, and another of smaller scale where a restoration was offered of the original colouring of the effigies based on extant traces (pl. XXXV).[143] The principal quality of Stothard's work here is its astonishing accuracy of line. Now Stothard must have worked in a similar way in the Painted Chamber, producing steely and precise line drawings in pencil, then massing in the colours to produce a legible effect, and finally articulating the forms with inked lines. The drawings, when completed by the clever use of raised surfaces to imitate the embossed compounds used in the original murals,[144] became inherently worthwhile pieces, lending themselves conveniently to clear coloured engraving of the sort resulting in their reproduction in the volumes of *Vetusta Monumenta*.[145] The adaptation of the copies to such reproductive techniques inevitably entailed that the awkward complexities of the originals had to be ironed out. Moreover, Stothard did not provide alternative versions of the Painted Chamber as he did in the *Monumental Effigies*, that is to say straight copies of the original and also a discreet restoration; rather, he merged the two. Thus, although the comparison is odious, his activity in the Painted Chamber cannot compare, in terms of its documentary value, with work done in the 1840s and 1850s under the supervision of the Commission des Monuments Historiques, on the painted medallions of the upper chapel of the Sainte-Chapelle in Paris.[146] Robert Branner rightly described Steinheil's copies of the medallions, made to the demanding standards of Prosper Merimée, as 'models of archaeological exactitude', making a clear distinction between documentation and restoration.[147] Stothard's copies, although more attractive than the later Sainte-Chapelle series, are certainly less intellectually tough, and reveal a more liberal and sentimental level of expectation among English antiquarians of the early nineteenth century.

Edward Crocker's copies of the murals, which were first taken into account by W. R. Lethaby in 1905,[148] are technically like those of Stothard, employing watercolours, gilded raised detailing and the same sort of scale. Crocker's palette is more full and rich than that of Stothard, and his copies are accordingly more gorgeous in appearance. Nothing important is known of his artistic training. As an employee in the Office of Works at Westminster, his principal concerns would have been with architecture and surveying; he was probably no more than an amateur when it came to copying antiquities. His figure drawing is rather less secure than Stothard's. But on the whole the general approach is similar, similar enough to raise momentarily the possibility of collusion. If proved, this would clearly compromise the value of one set of copies in confirming independently the account offered by the other. Unfortunately, only the sketches by Buckler are dated exactly, to October 1819,[149] and so the order in which the copies were made is unclear. Neither copyist refers in his written account of the murals to the work of the other artist. One piece of evidence shows that Crocker's copies must have been largely complete by the time that Buckler began work in October: Buckler copied Crocker's annotated elevation of the room.[150] Collusion between the copyists is ruled out by some internal features of the copies. In the first place, both sets disagree over some minor details in the murals; Nicanor, shown at the centre of one of the Maccabees scenes, has two different types of helmet (pl. Xa, b); Crocker differs from Stothard in showing a combination of trefoils and quatrefoils on a cornice from the story of the Famine in Samaria (pl. XIV), and so on. Second, Crocker recorded paintings not copied by Stothard, such as the soldier guardian by the Coronation of St Edward, the socle paintings beneath the Virtues, and perhaps most importantly the invaluable inscriptions from some of the Old Testament scenes on the north wall (pl. IX); conversely, Stothard copied the story of Joab and Abner from the south wall, and a scene from the Maccabees on the north wall omitted by Crocker. The two artists therefore had a different sense of what was sufficiently well preserved, or representative, to merit a copy. Iconographically speaking, the consideration that Crocker's copies are in some respects, however trivial, fuller than those of Stothard, together with the survival of his working drawings made on site (pl. I),[151] must argue against his dependence on Stothard; and it is impossible to see how the tentatively exquisite drawings of Stothard could derive from Crocker's spirited, but at times coarse, draughtsmanship.[152] Buckler's contact with Crocker must have been closer, yet his sketches of the paintings, notably that of one of the angels from a window soffit on the south side of the room not copied by either Stothard or Crocker (pl. XLI*b*), have all the first-hand qualities of an eye witness excited by novel discoveries.[153]

Despite minor variations of interpretation, the copies taken together present a convincing agreement as to the ostensible stylistic contents of the murals in the Painted Chamber. Crocker and Stothard arrive at similar conclusions about composition, coloration, architectural motifs and decorative devices. Crocker is perhaps more prone to offer a discreet restoration here and there, while Stothard holds back. For example, in representing a scene from the story of the Captivity of the Jews (pls. XVIII–XIX), Crocker completes the tracery details on the canopy shafting on the left-hand building, while Stothard leaves them blank; yet there can be no doubt that both are recording the same repertoire of architectural components. While Stothard's figure drawing is here neat, reticent and sharply defined, Crocker's is more crudely conceived, and more thickly coloured in; yet the groupings of the figures and their demeanour is instructively close in appearance. The copies illustrate the general truth that architectural devices are easier to copy than subtle figure styles; accordingly, they invite an art-historical judgement at a corresponding level. And, whereas our appreciation of the style of the Painted Chamber is contingent upon the nature of the copies and their period of execution, their documentation of the imagery of the room is invaluable.

Of the surviving eye-witness descriptions, that of Crocker is limited,[154] and Stothard's is incomplete; his early death prevented him from publishing the full survey of the paintings that he evidently intended. One letter of his on the subject, to Henry Ellis, is printed in the *Memoirs*; another among them includes remarks not dissimilar in tone to his writing on the Bayeux Tapestry and the effigies.[155] In this case, Stothard may have been preparing a fuller report for the Society of Antiquaries. In his letter to Ellis, Stothard included some preliminary observations on the date of the murals as he saw them:

> It has been supposed, that this apartment was destroyed by fire as early as 1263, when a considerable part of the palace of Westminster suffered; but I think it will be seen, that this was not the case, when I shall at future time enter more deeply into the examination of these antiquities. It is remarkable, that the subjects on the walls have been re-painted at least three times; and I have reason to believe, that the last time the subjects were so renewed, the gilder was more employed in exerting his skill than the painter. The additions were partial.[156]

He continued:

> Although some anomalies are created in these subjects upon the walls, by parts of former designs being retained, yet a tolerably correct idea may be formed about what period the *last* painting was executed; and I should state it to be in the reign of Edward I . . .

In addition to the 'anomalies' on the walls, Stothard noted that revisions must have taken place to the design of the medieval ceiling of the room; the ornamental *paterae* which adorned its length had been laid over a series of preparatory designs of heads executed over half the length of the room, the drawing for which was 'loose and free'.[157] In the fragmentary essay printed in the *Memoirs*, Stothard extended his enquiry:

. . . who were the artists capable of producing so magnificent a work at so early a period? . . . I am induced to think, that the artists who executed the principal part of these paintings were Italians . . .[158]

Stothard supported this conclusion by reference first to the architectural details painted in the murals; on their use of gables and crockets he observed:

> It may be justly said, that these forms are to be found in many of our cathedrals and churches in this country, but I feel convinced that they may all be traced to the Italians; and that it is to them we owe this feature, which was afterwards ingrafted into our own architecture. The purest examples of this particular style in England are to be found on the tombs of Edmund Crouchback, and his countess, Aveline, and on that of Aymer de Valence. I have purposely selected these, because it will presently appear that they are still more closely connected with the Painted Chamber.[159]

Stothard's last remark on the tombs in Westminster Abbey is an important one, but it was never to be more fully expanded.[160] He settled for the time being for a comparison between the Painted Chamber, the Crouchback tomb, and details drawn from architecture at Orvieto. In addition, he observed that the use in the Painted Chamber murals of certain technical specialities also supported Italian authorship:

> . . . the raised composition with which these works are adorned, is undoubtedly of Italian origin. Of this, Margeritori [*sic*] of Arezzo is said to have been the inventor . . . When these paintings before us were first executed, it does not appear that this composition was at all used . . . It is not improbable than the tinfoil found beneath the composition laid upon it, was used for the purpose of protecting it from damp.[161]

Furthermore, Stothard noted that documents of the 1290s for painting at the Palace of Westminster under Edward I showed that painters with Italianate names, such as 'Giletto', were paid more than those 'whose names were decidedly *English*'.

In making these judgements, Stothard shows that he was acquainted with Vasari's *Lives*;[162] Horace Walpole's *Anecdotes of Painting in England*, which included references to Italians, or those with Italianate names, among the royal painters in the thirteenth century;[163] Stow's *Survey*;[164] a letter to Walpole noting that some friars referred to the murals in the Painted Chamber in 1322;[165] and possibly also Smith's *Antiquities*, which published further documents for painting at Westminster in the 1290s.[166]

For Stothard, this material suggested cumulatively that the murals had been repainted in the early fourteenth century, but he added:

> Although it is a remarkable character in this work, that notwithstanding its having been twice repainted, it still retains in most places the original compositions, as well as some of the minuter forms; yet there is not sufficient existing of these to form any idea of the period at which the work was commenced.[167]

Having said this, Stothard was apparently inclined to accept that the paintings dated basically from the reign of Henry III and that later work was superficial.

This was a natural conclusion to arrive at, given that the selections of documentary material to which he had access, especially those assembled by George Vertue and Walpole in the previous century,[168] showed that Henry III appeared to be the first king to patronize wall painting in the Palace of Westminster, from as early as the 1230s. Indeed, Stothard went so far as to identify the material relating to King Antiochus in the Painted Chamber with a source with royal associations dating from 1250.[169]

Now, as Stothard's remarks constitute the principal eye-witness account of the murals, it will be valuable to consider briefly the two main issues to which they give rise. First, his impression was that the murals had been restored or repainted, and that in the process they had taken on a palimpsest appearance. This effect was also noted in the description in the *Gentleman's Magazine* for 1819.[170] Stothard is not precise as to which paintings had been so treated. In 1842, John Gage Rokewode, Stothard's contemporary, gave some instances: the figure of *Debonereté* (col. pl. II*b*) on one of the window splays of the south wall had (according to a lost source of Stothard's) been 'twice repainted'; a battle scene from the east wall showed 'perhaps a little difference . . . in the drawing and colouring, compared with the other paintings' (pl. XXV*a*); and within one of the scenes from the Maccabees 'there occurs a considerable ambiguity and apparent confusion, especially as regards the surcoat and hauberk, possibly occasioned by repaintings or subsequent alterations' (pl. X).[171]

What Stothard and Rokewode meant by these observations is not entirely clear. Both believed that the paintings had been repaired; but neither tells us to what extent these repairs had diminished the authenticity of the original style of the murals. Stothard's allusions to 'original compositions' and to the retention of 'former designs' can be taken in two ways: he might have been referring to older and iconographically distinct paintings visible under newer ones, so causing thematic confusion; or he might have had in mind areas where the underdrawing had come through, showing the various changes of plan that commonly occurred at this stage of executing a wall painting. We know that underdrawing was visible because Rokewode was able to trace a variety of underdrawing techniques.[172] It is likely that the witnesses in fact saw all these possibilities in the paintings: confused preparatory stages; true palimpsests; and signs of the simple repainting or a conservation that could occur on murals of this type.[173] The room had seen a good deal of painting activity in the course of the thirteenth century. The one telling question is why none of these possibilities is really apparent in the copies of Stothard and Crocker.

The second striking element in Stothard's writing is his attribution of the paintings to Italians. In principle, this attribution might cast doubt on the assumptions underlying Stothard's process of copying, and the neutrality of his observation. But Stothard never went to Italy, and his *Memoirs* do not suggest that he was especially well acquainted with Italian art; rather, it seems that his judgement was based upon an intellectual rather than a visual prejudice. His view on the primacy of Italian painting in the thirteenth century was conventionally held in the early 1800s and was compatible with the Walpolian utterances of many antiquarians of Stothard's generation. These were fed by a reading of Vasari and the Vasarian *Anecdotes* of Walpole, which cast doubt on the importance of the contribution of English painters in the medieval period.[174] That Italian art had had a major role in medieval England was accepted by writers such as J. C. Brooke,[175] and this assumption was further informed in the early nineteenth century by a rising interest in Italian medieval architecture. An exponent of this interest was indeed Stothard's principal mentor, Thomas Kerrich (1748–1828), who lectured to the Society of Antiquaries in 1809 on the subject of Italian Gothic architecture.[176] It is likely that Stothard's use of Italian architectural analogies for the Painted Chamber, however misguided, was prompted by his close contact with Kerrich, and his thinking in this respect does not of itself invalidate his copies.[177]

Some aspects of the comprehensive account of the Painted Chamber written by John Gage Rokewode shortly before his death in 1842, and published in *Vetusta Monumenta* with engravings of Stothard's copies, suggest that it too may have arisen from experience of the monument itself, and that it should also be considered as an early eye-witness account. Rokewode certainly had access to those parts of the old Palace of Westminster, and his description of some of the technical features of the Painted Chamber murals shows that he had seen fragments of the paintings.[178] While relying on Stothard's observations to some extent, it is clear that Rokewode's writing on the subject did more than simply pick up where Stothard left off. Stothard's fragmentary writings reflected the absence of an informed body of opinion on the appearance and history of English medieval figurative art. In the early 1800s, as Munby has shown, few people showed an appreciation of English manuscript painting of the thirteenth and fourteenth centuries; the most notable exception perhaps being Francis Douce (1757–1834), who not only owned the great Douce Apocalypse (Oxford, Bodleian Library MS Douce 180) and the Crocker presentation copies of the Painted Chamber in the Ashmolean Museum, but was also put forward as the most sympathetic candidate to continue Stothard's researches on this subject, a task which he declined to undertake and which as a result passed into Rokewode's unwilling hands.[179] Examples of early wall and panel painting at Westminster, as elsewhere, were usually treated as an addendum to the study of tombs and their polychromy, and not as a special area of enquiry.[180] What more specialized accounts there were concerned themselves primarily with the use, or non-use, of oil paint in the period before the innovations of Van Eyck.[181] Rokewode's essay, on the contrary, marks a considerable advance on the thinking of Stothard and his time. He retains some of the standard preoccupations of a generation of antiquarians nurtured on the writings of Joseph Strutt and Walter Scott and fascinated by the details of historical fashions in costume and armour.[182] But he rejects the Walpole-derived framework of prejudices found in Stothard with regard to the Italian authorship of the Painted Chamber murals; Italian analogies are rightly dispensed with and instead the sources called upon are northern European.[183] Striking comparative material is chosen from contemporary English manuscripts such as the Guthlac Roll, the Lives of the Offas and the Queen Mary Psalter, works which a generation or so earlier would have invited scorn, but which are here accurately reproduced.[184] Rokewode includes the first serious analysis of the fabric of the room and the documentary sources for wall painting pertaining to it from the 1230s through to 1308, which broadly confirmed Stothard's unsubstantiated opinion that the Painted Chamber had been worked on under both Henry III and Edward I.[185] Fragments of the paintings were examined by Thomas Phillips, R.A., and Michael Faraday for evidence of their technique.[186] And, perhaps more significantly, Rokewode is the first to compare the Painted Chamber to what remains the most famous single product of Westminster painting of the thirteenth century, the Westminster Retable (col. pl. VI), framed for viewing by Edward Blore in 1827:

> The folds of the drapery are better arranged than what are found in the figures of the Painted Chamber; and there is a more sober tone of colouring throughout, and an olive complexion, which time would hardly have given to the painting.[187]

In effect, Rokewode had a view recognizable to art historians of the milieu of medieval painting at Westminster, undoubtedly brought about by such considerations as the emergence of a more critical language of description and evaluation from within the field of architectural history,[188] the expansion of the study of English medieval manuscripts under authorities such as T. F. Dibdin, W. Y. Ottley (and, indeed, Rokewode himself),[189] a widening taste for accurate facsimile reproduction fed by the work of Madden and Shaw and J. O. Westwood,[190] and the increasing availability of printed documentary sources for royal patronage in the medieval period.[191]

Rokewode's account of the Painted Chamber attests to the remarkable progress in the study of English medieval art in the period 1820–40, although the nature of this progress, and of the studies of medieval art at Westminster which sprang from it, remains outside the scope of this work. The contributions made by Sir Charles Eastlake,[192] E. E. Viollet-le-Duc,[193] William Burges,[194] and especially W. R. Lethaby[195] were concerned primarily either with the technical aspects of medieval painting,[196] or with the stylistic origins of such extant works as the Westminster Retable and the attributional problems to which it gave rise, and cannot be said to constitute more than informed secondary sources for a study of the Painted Chamber itself.[197]

Conclusions

From this discussion of the fabric, documentation, and visual records of the Painted Chamber, some clear conclusions can be drawn about how and when the room was decorated. Yet some critical uncertainties remain. The principal area of uncertainty derives, inevitably, from our diluted, second-hand sense of the physical quality of the paintings. We know in a general way what the main features of these paintings were; it is impossible to agree with Rickert's statement that nothing is known about their style.[198] We know what imagery they contained. But the degree of their technical accomplishment is now lost from view. How would they have stood comparison with the superb Westminster Retable, which Rokewode evidently thought superior to them? The reports that the murals were repainted also leave us with a feeling of disquiet. How radical were the repaintings? Why are they not apparent in the copies to any significant extent? Did they occur in the course of the thirteenth century, or substantially after the completion of the cycle as a whole?

We can only guess the answers to these questions. As the documentary evidence for work on the paintings stops in the early fourteenth century, the question of the extent of later medieval repairs remains open. In fact, the paintings as copied show no details which suggest that a radical repainting occurred later on. It will be argued below that what revisions took place were primarily concerned with peripheral, ornamental detail, probably taking place as the mural cycle took shape in the campaigns of the late thirteenth century.

On the basis of what is known in general about the techniques used in English medieval wall painting, some hypothetical remarks may be allowed concerning the way the murals may have been constituted. The appearance of many of the paintings—particularly the Coronation of St Edward and the Virtues on the window splays—suggests a close affinity with panel painting executed in oil or tempera, such as the Westminster Retable.[199] The sedilia panels in Westminster Abbey, its murals, the painted surfaces of the late thirteenth-century tomb of Edmund Crouchback and the fragments of the murals from St Stephen's Chapel are analogous to the thirteenth-century Retable in using drying oils and a highly finished *al secco* pigmentation;[200] *fresco* technique is hardly ever found in English wall painting of this period.[201] The Painted Chamber murals were almost certainly not frescoes. It was noted at the time of their discovery that the pigments decayed or faded rapidly on exposure to the air, and were soluble in water, leaving the preliminary drawings exposed.[202] This suggests that the paint surfaces were superficial, and not bound up chemically with the layer of plaster beneath, as in *fresco* technique.[203] Although the nineteenth-century investigators were uncertain as to whether oil had been used in the colours, it seems likely that the painters were familiar with both oil and tempera media. Oil, size and eggs figure commonly in accounts for wall-painting purchases at court throughout the thirteenth century.[204] The salient point is that the Painted Chamber murals probably had a richness and density of coloration which allowed them to be repaired and refreshed periodically without total repainting, and it may have been this technical feature that conveyed to the eye-witnesses the palimpsest effects they refer to in such a vague way.

So far as the broad chronology of the work in the Painted Chamber is concerned, a general pattern undoubtedly emerges from the evidence considered so far. The copies show that we are dealing with murals executed at some time in the second half of the thirteenth century. Even granting that repairs took place, the documentary sources show that the date brackets for these paintings can be narrowed down to two alternatives: they must have been done either in the years after 1263 or those after 1292. The Old Testament scenes were plainly in existence by 1323, and there is no reason to doubt that they were the same as the *diversae historiae* repaired in 1307–8. They must therefore belong to one of the two thirteenth-century campaigns just outlined. In addition, the allusion of 1267 to paintings around the king's bed may well provide a guide to the date of the Coronation painting in the room, and so to those paintings allied to it stylistically and iconographically. In order to provide an even more accurate dating for the murals in the Painted Chamber we must now turn to their details, and begin with those paintings most compatible with the artistic tastes of the court of Henry III.

II. THE PAINTINGS IN THE GREAT CHAMBER OF HENRY III

Henry III has always been regarded as the greatest royal patron of the arts in thirteenth-century England. That his role was a significant one is beyond dispute. It is attested above all by his work at Westminster Abbey, with its French-inspired *chevet* and shimmering, imported Roman sanctuary floor. It is demonstrated, too, by the mass of documentary evidence for his interest in the decorations of his palaces and castles throughout his realm.[1] His projects were both grandiose and intimately domestic, broadly conceived in their lavishness and yet concerned too with the niceties of the appearance of his royal rooms, the location of their windows and wall paintings. Although so little of what he did survives, we know more about Henry's patronage than that of any king before him. Henry certainly appears at first sight to have overshadowed his son Edward in matters artistic.

It comes as no surprise to find that previous studies of the Painted Chamber at Westminster have attributed to Henry not only those paintings specifically recorded as being ordered by him for the room from the 1230s onwards—the lions in the gable, the Evangelists, a Tree of Jesse and so on—but also the remainder of the work copied in 1819: the Old Testament scenes, the Coronation of St Edward and the paintings of Virtues and Vices on the window splays. Cumulatively the range of images is an impressive one, remarkable in its diversity for the tastes of one man. Henry, it has been suggested, decorated the room in one way and then, after the fire of 1263, completely changed his mind; throwing aside the old murals, he replaced them with splendid biblical narratives and images of his patron saint and the courtly Virtues. Despite his declining years and the disturbances in the kingdom, Henry's work as an ardent francophile and ever-curious patron remained as marked as ever.

The argument put forward here will amount to a partial revision of this traditional view of Henry as a patron. So far as the Painted Chamber is concerned, it is clear that Edward I's contribution was no less significant than that of his father; the Old Testament scenes display an important number of stylistic and iconographic features which indicate that they cannot have been conceived much before the end of the thirteenth century, and that they are likely to have been the product of Edward's patronage. More generally, the fact that there is so much documentary information about the details of Henry's patronage may of itself have exaggerated his relative importance. Very much less of the sort of information we find under Henry is to be found under Edward; but this is as much a product of changing administrative practices in the thirteenth century as a reflection of the true roles of these kings. Edward simply did not use the Chancery administration in the way that Henry did, and so in documentary terms he seems to be a more obscure figure.[2] Again, the undoubtedly experimental and francophile elements in Henry's patronage have to be seen in the wider context of his work as a patron. While Westminster Abbey and the palace saw a strong infusion of French stylistic ideas as the reign of Henry advanced, Westminster Abbey is far from being a straightforwardly French building, the product, say, of an export package, in the sense that Cologne Cathedral is.[3] English traditions were not submerged under Henry. The records of the images chosen by Henry for his residences suggest that in iconographic terms he was insular and perhaps rather on the conservative side; we find an unsurprising prevalence of hagiographic and religious imagery, and no real signs that Henry was mechanically following French precedents.[4] Most of Henry's images can be accounted for in English, not Continental, terms. What French elements we can trace therefore take on a specific, rather than a general, importance.

   This chapter will show that some of Henry's work in the Painted Chamber can be identified. This will require an investigation of both the style and the iconography of the copied murals. Indeed, because of the problems of using copies to judge the style of the murals, the first hypotheses must rather be iconographic and functional ones. Which paintings in the room conform best with what is known of Henry III's particular preoccupations, and the way he may have conceived the function of the king's chamber? Although the execution of the images of St Edward and the Virtues and Vices is not explicitly recorded in the documentation, it can be shown that this imagery, rather than that of the Old Testament scenes, reveals conclusive signs of having been planned and executed under Henry before 1272.

The images of the king's great chamber in context

Quite how the *magna camera regis* functioned routinely in the thirteenth and early fourteenth centuries is largely a matter of conjecture. Few residential apartments of this order were devoted exclusively to a single, specialized activity in the thirteenth century, and it would be fruitless to try to define the king's chamber's workings too closely in the absence of so much evidence.[5] As Colvin has noted, a differentiation of a clear sort between the 'Great Palace', its public and official part, and the 'Privy Palace', the residential apartments of the household, only arose in the Palace of Westminster in the early fourteenth century.[6] Where the king's chamber fell in respect of this distinction in the thirteenth century is unclear. There are no formal records describing the use of the Westminster rooms surviving from the thirteenth century.[7] The Westminster Coronation Directory of the early 1270s notes such details as the setting up of thrones in the Great Hall prior to the ceremony of the coronation, but no mention is made of the king's chamber despite its apt iconography of the Coronation of St Edward.[8] Records of events taking place in the room are piecemeal, and for this reason may be unrepresentative. It emerges occasionally as the location for major state events, as when the homage of Alexander of Scotland was received there in 1279.[9] Parliamentary activity in the room was not formalized in the thirteenth century, and is known to us only in the form of partial, if suggestive, reports such as that of 1297, when the king imposed a tax with the consent of 'the *plebs* standing around in his chamber' at Westminster.[10] Edward II's construction of a private bed chamber may have entailed that after 1307 the great bed of estate in the Painted Chamber was no longer slept in, and retained only as a public symbol of authority.[11] We hear more of the public use of the room in the fourteenth century. Edward II used both the Painted Chamber and the adjacent Lesser Hall for state feasting, a practice which lasted well into the century when it was becoming more normal for great chambers to take over some of the functions formerly held in the Great Hall in important seigniorial residences.[12] In 1310, the reforming Ordainers were chosen in the Painted Chamber.[13] During the indictment of the Despencers in 1321, the room was reserved for the prelates.[14] Rolls of procedure for Parliament show that the Painted Chamber was used for more formalized parliamentary gatherings from the 1330s and 1340s as a convenient alternative to the chapter house of Westminster Abbey.[15]

By 1323 we have the explicit statement that the room was 'illa vulgata camera', and that knowledge of its splendid appearance was increasingly available to more than just the court circle.[16] Evidence that the king's chamber was put to public, if not exactly state, use in the thirteenth century is provided by the charitable works performed there under the auspices of the royal household. In 1243, for example, six thousand people were fed and entertained on a biblical scale in the palace, crowding out the Great Hall, the queen's apartments and the king's chamber.[17] The virtuous iconography of the paintings, and the charitable exhortations of the texts in the room would have acquired a clear enough significance under these circumstances. This type of public exercise, doubtless fostered by the growing influence of the mendicant orders at court in the thirteenth century,[18] must have imposed a degree of flexibility of use on the royal rooms, requiring, in addition to such permanent props as the great bed of estate, the use of movable trestle tables and chairs, arranged with respect to the points of highest status within the room.[19] More formal occasions were undoubtedly pervaded by ritual, and later medieval practices suggest that almost all feasting activity held in the presence of the king, whether in hall or chamber, would have obeyed strict codes of conduct.[20] In the absence of explicit information on the subject, it is hard to establish how such codes could have influenced the formally decorated room at Westminster. That considerations of status influenced to some extent the layout of its decorations is suggested by the topography of the king's chamber.[21] The room was entered at its west end, furthest from the royal bed with the kingly iconography of St Edward. In 1236 the text *Ke ne dune ke ne tine ne prent ke desire*—whoever does not give up what he possesses shall not receive what he desires—was painted in the gable next to the entrance, being therefore legible to the king as well as those entering and leaving the chamber.[22] This exhortation to charity anticipates the theme of the Virtues, notably *Largesce,* ornamenting the splays of the room, and parallels exactly the iconography of some of Henry III's great halls in the 1240s and 1250s, where the parable of Dives and Lazarus in St Luke's Gospel, xvi, was painted on the wall opposite the king's seat at the high table, similarly aimed at the point of highest status in the room.[23] Henry's sense of the impact of such moralizing iconography, when located strategically, was obviously marked.

The great bed in the *magna camera regis* is especially central to an understanding of its decorations. Placed furthest from the entrance, it presented a permanent, architectural focus in the room around which a systematic iconography could be composed. So much is implied by the statement that paintings around the king's bed were in existence by 1267.[24] This can be taken to mean that the bed and its surrounding walls were decorated; that the paintings were orientated around the bed. A contention of this argument is that the *picturae circa lectum* of 1267, which clearly comprised an expensive component of the work conducted after 1263, can be identified as the Coronation of St Edward behind the bed, the splay figures of St Edward and St John opposite the bed, and the figures of the Triumphant Virtues, eight in all, on the remaining window splays of the room (fig. 3). The coherence of these images as a programme is demonstrated by their identity of style, by their integrity of theme, and by their relationship to the room as a whole, reflecting the rules of social restraint and precedence which on the most formal level governed its use. The documentary evidence shows that the bed itself already possessed the salient features of later medieval beds of estate. In 1244 it is recorded that it had posts and curtains, implying the existence of a large *celour* or canopy which could have been of textiles or painted woodwork.[25] It was surrounded by rich textiles, a clear mark of its status.[26] Its tester, the wall at the head of the bed, was filled with the Coronation painting, a 'wide image' of the sort ordered by Henry for the royal bed at Havering in 1251, indicating the more widespread use under Henry of such big bed images.[27] The Coronation image, itself canopied with the same kind of arcading as that found over the royal pews in the Sainte-Chapelle in Paris of the 1240s (pl. XLIX), was presumably surmounted by the *celour* (fig. 2). This was iconographically appropriate, as canopies supported on posts were held over the king or queen during the ceremony of the coronation itself.[28] The panelling of the bed in 1253 could have opened the way to figural decoration too, perhaps with further material concerning St Edward, linking the Coronation image to the equally narrative-derived scene of St Edward giving the ring to St John on the splays of the window opposite the bed.[29] Thus envisaged, the bed would have been as cogent an assertion of Henry's immediate, physical identification with the saint-king as was his later occupation of the Confessor's old grave in Westminster Abbey.[30]

The symbolic importance of such large canopied enclosures cannot be overstated. The social use of royal beds as a focus of court activity can be traced in such accounts as Joinville's descriptions of the habits of St Louis, gathering together his intimates with him at the foot of his bed to discuss matters concerning the dispensation of justice.[31] By the fourteenth century such furnishings were central to, indeed defined, the formal royal *séance* in France. The paraphernalia of the French *lit de justice*—strictly speaking not a bed at all, but rather an elaborate seating-place—comprised a cordoned-off space in the king's great chamber, with inside a structure of canopy, backdrop, pillows and rich textiles specially constructed for the *séance*; the *lit de justice* was, like the earlier state bed at Westminster, a chamber within a chamber, the whole assembly coming to symbolize justice or judicial kingship.[32] The iconography of the Wesminster bed had a similar connotation to that of the formal *lit de justice,* not only because it was a prominent structure associated with the person of the king, but also because it possessed an imagery pertaining to just and virtuous kingship. Here, kingship was manifested in the imagery of coronation,

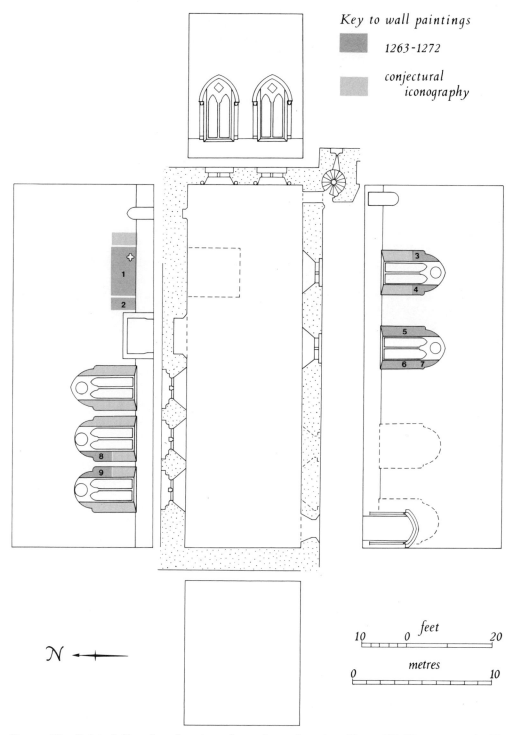

FIG. 3. The Painted Chamber: location of murals attributed to Henry III (Cat. nos. 1–9). The broken line indicates the site of the king's bed (east wall at top of page)

charity, wisdom—implied by the location to either side of the bed structure of the Guardians of Solomon's Bed—and the suppression of vice. The bed, lying at the heart of the English royal *séance* (and conceivably also the embryonic parliament, although the evidence is unclear here), drew together the highest values of the court circle. In being continuous with the splay imagery opposite the bed, the iconography of the Virtues extended the moral qualities of the royal audience out beyond the structure of the royal bed into that area of lower status towards the west end of the room. The Virtues were not, accordingly, shown facing each other across the window void; *Debonereté* did not turn to face *Largesce* in the south window; rather, both figures turned westwards to address those assembled in the western half of the room furthest from the bed (col. pl. II).

The Coronation and splay images were not, then, a loosely related series of images, but rather consisted of a formal systematic programme reflecting the internal disposition of the chamber and the symbolic content of the bed. They constituted a discrete unit, separable from the Old Testament scenes in the room in meaning and in the way they were read. The regular layout of the Old Testament stories in bands meant that they were read sequentially, the movement of the spectator in a sense blurring the distinctions of status inherent in the layout of the king's chamber as conceived by Henry III. The Old Testament scenes united the room decoratively in a narrative sweep, whereas the Coronation and splay paintings divided it up into sectors of status corresponding to the distribution of Henry III's furniture. Their strategic, as opposed to narrative, layout attests to the influence of some of the guiding principles of French portal statuary. The splay figures were architectonic in nature, constrained in each case by a canopy painted on the receding splay surfaces in the manner of French portal jamb statues. The Virtues borrow the common sculptural motif of trampling their opponents, the Vices. Above them, on the window soffits, were vigorously posed angels holding crowns, forming in effect an abbreviated voussoir, while beneath them were less consequential paintings corresponding to a figured socle. Similarly, the Coronation was prominent, frontal and static, and also climactic, the counterpart to the French non-narrative sculpted portal tympana of the period. It was visually separate from the splay paintings, but, as on a monumental sculpted façade, it enjoyed an iconographic relationship with them, much as a tympanum might to the jamb figures below. The juxtaposition of two seemingly disconnected sets of murals, one concerning an Anglo-Saxon saint-king and the Virtues, the other biblical narratives of a very different mood and order, each arranged separately, appears of itself to be suggestive of two campaigns of thought in the room, each responding to independent decorative needs. Is there, then, evidence that the imagery of St Edward and the Virtues was current at the time of Henry's redecoration of the king's chamber in the 1260s?

The iconography of St Edward (Cat. nos. 1–4)

The Coronation of St Edward (col. pl. I, pls. I, II) shows the frontally seated saint, with archbishops Aelfric of York and Eadsige of Canterbury and other ecclesiastics to either side. The whole scene is identified by the prominent uncial text CEST LE CORONEMENT SEINT EDEWARD. As he is crowned, Edward is given the dove-headed sceptre.[33] The scene as copied was imperfect, but its contents can be established from the fact that this iconography recurs in two later manuscripts containing coronation iconography, both associated with Westminster: the so-called 'Merton' *Flores Historiarum* (Eton College, MS 123) of *c.* 1300, which employs this imagery for its representation of the coronation of Edward I (fol. 237), and the Westminster Abbey copy of the *Flores* (MS 24) of the early fourteenth century, where the image is used for the coronation of King Arthur (fol. 83).[34] The Merton *Flores* version (pl. XXXVI) reproduces literally all the features of the central group in the mural: the deep blue ground, the poses and gestures of the figures, the position of the sceptre, and the crosses held aloft to either side (mistakenly painted over in the manuscript). The occurrence of just this coronation imagery in *Flores* manuscripts suggests the approximate date by which this iconography was formed. The other major repository of coronation iconography in this period is the Manchester *Flores* (Chetham's Library MS 6712), the compilation and illustration of which began in the mid-thirteenth century.[35] The Chetham manuscript's version of the coronation of St Edward (col. 433/34) belongs to that part of the manuscript executed before *c.* 1265 (pl. XXXVIIa). It is unlike the Westminster mural in being stylistically more conservative, in including the anointing (which appears not to have been represented in the king's chamber),[36] and also surrounding the central group with peers rather than ecclesiastics. But the general conception of the image is strikingly similar. The main group is extended by a throng of tall and slender figures, which are set off against a dark background held within the rectangular picture space, a pictorial format used in the contemporary saints' lives being produced at St Albans or Westminster.[37] There is little reason for doubting that the king's chamber scene derived its contents from a model of approximately the same form and date as the Chetham *Flores* picture; either from such an historical compilation, or a set of narrative pictures. The Chetham series of coronation scenes runs up to Edward I, but its earlier, pre-1265, representations are in a style which is immediately antecedent to that found in the Cambridge manuscript life of St Edward, *La Estoire de Seint Aedward le Rei* (Cambridge University Library MS Ee.3.59) of shortly before *c.* 1260.[38] The Cambridge manuscript has iconographically similar coronation imagery to the *Flores* compilations and the Westminster mural (pl. XXXVIIb).[39] There is, therefore, a series of manuscripts with a related iconography connected in one way or another with the St Albans and Westminster sphere. The Chetham *Flores* was associated with both St Albans and Westminster before finally passing into Westminster hands in the mid-1260s.[40] The text of the Cambridge Edward seems to be directed specifically to a Westminster audience, and is dedicated to the Queen.[41] The later 'Merton' and Westminster Abbey *Flores* manuscripts were in all probability Westminster compilations, using older iconography.

These works provide evidence for believing that the Coronation in the *magna camera* could certainly have been in place by 1267, or indeed rather earlier. It is not impossible that such a picture adorned the chamber before the 1263 fire, and that it was reproduced in a stylistically up-to-date form in the post-fire years. Henry's *penchant* for St Edward and his imagery was well established by the 1240s, from which period onwards serious work on provision for his new shrine was under way.[42] There is no documentary proof that this subject decorated the room before 1263. But its attendant iconography of the Guardians of Solomon's Bed and the splay figures opposite the bed, of St Edward and St John, could sustain this view. The image of the bed guard (pl. III) was drawn from the Song of Songs (iii, 7–10) and had already been used in association with the royal bed at Winchester in 1250.[43] Crocker copied one guard from the Coronation's right flank, surmounted by the same sort of cusped arcading as that over the Coronation, and presumably continuous with it as part of one decorative idea.[44] Space was available for a corresponding guard on the other side of the bed. The comparatively direct nature of this Solomonic reference may also be borne out by Henry's choice of green textiles and paintwork for the bed in the 1240s, perhaps in allusion to the text *lectulus noster floridus* (Song of Songs, i, 16). Thus, given that the location and decoration of the bed with which these paintings were associated were established in the 1230s and '40s, that the Coronation could have been using a mid-thirteenth-century iconography, and that the image of the guard was used at Winchester in 1250, it is possible that the *picturae circa lectum* of 1267 were at least in part an older theme in the room.

This is certainly supported by the figures of St Edward with the ring and St John in the guise of a pilgrim, painted on the splays opposite the bed (pls. IV, V). Although the splays were physically detached from the Coronation, their subject-matter enjoyed a programmatic relationship with it, and can accordingly be seen as a facet of the bed imagery. The bed acted in the same capacity as a focus of images as thrones did under Henry. Seats painted with kingly figures are recorded under Henry's patronage; even when unoccupied, they retained a sign of their symbolic importance.[45] St Edward and St John, two saints close to Henry's heart, were painted by the king's seat at Guildford in 1261, for instance.[46] This idea of confronting a royal seating-place with images of saints of special importance was not, of course, the sole preserve of Henry III. The location of St Edward and St John opposite the Westminster bed brings to mind the locating of key saints—St Denis and St Margaret—in the painted medallions of the upper chapel of the Sainte-Chapelle in Paris, directly opposite the king's and queen's pews (pl. XLIX*a*).[47] The paintings of Edward and John represent a pregnant moment from the life of St Edward when the king gave a ring to St John in disguise, who subsequently returned it to him as a token of his imminent demise. The ring brought back to St Edward corresponds to the palm of Paradise brought to the Virgin Mary before her death. Pictorially, the ring story was formulated in mid-century illustrations like that on fol. 26 of *La Estoire de Seint Aedward* (pl. XXXVIII*a*) in Cambridge.[48] The splay paintings conform closely to this type of model, and resemble, too, the public working out of the theme in sculpture beneath the rose window of the south transept of Westminster Abbey.[49] The image was ubiquitous, and would hardly have been remarkable in the king's chamber of the 1260s.[50] Indeed, of all the imagery in the room, that of St Edward would have had the most continuous history of interest to either side of the 1263 fire; especially so afterwards, as preparations intensified for the translation of the saint to his new shrine in 1269.[51]

The iconography of the Triumphant Virtues (Cat. nos. 5–9)

The scale, appearance, and presentation of the figures of Virtues on the remaining splays of the room show that they were part of the same sequence of images as those of St Edward and St John opposite the bed. Like the Coronation, the execution of this subject-matter is not explicitly recorded in the documentation; but its date and importance can still be inferred. Four of the original eight figures were copied.[52] On the south window splays were *Largesce–Covoitise* and *Debonereté–Ira* (pl. VI); amongst the figures from the north window splays only *Vérité* was identified by name (pl. VII), with one other Virtue, perhaps Fortitude (pl. VIII), bearing a spear and round shield.[53] The Virtues were tall and slender, crowned and holding their shields and attributes, and wearing mail armour. Their format was one derived from portal statuary, a genre which may have provided Henry with other, similar, themes, such as the Wise and Foolish Virgins painted amongst the pictures in the queen's chapel at Windsor in 1242.[54] The distinctive trampling motif was used, too, on the metal image of St Peter placed on the Confessor's shrine in the late 1260s *calcantis Neronem*.[55] *Largesce* stands over *Covoitise* (col. pl. IIa); she holds a long unstrapped purse between the third and fourth fingers of her left hand, from which gold coins spill out into the glutted mouth of the Vice. The Vice, laden with money-bags, writhes under the spear held in *Largesce*'s right hand. *Debonereté* displays her shield prominently, and holds a tapering bundle of rods over *Ira*; the Vice tears its hair (col. pl. IIb). In the spirit of the masculine decoration of the choir aisles of Westminster Abbey of the years *c.* 1260, the Virtues are surrounded by brilliant heraldic display.[56] The block borders by *Largesce* contained the arms of England and the Empire, while *Debonereté* had England, St Edward and St Edmund. Her shield was a differenced version of the arms of England.[57] The socle paintings beneath, copied by Crocker (pl. VI), were beyond useful identification, but seem to have comprised less consequential genre scenes identified by small texts.

The theme of the standing Triumphant Virtue was an old one, and can be traced in England back to the Romanesque sculpture of the Stanton Fitzwarren and Southrop fonts.[58] Seated Triumphant Virtues are found *c.* 1220 on the floor roundels once by the shrine of St Thomas at Canterbury.[59] The standing type was, however, the subject of new interest in the third quarter of the thirteenth century. A similar iconography to that at Westminster occurs within the Lambeth Apocalypse group of manuscripts. This is a significant inclusion, for these manuscripts represent an advance towards some of the stylistic features found in the Westminster murals. Folios 34^v and 39 of the Lisbon and Abingdon Apocalypses respectively illustrate Berengaudus's commentary on the Fourth Vision of the Book of Revelation, xiii, 1, concerning the Beast with seven heads.[60] The seven heads are said to signify seven Vices, over whom seven Virtues are shown in triumph. In the Lisbon Apocalypse (pl. XXXVIIIb), the Virtues are arrayed in two rows, and like those at Westminster are crowned, armed, and bear attributes. In the lower row *Largitas* wields a sword and showers coins from her left hand into the mouth of the corresponding Vice.[61] At Westminster, the Virtues are crowned; but they also had angels floating over them bearing crowns. This iconography could be said to correspond to the central theme of the Coronation in the room. It had Christological forbears; thus we find a counterpart to it in the illustration to Psalm 91, verse 13 on fol. 163 of the twelfth-century Eadwine Psalter, a copy of the Utrecht Psalter (Cambridge, Trinity College MS R.17.1), where Christ tramples on a lion and a coiled serpent and is crowned from above by an angel armed with a spear and shield. It may be more immediately related to an image in the contemporary English *Summa* of Vices by Peraldus (BL Harleian MS 3244, fol. 28) of a knight in emblematic armour confronting Vices, being crowned by an angel, an iconography with further points of contact with the Lambeth Apocalypse.[62]

The sculptures of the chapter-house portal of Salisbury Cathedral of *c.* 1280 (pl. XXXIX) also attest to this renewal of interest in the Triumphant Virtue theme.[63] The Salisbury sculptures, like those of the northern porch of the west façade of Strasbourg Cathedral of around the same time,[64] have in common with the Westminster images not only an architectural context, but also a certain refined meekness, far removed from the tough vision of conflict in the *Psychomachia*.[65] The Salisbury Virtues are arranged on the voussoir of the portal. Each stands beneath a canopy, armed, crowned, and trampling its respective Vice. Similar pairings to those at Westminster occur, notably *Largitas–Avaritia* and *Patientia–Ira*.[66] *Largitas* dispenses coins, not from a purse, but from a long ladle, into the mouth of *Avaritia*; nor does *Patientia* conform to Westminster's *Debonereté*. The switch held by *Debonereté* is instead the attribute of *Justitia* at Salisbury.[67] The iconography of the two cycles is therefore distinct.

The incomplete record that we have of the Virtues in the king's chamber means that we cannot reliably trace the source of this particular selection. The theme was comparatively rare. For this reason, its appearance in English illustrations of the commentary on the Apocalypse by Berengaudus executed *c.* 1260 or in the 1260s, and at Salisbury *c.* 1280, has some significance for the date of the Westminster group, if not its iconographic genesis.[68] The Virtues could very well have been on the walls of the king's chamber by 1267.

The images in the king's great chamber and the patronage of Henry III

The iconography of St Edward and the Triumphant Virtues in the king's chamber can reasonably be identified as the principal component of the *picturae circa lectum* mentioned in 1267, and probably under way after the 1263 fire. Viewed in the light of Henry III's patronage of certain themes, this assembly of images makes good sense as a programme. It can be seen in terms of the type of material brought to bear on the life of St Edward in the courtly Life of St Edward in Cambridge, the text and pictures of which certainly pre-date the work in the king's chamber of the 1260s. In *La Estoire de Seint Aedward* we find an eloquent account of the good state of the kingdom following the coronation of St Edward; the king is held up as the law-giver and virtuous monarch who imbues the court with wisdom and courtly bearing through the royal audience. He is compared to King Solomon. His tranquillity and largesse are celebrated.[69] The thematic interest, and indeed the mood, of the images in the king's chamber are encapsulated in such passages. The mood is calm, joyous and benevolent. Edward is sometimes shown smiling with spiritual satisfaction in *La Estoire*, a reminder of an episode of literal concern with the expressions to be worn by images executed for the court in the 1240s.[70] The kingdom is united by Edward's virtuous nature; this theme found further pictorial expression in the mural ordered by Henry in 1243, of a king and queen sitting with their baronage, to be placed over the dais of the new hall in Dublin Castle.[71] The Solomonic allusions in the text of *La Estoire* are striking.[72] Imagery associated with King Solomon as a type for wise and ideal kingship occurred at court in a number of ways under Henry: in the coronation order; in the appearance of the throne on the second Great Seal of 1259;[73] in the choice of the story of Solomon and the jester Marculph for a painting in one of the chambers at Westminster in 1252;[74] and perhaps also in the choice of shields to adorn the choir aisles of Westminster Abbey.[75] The theme retained its potency at court later in the century.[76] But it is surely significant that the Coronation in the king's chamber was closely associated with Solomonic ideals, through the presence by the bed of the Guardians of Solomon's Bed. We could go so far as to suggest that the Solomonic connotation of the bed placed the Virtues in the chamber in fundamentally the same relationship to this cumulative image of saintly and biblical royal authority as that of the Virtues and the Throne of Wisdom in that synthesis of Solomonic and Marian iconography of the high medieval period, the *Verger de Soulas*.[77] At Westminster, the Virtues represent the ideals of the court and household of Henry III envisaged in terms of the chaste presence of St Edward; Edward is, as the text of *La Estoire* demonstrates so amply, the debonair king *par excellence*, and it is his arms that are found in the block borders beside the figure of *Debonereté*. This is, perhaps, the sort of imagery adumbrated in a different context by the household of Virtues assembled with the Emperor Henry VI in an illustration in Peter of Eboli's *Liber ad Honorem Augusti* (Bern, Bürgerbibliothek Cod. 120, fol. 146).[78]

The scheme of paintings in the king's chamber of the 1260s represents, then, a cogent illustration of Henry III's view of his kingship, and the content of this scheme is all the more telling when we recall that it was shaped in the midst of the political upheaveal of the Baron's War. Whether or not these murals were conceived in the light of the political events of the 1260s depends to some extent on whether their iconography represented a genuine innovation of these years. As we have seen, it would have been iconographically feasible for at least some of these paintings—notably the Coronation and Guards—to have been present in prior form before the 1263 fire. We cannot be certain, as there is no documentary proof for this supposition. The scheme of things in the 1260s certainly suggests one thing: that the king's chamber murals were gaining an increasingly formal content. What is recorded of the pre-1263 murals implies that the initial scheme was much more loosely arranged, and in a sense thinner of content: we have the Evangelists, one on each wall, specified in 1243; lions in the gable; and the Jesse Tree executed in the late 1250s.[79] There is the additional problem of the *magna historia* referred to in 1237. What this was is a mystery. The term itself denotes something with a narrative content; and the term is all we have. There are two general possibilities. As no mandate for its execution was given out in the 1230s, and as Henry ordered that it should be conserved, it is conceivable that this was one of an earlier set of paintings in the room—perhaps pre-dating Henry's accession—which Henry wanted to retain in his conservative phase, much as he wanted to retain older murals at Winchester and Rochester in the 1230s.[80] On the other hand, the *magna historia* may have been the same as the *mappa mundi* which is incidentally mentioned as in the king's chamber at Westminster in a source connected with Matthew Paris (Paris is in fact held to have copied the *mappa mundi* in his ordinal); a date in or before the 1230s could not be ruled out for such an image, but there is, of course, no guarantee that the Westminster map was actually a wall painting.[81] Yet however we interpret the first work of Henry in the room, it seems in principle to have been less high-minded than the post-fire scheme, nor was it so organically tied to the topography and function of the king's chamber.

Henry's last scheme represented the culmination of his precise sense of image-placement; a sense that emerged in the 1230s with his early maturity, and remained in many essentials constant to the end of his reign. Of this sense there is much documentary proof. In 1236, Henry ordered that a Wheel of Fortune should be painted in the Great Hall at Winchester Castle in the gable over the dais.[82] In 1235–6 the story of St Edward was painted in the chancel of the chapel of All Saints at Clarendon, and the pictures around the king's seat were illuminated and varnished.[83] In 1236, at the time of the king's marriage, curtains were painted behind the king's and queen's beds at Woodstock, like those behind the king's seat and bed at Marlborough.[84] In 1234–5 a glass window with a Crucifix and St Mary and St John was placed in the window at the head of the bed at Ludgershall.[85] In 1240 the roof of the king's chamber at Geddington was to be repaired, as the paintings over the king's bed had been damaged by rain; in 1242 the Wise and Foolish Virgins were painted *inter alias picturas* in the queen's chapel at Windsor.[86] In 1246 a picture of a city was to be painted opposite the door of the queen's chamber at Winchester.[87] In 1247 a new fireplace with a Wheel of Fortune and a Jesse Stem was made at Clarendon.[88] In 1250 paintings of the Guardians of Solomon's Bed were painted by the king's bed at Winchester.[89] In 1256 an image of St George was placed over the king's entrance to the Hall at Winchester.[90] In 1259 a pall was painted over the king's bed in his chamber at Guildford, while in 1261 a screen was made at the end of the king's table in his hall there, towards the entrance to the king's chamber, with painted figures of St Edward and St John; the same images were painted by the king's seat in his chapel.[91] In 1269–70 the image of a king was painted behind the king's seat in the Hall at Geddington.[92]

Similarly for Westminster. In 1236 crosses were painted next to the green seats of the king and queen in St Stephen's Chapel.[93] In 1238 the story of Joseph was to be painted above the royal seat in the small chapel by the king's chamber.[94] In 1245 Henry ordered that St Mary should be painted on the outside of the king's seat in St Stephen's Chapel, in such a way that her image could be seen by the king as he came down from the Great Hall.[95] In 1240 the image of Winter was painted by the fireplace in the queen's chamber.[96] In 1256 the story of the King of the Garamantes, rescued from his seditious subjects by his dogs, was painted in the garderobe where the king was wont to wash his head.[97]

From these and many other instances, a pattern emerges in Henry's thinking.

He thought in terms of a central repertoire of images—principally hagiographic ones—which remained constant throughout his life. He extended this repertoire to almost every significant royal residence, in much the same way that he was content to reproduce certain practical arrangements over and over again: witness the similarity of the bed arrangements at Westminster, where a painted chapel was located by the king's bed, with a glazed window in between, to those at Winchester, Woodstock and also probably Ludgershall, under Henry.[98] He was constant in his love of the imagery of St Edward.[99] He liked a fairly direct form of moralizing, parable-derived iconography, such as Dives and Lazarus and the Wise and Foolish Virgins, and ordered surprisingly little narrative biblical material. He was especially specific about the location of images by beds or seats, or at other significant points in a room. For Henry, their meaning was not self-contained, but was shaped by their physical application. He wished to look upon the humbling, suspicious, message of the story of the King of the Garamantes while he was, in a sense, humbled by the act of head-washing. Dives and Lazarus were to preside over his feasts.

Henry's mandates reflect a conservatism and a sense of ritual no less apparent in the murals in the Westminster king's chamber of the 1260s. What marked these paintings out was that their content was geared more specifically than at any other residence to the expectations of a Westminster audience. Henry's choice of the iconography of St Edward and the Virtues is understandable in terms of his desire to root his kingship in the person of a sainted royal ancestor whose cult was especially associated with Westminster.[100] With this desire went a growing sense of the true location of English government. Westminster was emerging not only as the administrative heart of the realm, but also as the focus of its historical identity; the *Flores Historiarum* was continued there in the same way as the official French royal chronicle, the *grandes chroniques,* was continued at the abbey of Saint-Denis.[101] Colvin has remarked with reason that, in these years, 'what Reims and St Denis were to the house of Capet, Westminster should be to the House of Plantagenet'.[102] The Coronation and Virtues accordingly combine ideas present in the historical imagery of the *Flores* manuscripts; and in current royal hagiography, particularly the virtuous and unifying example of the life of St Edward celebrated in contemporary court literature. Coronation imagery was appropriate to this time and place, for Westminster's coronation order was a matter of active interest.[103] Taken together, the images in the great chamber attest to that sense of the theatricality of monarchy that has been attributed to Henry III; a sense that triumphed even in the midst of the struggles of the 1260s. The murals in the king's great chamber resolutely and calmly asserted that 'at Westminster with its great hall, palace and abbey, the monarchy stood at the centre of a strife-torn but resilient community'.[104]

The style of Henry III's murals: introductory remarks

In iconographic terms the case for identifying the paintings concerning St Edward and the Virtues in the king's chamber as works of Henry's reign is a strong one. In principle, it should allow us to narrow down their date with considerable precision. What was copied in 1819 is likely to have been executed after the fire of 1263. By November 1263, 10 months after the fire in the chamber, paintings were already projected for it as well as the chapel behind the king's bed, a scheme consonant with the report in the *Annales Monastici* that both rooms were damaged by the fire. The paintings were plainly in progress by the autumn of 1264, when attention was turned to the financing of their gilding; and work continued on them throughout the years 1264 to 1272. The most specific clue to the progress of work is provided by the large payment in 1267 for work including the paintings around the king's bed; from this time onwards, resources were increasingly divided between the decorations in the palace and the abbey, approaching the time of its dedication.[105] This means that the planning, drawing and painting of the Coronation of St Edward and its attendant paintings on the window splays must have been primarily the work of the period 1263 to 1267. By implication, the style of these murals should therefore have been one representative of the early to mid-1260s rather than the early 1270s.

Such a dating, if tenable, would provide a chronological landmark of the greatest value for our understanding of developments in English painting in these years, lying as they did in a period of undisputed importance in the emergence of Gothic figural styles. In practice, however, ascertaining the appearance of the earliest work copied in the chamber is not entirely straightforward, as Wormald and others have noted.[106] Here we confront two related problems. Bearing in mind that Edward I was active in the chamber in the 1290s, is it possible that he, rather than Henry, was responsible for the imagery of St Edward and the Virtues? Second, to what extent may Henry's murals have been reworked during later campaigns under Edward? A premise of this discussion has been that the iconography of St Edward and the Virtues in the king's chamber was particularly fitted to the known interests of Henry III, and that a corresponding date should follow. But we have also noted in passing that Edward's tastes were not so well documented as those of his father, owing to his different use of the Chancery administration. Thus it could be objected that there is no intrinsic reason why Edward should not have liked the imagery of the royal saint as much as did his father, and why he should not have executed such imagery in, say, the 1290s. Such an attribution would, of course, undermine the chronology of the oldest work in the room outlined here. But there are, in turn, good reasons for disposing of this problem. In the first place, it would be based on argument *e silentio*. There is no evidence that Edward was as prone to the public celebration of the royal cult as was his father. Second, the documents make it plain that Henry III planned significant paintings for the bed area of the chamber of the 1260s. If we attribute the Coronation of St Edward and the Virtues as copied to the reign of Edward I, we must suppose either that Henry's bed-images were not concerned with St Edward and the courtly Virtues, or that they were, and that Edward radically revised their appearance. So far as the first point is concerned, the balance of evidence is strongly in favour of Henry III having had such themes in the king's chamber at around the time of the translation of the saint and maximum royal interest in the cult, and so in close association with the chamber's central feature: its bed. Iconographic discrimination is essential to the matter; what was fashionable, even topical, in the 1260s may not have been so towards the end of the century. If we attribute the St Edward material to the 1290s, we would have to offer some account of why it was only then that imagery of this type was introduced into the scheme. On the other hand, the notion that Edward retained older imagery is not problematic. How else can we explain the repairs that did take place in the 1270s and late 1280s? There is no evidence that the layout or function of the king's chamber changed during his reign, or that older murals would have ceased adroitly to express that layout or function.

The extent to which Henry's paintings were subsequently revised is a separate question from their attribution. We know that Henry's murals were repaired twice under Edward, in the 1270s and again in the 1280s, as well as in 1307–8, when the accounts refer specifically to repairs to windows—presumably the window splays—as well as the walls in the *camera depicta*.[107] Stothard included the figure of *Debonereté* on one of the south window splays amongst those works he thought repainted. Whatever value we attach to his somewhat cryptic remarks, it is possible that the window splay paintings may have been the most physically vulnerable of all those in the room, being most nearly exposed to the elements; repairs to the paintings in the 1280s took place at the same time as repairs to the glazing of the room.[108] They were potentially the most susceptible to repair. As to the exact physical constitution of such repairs, the copies are evasive, for they project to us works by and large of smooth consistency rather than vigorous palimpsest. The copies show no signs of the type of *pentimenti* we might expect to find in murals that had been subjected to radical alteration. Despite this, the documentary evidence for activity in the king's chamber in the 1290s has led previous writers to suggest that the stylistic identity of Henry's work could have been submerged by late thirteenth-century repairs; as Wormald succinctly put it, 'these monuments can, therefore, be as late as the 1290's or as early as 1265'.[109] While the iconography of these paintings may have been a product of the 1260s, their style might not.

In the absence of the paintings themselves, we can hardly make dogmatic statements as to the original appearance of Henry's scheme. Certain considerations should lead us to question the idea that its original appearance was wholly lost. In the first place, by 1292, when Edward certainly turned his mind to an extensive redecoration of the chamber, his father's murals were only two decades old; it is improbable that they would have decayed so badly in the period 1272–92 as to require wholesale repainting, especially as they had been repaired by Edward in the intervening years. Secondly, it is most unlikely that the documented work of the 1290s in the room was concerned solely with the repair of paintings; a contention of this argument will be that this campaign saw the execution of the very extensive cycle of Old Testament scenes, and so the intervention of an entirely new programme of murals. The dating, and indeed the importance, of this cycle has been neglected by authorities such as Wormald and others, who simply regarded the activity of the 1290s as conservative in nature.[110] The Old Testament scenes reveal the true direction that Edward's mural iconography is likely to have taken in the last years of the century. So costly must this scheme have been that it is hard to envisage more than marginal outlay on earlier, but not very old, murals in the room. Finally, the theory that work of the 1260s could have survived later repairs in essentially its original form is supported by the extensive evidence that one master painter was employed regularly at the head of the workshop in the Painted Chamber from the 1260s right through to the 1290s: Walter of Durham, *pictor Regis*.[111] Walter is first mentioned by name in 1265, working at both the palace and the abbey, and is linked to the king's chamber as master from 1266.[112] His last work there was in 1297. So dominant was his position that it is probable that he was responsible for planning all the schemes carried out in the room in the 1260s and 1290s, and that whatever developments took place there occurred under his aegis. His employees certainly changed; but he must have been in a position to control whatever repairs took place to earlier paintings that had initially been his responsibility. If the documents showed that a radically different workshop intervened in the king's chamber in the late thirteenth century, we would have good grounds for supposing that the history of its paintings was discontinuous, and that older paintings there were unsympathetically revised. But no such circumstantial break in their history occurred. On the contrary, when a new master was finally employed in the room, in 1307–8, it was Walter's son, Thomas of Westminster, *magister in officio pictorie*. Thomas inherited the work of his father's career and perpetuated a family interest in it, for he had been employed as an assistant in the king's chamber under his father in the 1290s. These are all signs that the Painted Chamber embodied a tradition; that the paintings were marked by the sustained preferences of those who executed them, as well as by the changing tastes of kings. It may be significant in this respect that Stothard's remarks betray a certain ambivalence as to the radical nature of the repaintings in the room, for he remarked that 'notwithstanding its having been twice repainted, it still retains in most places the original compositions, as well as some of the minuter forms'.[113] Even if we concede that the style of Henry's murals may have become marginally more impure as the century drew to a close—and there are reasons for our doing so—we could also argue under these circumstances that the first work of Walter of Durham of the 1260s exerted a powerful influence on what was subsequently added; that the style of the Painted Chamber was shaped by advances made there at the end of Henry's reign, revealing both continuities and discontinuities in style.

The most important single argument for attributing the style of the Coronation of St Edward and its relatives to the 1260s is a comparative one. A number of features of these works can be paralleled in both English and French painting that may, with reasonable confidence, be dated to the third quarter of the thirteenth century. Here again, the issues are complex ones, many of them going beyond the scope of this work. Few of the examples of manuscript and panel painting that bear on the Painted Chamber at this stage of its development are precisely dated, and for none can the documentary precision of the dated campaigns in the Painted Chamber be produced. The dating of these works is still contingent upon current opinions as to their style. This is particularly true of the two works that bear most closely on the murals in question: the Westminster Retable and the Douce Apocalypse in Oxford. Both shed light on the Painted Chamber to the extent that they are surviving instances of a similar idiom produced under royal patronage. Yet both present controversial problems of stylistic interpretation and dating; indeed, the dating of these works has depended to some extent on how the chronology of work in the Painted Chamber has been understood. To avoid this vicious circle of argument we must try first to place Henry III's murals in their most specific context before considering them in the light of more general developments in English painting in the second half of the thirteenth century.

Stylistic parallels

The Coronation and splay paintings (col. pls. I, II, pls. I–VIII) formed a tightly knit stylistic as well as an iconographic group. In each case the figures were of considerable size, the Coronation mural being 1·73 m. in height, the Virtues filling the window splays to a height of about 3·05 m. These paintings were all placed just above eye-level, their scale calculated to make an impression on the walls of the king's chamber. Their colour palette was similar and distinctive, using subdued crimsons, olive greens and deep blues; flesh tones were dense but subtly modelled. The garment forms were conceived in the same way. In the Coronation the robes of the ecclesiastics fell in heavy broad folds, while the garments of the Virtues had crisp angular pouches of cloth, the hemlines pulled into straight and taut lines. The stress on straight and angular hemlines was enhanced in all these figures by the use of broad gilt geometric patterns on the hems, comprising scrolls, roundels or diapers of varying complexity. This criss-crossing of the figures with sparkling embroidered hem patterns counterbalanced their sombre coloration. The heads and hands were delicately and elegantly executed. The mass of ecclesiastics in the Coronation was enlivened by placing the heads not only frontally, but also in strict profile and three-quarter profile. Male heads, such as those in the Coronation or that of the pilgrim St John, had broad brows, narrowly placed eyes, long noses and quickly narrowing chins; the mouths turned gently downwards. Beards were softly curled and bulged outwards from the jawline. Hair was twisted up into complex convoluted curls. The left hand of *Largesce* made an affected gesture whereby the second and third fingers were spaced widely from the fourth and and fifth. In all the figures the irises and pupils were pushed into the far corner of the eye, lending to their gaze an intense form of squint; irises were prevalently pale, perhaps grey-green or blue.

All these distinctive features can be exactly matched in the illustrations in the Douce Apocalypse (Oxford, Bodleian Library MS Douce 180) and on the Westminster Retable in the south ambulatory of Westminster Abbey. A close analogy exists, for example, between the Coronation painting and the illustration of Revelation, xviii, 15, on page 75 of Douce.[114] The Douce picture (pl. XL) has exactly the same tight grouping of tall figures, whose garments fall in big, simple folds; the heads are small and elegant, turned in dialogue and shaped in the same ways as those in the Coronation painting; the hands are composed with mannered and calculated gestures, a celebrated feature of the figure style of this work. Douce also provides a convincing parallel for the angels located on the window soffits over the Virtues at Westminster, sketched by Buckler in 1819 and included in a drawing of the room in the 1820s by Stephanoff.[115] The angels were cramped into an awkward site, but their location was turned to advantage by the painters to set off figures composed with the vigour and peculiar complexity favoured by the Douce artist, especially in drawing angels (pl. XLI*a, b*). The head of the copied angel was small and framed by tight curling hair. The left arm swept across the right to hold a crown over the Virtue. The feet were large with spread toes, and the hems wide and simple, filled with the same sort of geometric devices as those garnishing the hems of the Virtues beneath. The pose of this figure is strikingly similar to that of the angel floating at the top of page 45 of Douce illustrating Revelation, xii, 10–12, and the overall composition of the angels over the Virtues (pl. XXVIII) is reminiscent of the angel and the Woman on page 46 of the same work. The brittle profiles of the figures of the Virtues and ecclesiastics and the broad, hard edges of the folds of their garments, are characteristic of the figures in Douce, which provides parallels, too, for the use of a very similar repertoire of hem patterns, as well as for the contortions of the fingers of *Largesce*'s left hand.

Although the range of stylistic information provided by the murals was relatively small, there can be no doubt as to the immediate similarities these works had to the Douce Apocalypse. The paintings on the Westminster Retable provide even closer parallels. The Virtue *Largesce* appears to have been a monumental counterpart to the figure of the Virgin holding a palm on the central section of the Retable (pl. XLII*a, b*). Each figure is constrained in a narrow, architecturally defined space in the manner of the figures of St John peering into his vision of Revelation in Douce. The capitals of the canopy arch over *Largesce*, although shrivelled in scale, are similar in design to the capitals of the tabernacles on the Retable. The heads of *Largesce* and the Virgin are covered with a veil and are bent slightly forward; the right arm is raised at the elbow. The head of the Virgin is executed in a very similar way, with gently arching brows, softly modelled flesh, and with the irises and pupils characteristically pushed into the far corner of the eye. In each case the iris is pale and the eyelids delicately defined. The Virgin's mantle is cast around her right arm and elbow in precisely the same way as that of *Largesce*. The lining just peeps out and the hemlines are adorned with a gold pattern of foils; the hem pattern on the upper part of *Largesce*'s mantle is almost identical to that running around the collar and cuffs of Christ in the scene on the Retable of the Raising of Jairus's Daughter. The Virtue's gown is gathered up and pinned, claspless, to her body by her right elbow, and thence the folds pull straight downwards into a cone-shaped flare which turns swiftly and abruptly over to cross the figure's lower portion. The cloth and folds have a stiff, shiny, almost metallic quality, shaped as if the hems were so heavily embroidered as to obstruct their free movement. They form sharp points when curled over. These fold conventions are precisely reproduced on the figure of St John opposite the Virgin on the Westminster Retable (pl. XLII*c*). Here the hems have a Cufic-derived pattern similar to those used in the sister manuscript of the Douce Apocalypse (Paris, BN MS lat. 10474) and recorded also on the figure of St Edward on the window splay opposite the bed in the king's chamber. As on *Largesce*, St John's mantle comprises complexes of big conical forms, all subtly modelled. Other figures on the Retable provide counterparts to the drapery forms used in the Coronation. The slow and straight fall of the hems on the figure of Christ from the centre of the Retable matches those of the Coronation. The figure of Christ in the medallion showing the Feeding of the Five Thousand on the Retable has a long, massive body and tiny, shapely head. The profile of his back is dead straight and vertical, and the garment falling from his right arm has a simple diagonal hem which forms a long, downward-pointing triangle, the short side formed by his collar. This is extremely close to the second bishop from the left in the foreground of the Coronation painting (pl. XLIII *a,b*). Indeed, the general composition of the scene of the Feeding of the Five Thousand bears comparison with that of the Coronation, for the heads of the Apostles, like those of the various bishops, are disposed on a horizontal line, and are relatively small and neat by comparison with the dark and massive garments beneath. The heads in the Coronation are not only constructed in the same way as those on the Retable, but are also turned hither and thither like their counterparts on the panel.[116]

The colouristic and decorative tendencies of the Coronation and splay paintings are also directly related to the Retable (col. pls. I, II, VI). The colours used on the Retable figures are dominated by a dark wine red, olive green and a deep greenish-blue, with isolated notes of orange and suave, brown-grey flesh tones. Highlighting on the garments is distinctive, and was achieved by building up glazes of lighter tones on darker. The rich body of the Retable colours and their subdued quality is strongly suggested in the Painted Chamber copies. Decoratively, the Coronation and splay paintings had more in common with the Retable than with the Douce Apocalypse. The repertoire of gilt (and slightly raised) ornamental patterns on the Retable garments is almost identical to that recorded in the Coronation painting. On a few occasions these patterns can also be found in the Douce Apocalypse. The cusps of the canopy arches over the Virtues are shown bearing a series of small studs set along the lines of the tracery which match the glass beading used on the cusps of the three principal arches on the Retable. The spandrels of the splay-painting canopies had red fields surrounding tracery oculi, ornamented with fine gilt ivy-leaf scrolls. These are close to the splendid red and blue glass inserts in the frame of the Retable, likewise covered in comparable gilt foliage and treated with the same taste for detail. The gentle texturing of the shafts of the splay canopies is matched on the central columns of the middle section of the Retable, although the patterns are different. The frame of the Retable is adorned with numerous artificial enamel plaques set under glass. These, together with the lavish gilding, create the effect of metalwork noted by Wormald.[117] They are of a brighter and more acid hue than the paintings themselves. But they can be matched satisfactorily on the canopy cusps of the Coronation painting, where painted enamel patterns alternated with plaques of scrolled foliage, the fields of the cusps being darkly coloured like the Retable's glass inserts.

The Coronation and splay paintings thus shared with the Retable not only a significant number of precise stylistic features, but also the same decorative taste, a taste revelling in rich material substance, combining sophisticated paintwork with colourful gilded surrounds, favouring the same strong sense of actuality and detail of information. All these features argue for production in close practical proximity of the murals and the panel and perhaps other items of furniture—such as the king's bed—arguably enriched in a way similar to Westminster Abbey's ecclesiastical furnishings.[118]

Comparative dating

The close relationship between the murals in the king's chamber, the Douce Apocalypse, and the Westminster Retable, is not hard to demonstrate, and has been generally accepted in the literature on the subject.[119] The analogies to the Retable tell all the more when we recall that the panel was unknown to the copyists, having been rescued from oblivion only in 1827. The dating evidence for the chamber could suggest that this style was developed in the court circle in the 1260s; but this requires at least tentative confirmation from the point of view of Douce and the Retable, as well as of those works providing a general context for this remarkable series of paintings. The murals in the king's chamber, Douce and the Retable, are but three instances of a style which emerged rapidly and widely in England, but especially—and indeed seminally—in France, in the mid-thirteenth century; a style that was undoubtedly coming to transform the appearance of the figurative arts in England in the 1260s. This style was marked principally by the development of the so-called 'broad-fold' idiom of depicting drapery, whereby garments were no longer shown hanging in soft, troughed loops (as in the manner of those drawings attributed to Matthew Paris in England, or Villard de Honnecourt in France), but instead hardened into flat, angular surfaces often articulated by strong modelling of the forms. The Westminster paintings under discussion are celebrated instances of the broad-fold style, and their dating must take this into account.

This style was associated internationally with tall figures, elegant suave postures and small heads with neatly curled hair. The emergence of these features in first French, and then English art from the mid-thirteenth century has been described elsewhere.[120] In France, the broad-fold style was stimulated in painting by a strong wave of influence from the innovatory sculpture *ateliers* of the Île-de-France employed at Paris and Reims, and elsewhere, in the second quarter of the century.[121] Robert Branner observed that this style penetrated French wall painting as early as the 1240s, the central evidence being provided by the wall paintings produced under royal patronage in the upper and lower chapels of the Sainte-Chapelle in Paris in the 1240s.[122] Parisian book-painting soon followed suit,[123] as did French glass-painting at, for example, Amiens in the 1260s, Saint-Urbain at Troyes, *c.* 1270, and Beauvais before 1284.[124]

The first signs of this style appear in England in the late 1250s. This is attested by sculpture and manuscript painting. An early instance is provided by the seal of Hugh de Balsham, Bishop of Ely, dated 1257.[125] Progress in sculpture was rapid, for further evidence is provided by the effigies of Bishop Bridport (d. 1262) and Bishop Walter de la Wyle (d. 1271) at Salisbury, the heart memorial to Bishop Aymer de Lusignan (d. 1260) at Winchester, the effigy of Bishop Aquablanca (d. 1268) at Hereford, and the sculptures in the Angel Choir at Lincoln, before 1280.[126] Little precise dating evidence survives for the acquisition of these new traits by English wall painters. The sole example of wall painting that can be attributed to court patronage of the 1250s, the remnant of a series of royal figures painted in the Dean's Cloister at Windsor, seems to reflect a style also found in the courtly *La Estoire de Seint*

Aedward le Rei in Cambridge.[127] This shows that some *rapprochement* pertained at this stage between miniature and monumental painting, comparable to Douce's later relationship to the king's chamber at Westminster. Save for a series of poorly preserved murals, perhaps attributable to Edward I, recently noted at Chester Castle,[128] all significant wall painting of the court from this period has been destroyed. Very tentative influences from the broad-fold style can be seen in the murals executed in the nave of St Albans Abbey, and on the vaults of the chapter house of Oxford Cathedral, but these are not precisely dated and fall outside the immediate sphere of court patronage.[129] It is conceivable that court wall painting was moving in this direction in the 1250s; but it is also no more than hypothetical.

The antecedents of Henry's work can best be traced in miniature painting. The influence of the broad-fold idiom has been noted in a series of manuscripts worked on in the 1250s and 1260s, which exhibit marked French influence. The most outstanding of these are the Trinity College Apocalypse (Cambridge, Trinity College MS R.16.2), *La Estoire de Seint Aedward,* the Lambeth Apocalypse (Lambeth Palace Library MS 209), the Lisbon and Abingdon Apocalypses, the Oscott Psalter (BL Add. MS 50000), the Metropolitan Psalter (New York, Metropolitan Museum MS Acc.22.24.1), and a series of biblical illustrations belonging to a psalter in Cambridge (St John's College MS K.26).[130] Of these, five in particular are related stylistically and iconographically to each other and to the Westminster murals: *La Estoire de Seint Aedward,* the Lambeth, Lisbon and Abingdon Apocalypses, and MS K.26 in Cambridge. We have already noted that the coronation iconography in *La Estoire de Seint Aedward* is related to that in the king's chamber, while the imagery of the Triumphant Virtues there is close to that in the Lisbon and Abingdon Apocalypses (pls. XXXVII*b*, XXXVIII*a, b*). In terms of their style, *La Estoire de Seint Aedward* and the Lambeth Apocalypse are strictly speaking transitional, for the broad-fold idiom can be seen emerging in them in the course of their production (so attesting to the innovatory impact of the new style). One hand employed in the Lambeth Apocalypse, that responsible for the Antichrist scenes on fols. 11^v–13 as well as the series of narrative and devotional illustrations appended on fols. 40–53^v of the manuscript, employs the broad-fold style in a particularly mannered and hard way, depicting figures with extreme proportions, unnaturally lengthened limbs, and garments forged into ample, but angular and strongly shaded folds.[131] The Westminster murals do not resemble this style especially closely. Their figures are comparably monumental, but are smoother and more elegant in manner, their garments having a more lustrous and composed finish. Much better analogies to this style are to be found actually within the sequence of Apocalypse illustrations in the Lisbon and Abingdon manuscripts, whose iconography depends closely upon the stylistically less advanced Lambeth Apocalypse. Their similarities to the murals are both technical and stylistic. Unlike *La Estoire de Seint Aedward* and the bulk of the work in the Lambeth Apocalypse, the Lisbon and Abingdon Apocalypses make extensive use of full-colour paint rather than bistre washes laid over the preliminary drawings. The pigments, especially in the garments, are sometimes thickly laid on, and modelling is achieved by building up light tones on darker ones in a manner similar to fully painted *secco* mural painting, or panel painting.[132] The smooth and confident tonal gradations found in the Lisbon manuscript (pl. XLIV) are related to the lush effects in the Westminster murals and the Westminster Retable. The drapery forms of the Westminster murals correspondingly resemble closely those within the Lisbon and Abingdon Apocalypses, for both employ the rather stiffened conical and triangular fold-forms present on *Largesce* and on the figure of St John on the Retable (pls. XLII, XLIV). The murals are therefore allied both to the first phase of the broad-fold style, present in the popular Apocalypses, and to its more polished second manifestation in Douce and on the Retable.

The odd illustrations in MS K.26 in Cambridge fall precisely into this stylistic milieu, for they are related to the Lambeth Apocalypse group and the Oscott Psalter while also presenting us with idiosyncrasies found in the king's chamber.[133] In common with the Westminster group is a certain lugubriousness of manner; but of more particular importance is the use in this manuscript of dark, fully painted broad-fold draperies which employ a broad band of geometric ornamentation on the hemlines, coarser in detail than the murals, but contributing to a similar overall effect. The garments of God from a Creation scene on fol. 3 of MS K.26 (pl. XLV*a*) are composed in a manner close to those of *Largesce* at Westminster, the cloth tugged around the arm with the hemline jabbing down to a point by His left knee. The construction of the male heads in MS K.26 also compares with those on the Westminster Retable; the swept-back hair of God on fol. 3 is not unlike some of the bearded faces on the Retable (pl. XLIII*a*), and in common with the Retable small strokes by the nose are employed to depict the nostrils; and amongst the beardless youths in the miracle scenes on the Retable can be found the round, podgy features of the extraordinary angels with Abraham on fol. 9 of MS K.26 (pl. XLV*b*). The richly modelled and adorned mode of MS K.26 seems to be little more than a coarsened version of the Westminster murals and the Retable in the abbey, and could even imply their existence.

Do these manuscripts, which cumulatively present a number of the essential features of the murals, shed any light on their date? Formally speaking, these works tend to suggest a fairly close formation in time, and it may be worth noting that some features of the mature style of Douce, such as the splendidly coiled hairstyles of its male figures, have already emerged on certain figures in the Lisbon Apocalypse (notably one of the angels on fol. 15^v; pl. XLIV*b*). However, the absolute chronology of this sequence is disputed, nor is it at all certain where all these manuscripts were made. Of them, only *La Estoire de Seint Aedward* can confidently be ascribed to an *atelier* either at Westminster or, less probably, at St Albans.[134] On stylistic and textual grounds this book could have been prepared for a court audience (it is dedicated to Eleanor of Provence and compliments Henry III) shortly before 1260.[135] More valuable circumstantial evidence is provided by the Abingdon Apocalypse, which it has been convincingly argued was commissioned and owned by Bishop Giles Bridport of Salisbury before his death in 1262.[136] As the Abingdon Apocalypse is more advanced stylistically than the Lambeth Apocalypse, and depends upon it iconographically, there is therefore a presumptive case for dating both the Lambeth and Lisbon Apocalypses before 1262 as well; on internal evidence, Lambeth must date to before 1267 and could be taken to date before 1264.[137] It has also been proposed persuasively, if not conclusively, that the Oscott Psalter was commissioned in the mid-1260s, in which case a corresponding date for MS K.26 cannot be ruled out.[138]

The history of this group of manuscripts, in so far as it can be ascertained with any precision, suggests that the broad-fold style emerged in miniature painting at the same time as it did in sculpture, in the late 1250s and 1260s. In the light of this, there is every reason to believe that this idiom was available, in turn, to the *atelier* of wall painters that assembled in the king's chamber for its post-fire redecoration in 1263. The date of *c.* 1263–72 proposed here for the king's chamber murals would conform admirably to the maturing period of the broad-fold style in England. It would also make sense in the context of French metropolitan painting. An antecedent broad-fold style had already appeared in the murals of the Parisian royal chapel in the 1240s, and it attained a stage of maturity parallel to that of the Westminster murals in Parisian work of the period 1250–70, notably the Padua Psalter (Padua, Seminario MS 353), the Assisi Missal of *c.* 1255–6 (Assisi, Museo del Sacro Convento), the Saint-Denis Missal of after 1254 (BN MS lat. 1107) and the St Louis Psalter of *c.* 1255–70 (BN MS lat. 10525).[139] Having noted that the Westminster murals are related to some of the first examples of the broad-fold style in England, we can also argue that their relatively greater refinement was in part a product of a particularly fertile period of contact between the French and English broad-fold styles falling in the 1260s, and owing some of its momentum to the patronage of the court circle. If so, then we may have a case for supposing that the related style of the Douce Apocalypse and the Westminster Retable, understood separately from the works themselves, was also a creation of the 1260s.[140] Since the style of the murals must have been basically established by the time of the reference to the programme in 1267, we may assume that the point of departure for this style in other media was related not to the approximate completion date, around 1272, but rather to the period of the preparation of the murals, here attributed to the years *c.* 1263–7.[141]

Opinion is divided over the date of the Douce Apocalypse itself (pls. XL, XLVII, LVII). Its pictures have been dated on stylistic grounds to the 1260s or 1270s, but not later.[142] The manuscript is dated circumstantially to the extent that its prefatory, but unillustrated, French Apocalypse text has an opening initial depicting the Lord Edward and Eleanor of Castile heraldically appropriate to the years 1254–72.[143] This indicates that the French part of the book at least was begun before 1272, and this date margin can be slightly narrowed when Edward and Eleanor's departure from England on crusade in 1270 is taken into account; they remained abroad until 1274.[144] Douce's pictures belong to the second, Latin, text to which no internal dating evidence really applies.[145] As the script and ruling of the French and illustrated Latin parts is extremely close, the 1254–72 date for the French part could also apply to the Latin one; but on the most pessimistic analysis it could be maintained that the whole of the Latin part was begun after 1272 or, at least, that only the text of the Latin part was begun before 1272.[146] It is quite uncertain how long after 1254 the texts were begun. The style of the opening Edward–Eleanor initial differs from that of the pictures, and could point to a date well inside the 1260s; but this is not a strong argument for a much later start on the pictures.[147]

The painting of text initials and of narrative illustrations are activities of a different order of status which could exist closely in time; thus, the facts that the style of the pictures differs from that of the opening initial, and also that the pictures and some of the remaining initials in the text are incomplete, are not evidence for separate campaigns of work on the book.[148] The incomplete state of the Douce Apocalypse could be explained by an interruption in its financing, loss of interest by the patron, or indeed the departure of the patron from the country, as occurred in 1270. The evidence of the king's chamber implies that the style of Douce could well have appeared before, rather than after, about 1270. Peter Klein, on the other hand, has argued that Douce post-dates the murals, on the grounds that Douce may have been accommodating new features of Parisian miniature painting appearing in the 1260s or 1270s which account for its sharp elegance and mannerism.[149] The mannered tenor of Douce's illustrations must, of course, also be seen in the context of the artist's particularly rich and vivid conception of how the text of *Revelation* should be communicated pictorially, an intrinsically different exercise from composing formal, monumental decorations for a king's chamber. Again, a style like Douce's was known to the artist of BN MS lat. 10474, a book intimately tied in style and iconography to a work of the 1250s, the former Dyson Perrins Apocalypse.[150] How much experimental material pertaining to the emergence of the mature and accomplished style of Douce and the murals has been lost from the court circle of the 1260s? Douce offers us qualities which set it and the Retable to one side of contemporary English and French painting; it has a clarity of vision, a love of direct observation and an almost mocking propensity for facial caricature, indicative not so much of particular sources, as of the workings of an unusually ingenious artistic imagination. So talented and incomparable is the Douce artist in the execution of his task that we cannot be sure that this work was not under way before 1270, and that it did not constitute a skilled and cosmopolitan variant of the style of the king's chamber.

The dating evidence for Douce does not, in any event, cast doubt on the attribution of the king's chamber murals to the period 1263–72 proposed here. With the Westminster Retable we are presented with problems of a greater order of magnitude. It is a unique instance of its type; and it is quite undated circumstantially. If it could be shown that it was originally intended to adorn the high altar of Westminster Abbey, there would be strong presumptive reasons for supposing that it was in place by 1269, the date of the dedication of Henry III's new fabric. If so, then the Retable would be a product of the same phase of royal patronage as that responsible for the murals in the king's chamber. The evidence for linking the Retable to these particular functional and historical circumstances is, however, so complicated as to extend beyond this survey of the Painted Chamber. The Retable's position in the history of painting styles in this period is understandably disputed; wherever we locate it in time, we seem to be presented with inconsistencies which suggest that no definitive solution to the problem will be found.

One of the hardest questions to be resolved is the nature of its relationship to Douce, and so by implication the nature of the relationship of manuscript and panel painters employed by the court. There is no reason to doubt that both come from the same stylistic milieu. The general similarities of figure style in the two works are celebrated.[151] Both use a certain type of pattern on the hemlines of garments. The architectural details employed on the Seven Churches on the opening pages of Douce reveal incidental points of contact with the Retable. The gabled canopy over the Son of Man on page 3 of Douce is close to the architecture of the central section of the Retable, reproducing its rhythm of wide and narrow bays, weighty arches, capitals and curled crockets (col. pl. VI, pl. XLVII). The cusps of the arches are filled with dark pigment corresponding to the deeply coloured glass inlays in the Retable's architecture. Page 34 of Douce, illustrating the Measuring of the Temple, Revelation, xi, 1, also reveals the proximity of motifs in Douce and the Retable (pl. XLVI*b*, *c*). The bases of the shafts supporting the canopy of the Temple are supported on tapering brackets identical to those found propping up the thick shafts of the Retable canopies which project from the plane of the painted surfaces and are lifted up over the cavetto of the frame. Tucked into the scene of the Raising of Jairus' Daughter on the Retable is an aedicule with the same type of curled crockets and heavily inscribed foil as those represented in Douce's Churches (pl. XLVI*a*). Also, the spatial sense of the medallion scenes on the Retable has numerous parallels within Douce's narratives: compare the manner of composing crowds, such as the Five Thousand on the Retable, with the worshippers gathered in the Temple as in Revelation, x, 1, on page 34 of Douce. The physiognomies of the Retable are fundamentally those of Douce: compare St Peter with the standing Witness on page 35 of Douce, or the hooded, dome-headed figure on the left of the scene of the Healing of the Blind Man on the Retable with the whiskered and prostrate Witnesses on page 38 of Douce. On the other hand, there are discrepancies. The heads and hair on the Retable are more softly drawn. There is no exact parallel in Douce to the soft coiffures of the beardless figures in the Feeding of the Five Thousand scene. The hair of the bearded figures on the panel is swept back from the brow rather than being knotted up tightly like the hairstyles in Douce. The hair of the Blind Man on the Retable falls onto his shoulder in the same type of curls as those of St John to the right of the scene of the Angel with the Millstone on page 77 of Douce; but the finish of the curls is more material, more sensual. The anatomy of the Retable figures is considerably less tough and vigorous than Douce's; the figures are looser of limb and the joints less securely articulated. Although conspicuously masterly in its painting technique, the Retable has an element of limpness not related to the agile, objective style of Douce.

These are good reasons for believing that Douce and the Retable are not products of the same hand, or at least one hand at the same stage of its development. With the king's chamber murals, we have in effect four variants of this basic Westminster idiom, including the Retable, Douce, and Douce's sister manuscript (BN MS lat. 10474).[152] The stylistic evidence tends to suggest two groupings for these works: the king's chamber murals and the Retable; Douce and its sister manuscript in Paris. Thus there would seem to be evidence for separating off the activities of the panel painters from those of the miniaturists, and placing them very much nearer the wall painters. Documentary evidence from the period reveals at least two cases where court wall painters—Peter of Spain and Walter of Durham—were directly associated with the production of painted panels for the abbey; there is no corresponding evidence that panel and manuscript painters were so linked.[153] The similarities between the Retable and the palace murals indicate that the remarkable finesse of the panel represents a compromise between the technical and decorative procedures of contemporary court wall painting and the small-scale handling of miniaturists' work (obviously suggested by the incised gilt grounds of the paintings). The Retable specializes in the minute treatment of facial features, curls of hair, glossy fingernails and (within the globe held by the blessing Christ) landscape, which lends to its images a detached, mystical luminosity and clarity. By comparison, the images in Douce are harder and drier, more generalized. Douce's style is linear where the Retable is painterly. The panel's colour range is markedly different from Douce's. The manuscript uses a bright red, browns, blue-greys, a kingfisher blue and orange, whereas the panel has a stricter and so more sophisticated palette of dark reds and greens with milky, opalescent highlights not found in the manuscript. The most dynamic aspect of the Retable's coloration is provided by the heraldic reds, greens, blues and golds of its ornamental frame. The later monumental paintings in Westminster Abbey, the sedilia, St Faith and the saints in the south transept,[154] employ the same repertoire of reds and greens as the panel, suggesting again that the Retable can be viewed not only in a miniaturist's, but also in a monumental decorator's, context. The tonalities of the panel accordingly resemble, as do its decorative methods, those of the king's chamber paintings, and it is from this sphere that the character of the Retable as a public object must derive. The Retable shows that certain forms of painting were capable of miraculous reductions in scale, reminding us almost of the flexibility of French Rayonnant architecture in expanding in scale here, and shrinking there, without diminishing its effect.

The differences between the Retable and Douce may arise, therefore, not so much from different dates as from a technical or institutional separation of panel and manuscript painters at court, which could nevertheless allow for cross-fertilization. However, a further area of debate has been opened up in recent scholarship which presents a different view of the date-relationship of the two works. What may be called the orthodox dating of the Retable to *c.* 1270 has been questioned on the grounds that its exquisite paintings compare not only with Douce, but also with certain north-eastern French, and especially Parisian, miniaturist styles of the period *c.* 1280–1300. Parallels have been adduced with a particular group of manuscripts representing the high point of the so-called *style Honoré*, named after the obscure *Mestre Honore d'Amiens* mentioned among book painters in Parisian tax documents of the 1290s:[155] a copy of the *Somme le Roi* in London (BL Add. MS 54180), the Breviary of Philippe le Bel (BN MS lat. 1023), and the Nuremberg Hours (Nuremberg, Stadtbibliothek MS Solger in 4°, 4).[156] The most tangible and impressive of these parallels is provided by the Moses scenes on fol. 5ᵛ of the London *Somme le Roi*, wherein we recognize remarkably similar softly curled and shaded hairstyles and physiognomies to those of the Retable, and equally smooth modelled garments (pls. XLIII*a*, XLVIII). At first sight these similarities are so plausible that the dating evidence for the London *Somme*—before 1295 but in the 1290s—beckons also for the Retable.[157] The *style Honoré* represented by this small group of late thirteenth-century manuscripts indeed forces us to return to the question raised at the start of this section on the style of Henry III's murals; namely, to what extent could their style have persisted and developed into the last decades of the century?

A central issue is whether the Retable is to be seen as a dependant of the *style Honoré* (which, if true, would imply a very late date for it), or as an independent and earlier manifestation of the same general idiom drawing on English prototype styles. The idea that English court art could have anticipated certain aspects of Parisian manuscript painting is hard to square with the orthodox view that initiatives were taken only in France and were merely followed in England in this period. Some authorities have, nevertheless, supposed that a measure of influence from England can be traced in north-eastern French and Parisian miniature painting including the Honoré group.[158] A number of features of the Retable suggest that it need not have been literally dependent upon the *style Honoré* proper, of the 1290s. First, there is evidence that a form of the Parisian soft styles was emerging in miniature painting linked to London or Westminster in the period before *c.* 1290. Notable in this respect is the work done on the *Beatus* page (fol. 11) of the courtly Alfonso or Tenison Psalter (BL Add. MS 24686), dated before 1284.[159] The elaborate coiffure, softly formed garments and fiddly fingers of the princely harping David inside the *Beatus* initial suggest some connection with an idiom like that of the beardless figures in the Feeding of the Five Thousand medallion on the Retable. The Retable is also linked to London work of the period *c.* 1270–90 represented by the Windmill Psalter (New York, Pierpont Morgan Library MS M102), which, although not strictly in the soft style of the Retable, employs some of its characteristics, particularly the broad, gilt hem patterns, a curious and self-conscious tautness of posture, and the tendency to place the eyes close together with the pupils squinting into the far corner of the eye.[160] Secondly, close examination of the Retable reveals important discrepancies with the *style Honoré* which militate against dependence on it. While figures in the *Somme le Roi* have relatively broad proportions, those on the Retable are extremely elongated, notably from the hip downwards. The Retable figures are also considerably more dynamic; there is nothing in the *style Honoré* to compare with the extraordinary squirming and writhing of figures on the panel such as the hooded man to the left of the scene of the Healing of the Blind Man, or the youthful Apostle to the left of the Feeding of the Five Thousand, whose right shoulder-blade is inventively thrust towards us, his face almost hidden away like that of the crouching capped figure in the bottom right of the scene. The comparable groups in the London *Somme* or the Dormition scene on fol. 22 of the Nuremberg Hours are much less preoccupied with this sort of self-conscious posing; they seem to be more conventional, blander, more spent of energy. In this sense the Retable betrays its absolute dependence not upon the *style Honoré*, but rather upon that taste for contrived postures, emphatic gestures and swivelling stances typical of the earlier Apocalypses, notably Douce and lat. 10474.[161] The Retable's eschewing of mere prettiness, its mobility and piquancy of style, is stamped most clearly on the physiognomies of its figures. Unlike the round, practised smoothness of the faces in the London *Somme* or the Nuremberg Hours, the features are pinched, eyes are small and exceptionally close together, noses are long and brittle, and the features slither around regardless of bone structure. Finally, while the garments of one figure on the Retable, St Peter, have the softer flexible hemlines of the later styles, the fold forms are in general heavier and firmer, more inclined to form straight hems, and so are closer to the king's chamber murals and other initiatory examples of the broad-fold style. Thus, while the Retable shows some signs of the softer aesthetic of the Parisian miniaturists, it is not certain from this that the panel represents a parallel to the *style Honoré* so much as an adumbration of it, building skilfully on advances made in works properly datable to the third quarter of the century.

A further (and neglected) dimension to this question is added by the style of the Retable's decorative frame. While the narrative scenes were disposed in eight-pointed stars in the manner of metalwork or *opus anglicanum,*[162] each of the standing figures, St Peter, the Virgin Mary, Christ, St John and one lost figure (St Paul?), is placed under a gabled trefoil arch supported on strong shafts, with robust capitals and tall spires (col. pl. VI).[163] As Viollet-le-Duc implied, and Lethaby noted, the style of the frame is more French than English.[164] It resembles the fabric of the abbey only at those points where notably French details are used. The location of a rounded trefoil in the three main gables of its canopy-work was a feature of the original gable of the north transept of the church completed *c.* 1260, and based generally on a design such as the west front of Amiens.[165] The tracery painted in gold on the glass inserts of the spires is like that of the apsidal chapels of the abbey, and so shares its *Rémois* orientation.[166] The decoration of the gables with foliage motifs, and the use of small rectangular devices painted along the outside of the gable over St John, are reminiscent of the treatment of the gables on the west front of Reims.[167] In fact, were it not for its paintings, the Retable could legitimately be classed as a pure instance of Parisian applied architecture, and, most importantly, architecture not of the 1280s or '90s, but rather of the 1240s or '50s. The uniformly rounded foil forms, the tough comma-shaped crockets, the spires, square or polygonal capitals and bases, are close to examples of French metal micro-architecture; especially to datable works such as the *châsse* of St Taurin at Évreux, completed by 1255, the reliquary of three saints from the Sainte-Chapelle in Paris dated 1261, and the great *châsse* of the Sainte-Chapelle destroyed in 1791, but known from old drawings.[168] The Retable is as well attuned to the standards of metropolitan—one is tempted to say court—design in France as the canopy-work over the Coronation painting in the king's chamber, which alludes in its rhythm of pointed and broad segmental arches and big quatrefoil shape to the dado arcading of the Sainte-Chapelle itself (pl. XLIX). Taken as an ensemble (as it should be), the Retable therefore confronts us with a paradox, its paintings bearing comparison with the *style Honoré*, its decorative surrounds consistently rooted in French practices of the mid-thirteenth century. It copies faithfully the type of enamel and gilt ornamentation found on French metalwork such as the Évreux *châsse*. The honeycomb of blue glass over its central gables is identical to that found on one of the mid-thirteenth-century retables at Saint-Denis.[169] The foliage-tailed, two-legged wyverns painted in gold on blue on the central gable are like those in the frames of certain miniatures in the Isabella Psalter (Cambridge, Fitzwilliam Museum MS 300) made for the royal French *capella* shortly after *c.* 1255.[170] Lethaby was undoubtedly correct in relating the panel to the rich, metalwork-derived applied polychromy of the interior of the Sainte-Chapelle of the 1240s.[171]

This consideration is at odds with the view that the panel should be dated substantially later than Douce or the king's chamber murals simply on the grounds of its advances towards the *style Honoré* of the 1280s and 1290s. The architectural details of its frame are quite uninformed by later thirteenth-century, French-inspired metalwork such as the (now largely destroyed) shrine of St Gertrude at Nivelles (after 1272), which shows that in this period Continental *ars sacra* was responding punctually to tenets of contemporary Rayonnant architecture.[172] The *style Honoré* itself (pl. LVIa) uses impeccably up-to-date, late thirteenth-century French designs which should have been picked up by dependent or closely related works.[173] In contrast, the Retable is responsive rather to those forms used by French court miniaturists of the 1260s.[174] Is there then a case for supplying a late date for the Retable and excusing its undoubtedly early features on the grounds of wholesale, perhaps even self-conscious, conservatism? Such a case, which has the ring of special pleading about it, has to be examined in the light of developments at Westminster in the last years of the century considered in the next chapter. Even in English terms the Retable is considerably more archaic than products of the Westminster court masons of the 1290s, such as the tombs of Aveline, Queen Eleanor and Edmund Crouchback in Westminster Abbey.[175] The Coronation Chair, made in 1300–1 under the supervision of Master Walter (pl. LIIIb), is no more *retardataire* than any other instances of applied architecture of the period in the abbey such as the canopy-work of the sedilia in the sanctuary.[176] These, and other, examples will be examined in the context of the Old Testament scenes in the Painted Chamber, which show that by the 1290s court painters were absorbing those design forms characteristic of the *style Honoré,* and putting them to new and refreshing use. The emergence of the new Edwardian court styles in the 1280s and '90s does not provide a suitable visual environment for the Retable, which is by any standards a sizeable and prestigious object, an object which should have reflected the latest trends, and yet which, viewed decoratively, is quite out of keeping with examples of court micro-architecture of the 1290s such as the Westminster tombs. The detailing of the Retable finds no counterpart on the tomb chests of Aveline or Crouchback (pl. LXa), with their repertoires of square-section traceried buttresses and pointed trefoils.

Nor is this argument vitiated by the fact that we find some examples of Westminster painting of the years towards 1300 which employ older forms in a piecemeal fashion. Gables with comma-shaped crockets and trefoil arches retained their popularity, not only in the Old Testament scenes, but also in the case of the canopy over the figure of St Faith in St Faith's Chapel in Westminster Abbey (pl. LXII), here believed to be a substantially later work than the Retable because of the highly developed, meandering hemlines of the garments on the figure which resemble the sedilia paintings in the abbey (pl. LXIII).[177] The important point to note is that these forms were being used by now within the context of an architectural aesthetic increasingly foreign to that represented by the Retable. St Faith's gable type, with its fleur-de-lis finial and crockets, compares well with an example copied from the story of Hezekiah in the Painted Chamber, of the 1290s (pl. XVa), while the bulging capitals are extremely similar to those of a building in the story of the Famine in Samaria (pl. XIVa). But in all these examples, the architectural members now comprise skinny, grey or white tracery lines; the effect is essentially buoyant and delicate, unlike the heavily polychromed metalwork-like language of the Retable. The fact that the painters could employ older motifs to enrich their already considerable range of architectural devices is something that could perfectly well argue for the influential nature of the Retable's forms, rather than for the lateness of the Retable itself. Indeed, the Retable can only be described as relatively late if conclusive proof that its painting style was only possible by the 1280s or '90s can be found; and to date no such proof has been forthcoming. The evidence of the Old Testament scenes in the Painted Chamber is important in this respect in showing that, by and large, the compositional techniques and vivid mannerism typical of the Retable had already passed out of use by the 1290s. Some of the decorative features of the Retable inevitably persisted in the Old Testament scenes: notably the use of geometric gilt hem patterns. But this suggests only that the long career of Master Walter of Durham, from the 1260s through to the 1290s, saw a build-up in this workshop's repertoire of small-scale devices. In these terms, the Retable could very well have fitted into an earlier phase of Walter's œuvre linked in time to his first work in the palace in the 1260s. It is so wholly archaic in its decorative outlook, so narrowly concerned to reproduce the effects of French metropolitan art of the third quarter of the century undiluted by their later interpretations in the hands of the Edwardian court masons, that we have a strong case for placing it near the start of a phase which saw the gradual adaptation of French micro-architectural forms in England.

That this phase was under way by *c.* 1270 is surely proved not only by Douce, but also by the king's chamber murals. The taste for enclosing tall figures in surrounds composed of slim gilt members, so typical of the splay paintings there, is fully in accord with the use throughout Douce of gilt lines to circumscribe its strongly patterned figure compositions. The rose windows in the spandrels by the heads of the Virtues compare as closely to contemporary tracery designs in use at Lincoln Minster as the two-light windows surmounted by a quatrefoil next to them do to the windows in the lateral wings of the façade of Binham Priory, now dated by Bony to *c.* 1270.[178] The plain crenellations at the top of the splay compositions, lacking the rows of foils characteristic of English work of the 1290s, are used throughout Douce and its sister manuscript in Paris. We have already seen that the French idiom of the Retable is reflected in the canopy-work over the Coronation painting and in the detailing of the surround of the quatrefoil window within it. The use of these small-scale, but up-to-date, motifs provides a convincing prototype for the more fully fledged, and indeed dominant, use of such forms to shape the compositions in the later Old Testament scenes, newly enriched by motifs emerging in English court art and elsewhere in the years around 1290. As some details in the Old Testament scenes show, notably the small rose windows set into the citadel of Thebez in one of the Judges stories (pl. XX), which reproduce the rose forms in the gables over the scenes in the St Louis Psalter, court painters of the 1290s owed a considerable and continuing debt to earlier Parisian sources. It is likely that this sensitivity to ultimately Parisian forms had already appeared in work undertaken in the last years of the reign of Henry III.

Conclusions

The arguments presented in this chapter amount to the following. In the first place, there are sound documentary, iconographic and stylistic reasons for attributing the murals of the Coronation of St Edward and the window splays of the king's chamber at Westminster to the period 1263–72. Second, it follows from this that the style of not only Douce, but also the Westminster Retable, was formed in this period. The Retable's likely place in the sequence of styles in this period is naturally, and properly, a matter of debate. The more developed elements in its style, notably its relaxed and mobile figure compositions, may lend some weight to the view that it should be placed either at the end of the 1263–72 campaign in the king's chamber to which it is related, or somewhat later; but how much later is not something which the available evidence really allows us to decide. In architectural terms, as we have seen, the Retable could well belong inside the third quarter of the thirteenth century. The chronology proposed here certainly casts doubt on the view prevalent in much writing on the problem that the Retable is to be seen wholly in terms of the *style Honoré,* and should be dated accordingly. On close inspection the analogy with the *style Honoré* does not survive especially well, and, more importantly, begs several questions. Is the magnificent quality of the Retable a criterion of its date, or of the abilities of the workshop that produced it and the status of the patronage that brought it into existence? To what extent does the analogy with the *style Honoré* considered generically as embracing developments in northern France and the Paris region obscure the Retable's evident debt to the mature and vivid visual world of the English Apocalypses, so peculiarly fashionable in the third quarter of the century? Is it legitimate to base any speculation as to the date of a panel painting on the evidence of miniature painting produced under quite different circumstances, in the absence of any serious consideration as to how panel and manuscript painting related in this period, or even as to what the Retable was? Indeed, is the *style Honoré* itself to be seen as the beginning, or the end, of a series of developments which started in France and England in the 1260s and '70s; if the end, should it be taken as the standpoint from which to assess the history of developments throughout the late thirteenth century?

At the start of this chapter, the extent of French influence at the court of Henry III was deliberately questioned, partly because there is no evidence that Henry (unlike Edward I) chose specifically French themes for the decorations of his residences, and partly because the dating and significance of his work at Westminster in the 1260s can be assessed to some extent in terms of English art of the 1250s and '60s. But it would be misleading to suggest that French influences were not felt at all. The Westminster Retable illustrates the close, if problematic, relationship between French and English art in this period; in this sense it, as much as the murals in the king's chamber, stands as the central problem of English painting in the second half of the thirteenth century. From

this time onwards, the authority of French standards was increasingly acknowledged by English architects, painters and sculptors, and it is in this context that
we must shortly examine the work of Edward I in the Painted Chamber. The
transformations in English painting of the third quarter of the century,
although ultimately producing masterpieces such as the Douce Apocalypse,
whose style and imagery have no true French counterpart,[179] must nevertheless
be seen against a more cosmopolitan background. There is no reason to doubt
that the English court was in a position to act as a focus of international ideas.
Thus, the style of the king's chamber murals considered so far is generally
compatible with those miniature styles selected by Robert Branner as being
representative of Parisian manuscript painting of the years 1250 to 1270,
culminating in the increasingly fluid styles of the French royal psalters.[180] It is
tempting to suggest that this Westminster style originated in episodic or more
sustained contacts between English and French painters, of the sort proposed
by Branner between the William of Devon Bible style—in a sense the most
French of all English bookpainting styles of this period—and the *Grusch atelier*
in Paris.[181] All that is lacking is any documentary proof; the Westminster court
painters of the 1260s and 1290s appear to have been English to a man.

What is also lacking is a solid body of evidence for the appearance of French
court wall and panel paintings from this time. The only basis for comparison is
provided by the somewhat earlier decorations in the Sainte-Chapelle, executed
in the 1240s, especially the figures in the lower chapel and the medallions in the
dado arcade of the upper chapel.[182] Although badly affected by the ravages of
time, and now known principally through good nineteenth-century copies,
these seem to have anticipated features of later Westminster painting in their
use of a broad-fold style, increasingly active and complex postures, and an
elaborate range of decorative additions. But the links between this idiom,
presumably typical of French royal taste and adumbrating a number of features
of the royal psalters, and that of Henry, are missing, and can only be recovered
imperfectly from the evidence of miniature painting. One of the most
tantalizing questions is whether the Westminster Retable could have been as
closely related to French panel or wall painting as it is to French architecture.
A long and respectable tradition of thought, extending from Viollet-le-Duc and
Lethaby, asserts that the Retable is indeed wholly French in origin, and that its
importation profoundly influenced the subsequent development of English
painting.[183] Serious difficulties, of course, hamper this theory. It would imply
that the Retable pre-dated and influenced the murals in the king's chamber,
and the Douce Apocalypse; but while the Retable's architecture could support
such a dating, there is no corresponding evidence that painting styles of this
order existed in mid-century France. It is hard to see how a work such as
Douce could derive from the Retable alone its mature and rich pictorial
language while at the same time not picking up the more mellifluous elements
in its style. Douce and the king's chamber murals can be accounted for in style
and iconography by pre-existing English modes of painting, and by contacts
with French miniaturist styles known to us. It is improbable that Henry III
would have had to turn to French painters to create such a subtle piece of
imagery when a large and talented workforce was already available to him
under the obviously English Walter of Durham. But the general idea of close

rapprochement with French painting still cannot be excluded. One way out of the impasse confronting us in the Retable's mid-century architecture but relatively late painting style, when judged in French terms, is to suppose that the Parisian *style Honoré* of the 1290s had been anticipated in French panel painting of the period broadly *c.* 1260–80 which was simultaneously influential in some circles in England. Such work could have been linked with the architectural style of the Retable while at the same time bridging the gap with the soft styles of the last decades of the century. Here the art historian faces simple lack of evidence. We cannot safely presume that panel painting was in advance of manuscript painting, and that the slow shift of initiative away from miniature painters towards wall and panel painters characteristic of the later medieval period had already begun. The one French panel painting (actually executed on vellum laid on beechwood) which bears any comparison with the Retable, the diptych in the Musée de Périgord executed between 1293 and 1306 for the priory of Rabastens-en-Albigeois (Tarn), is relatively conservative by the standards of late thirteenth-century Parisian miniature painting.[184] Whatever stylistic links may have existed between objects like the Retable and its lost French counterparts are therefore obscure.

W. R. Lethaby noted that many of the marked decorative preferences of Westminster court art have to be seen in the context of Parisian fashions.[185] The Retable and the Painted Chamber illustrate the close cooperation of pure painting and rich applied decoration established in the Westminster *ateliers*. The cream-coloured shafts of the central section of the Retable are delicately textured to suggest the surface embellishment of goldsmiths' work (pl. L*a*), and its frame is adorned with various artificial, but superbly contrived, items—false cameos, glass beads, imitation enamels and plaques of glass—suggestive, but only suggestive, of metalwork. The Retable illustrates well Ovid's sentiment *materiam superabat opus*.[186] This form of technical trickery is not to be explained by the poverty of royal patrons; many of the more highly coloured objects found at Westminster of the period 1260–1310 use this form of applied work, including the palace murals, the Aveline and Crouchback tombs erected in the 1290s, the sedilia, the Coronation Chair and so on.[187] On the contrary, the common occurrence of these effects shows that they were but a facet of a taste which liked the juxtaposition of detailed painted surfaces and the harder effects of structural polychromy (notably cosmatesque mosaics, inlaid brass lettering and cast bronze in the abbey). They also had glamorous models. Similar effects, drawing on painting, metalwork, glazing and textiles, characterized the interior decorations of the Sainte-Chapelle in Paris, of the 1240s.[188] The painted medallions of the upper chapel have diapered, gilt and inlaid grounds; false enamels were set into the fabric of the architecture itself.[189] The slightly later relic platform and screen—in place by the 1260s—were also ornamented in a way similar to the Westminster objects, their thin tracery members decorated with minute applied patterning.[190] Viollet-le-Duc's sentiment that the ensemble of the Sainte-Chapelle was honourable not because of the intrinsic worth of the materials used—which was negligible—but because of 'la beauté du travail . . . la perfection de la *main-d'œuvre* . . . l'extrême perfection du travail de l'artiste' is no less appropriate for Westminster, for it is from the Parisian sphere that the aesthetic of the Retable and the brilliantly coloured tombs in the sanctuary of the abbey, no less aptly described by Stone as having 'an air of meretricious *chichi*', may have derived.[191]

The lavish applied effects which dominated Westminster painting well into the fourteenth century can be seen in Parisian terms; but they also had innovatory features. The Painted Chamber murals employed a raised composition to adorn the decorative surrounds of the paintings, and indeed some objects contained within the pictures themselves.[192] Stothard noted that this material was laid upon tin foil,[193] perhaps to protect it from damp or to provide a barrier against the absorption of the oil used in this compound by the plaster base on the wall. The copies by Crocker and Stothard show that the croziers and the box held by the right-hand archbishop in the Coronation scene were done in gilt relief (col. pl. I, pl. II). Buckler's sketch of the opening through the Coronation painting notes that it was 'painted and adorned with stucco'.[194] The crowns of the Virtues are shown projecting from the plane of the paintwork, as are the decorative surrounds of all the splay figures. The same features occurred in the Old Testament scenes. Crocker's version of the encounter of Judas Maccabeus and Nicanor shows a tumbling figure holding a round shield delicately ornamented with a reticulated pattern of foils (pl. X*b*). His copies show that the many aedicules in these scenes were sometimes picked out with embossed work. The eye-witness accounts of the murals were drawn to the mixture of relief work and painting; even mail armour was textured.[195] Some of the real architectural features of the room were similarly treated, creating a decorative continuum with the murals.[196]

These artificial adjuncts must, by their nature, have compromised the flat effects of pure wall-painting technique, and so illustrate supremely that drawing together of wall painting with effects typical of other media—goldsmiths' work, painted altar panels like the Westminster Retable aiming at the aesthetic of textured and inlaid metalwork, and ultimately tapestry—so characteristic of interior decorations from this time onwards. In these adjuncts we may also see a sign of the rising importance of panel painting itself. The encroachment of relief into the actual picture-spaces themselves occurs in two English panel paintings of the 1330s or *c.* 1340, the Thornham Parva Retable and the Musée de Cluny Frontal, where items such as morses and book-covers stick out from the plaster surface, and use the same stamp designs as those found on the grounds beside the figures.[197] The same habit of mind was clearly at work in the king's chamber murals, for Crocker's copy of the Coronation scene shows that the box held by the archbishop had a raised gilt pattern identical to that found on the flat surfaces of the window splay by St Edward, opposite St John, showing the same tooling at work (pls. II, V*b*). Again, the most important monument of fourteenth-century Westminster painting, the programme of murals in St Stephen's Chapel dating to after 1350, has been shown to have used painting techniques typical of panel painting, and also uses embossed details prominently.[198] In the context of thirteenth-century wall painting, the king's chamber murals are in this respect unusual, but they are not wholly isolated. Relief decoration was characteristic of some Romanesque wall-painting traditions, and this may explain isolated occurrences of such adornment in some early Gothic schemes, such as the vault paintings in the Chapel of the Guardian Angels at Winchester, where gilt relief stars are to be found, anticipating the decorative methods of *c.* 1260–70 employed on the vaults of the lower church of San Francesco at Assisi. Here the grounds were set with small mirrors in imitation of twinkling stars (this also brings to mind the possibility that the *paterae* on the ceiling of the king's chamber were set with reflective glass of some sort).[199] Relief patterning is a distinctive feature, too, of the murals executed *c.* 1260–70, and so contemporary with the Westminster scheme, in the west gallery of the cathedral at Gurk (Carinthia), for the magnificent Throne of Solomon mural there has relief work on crowns, architectural surrounds, morses and even hems, which provides probably the closest analogy of the period to the techniques used at Westminster.[200] A cross-section of European art in the middle years of the thirteenth century—in France, Austria and Italy—indicates the rise in sophisticated circles of a new cooperation between wall painting and the decorative arts; indeed, so close did this cooperation become that it casts doubt on the validity of any distinction between 'pure' and 'applied' arts in this period. And this tendency continued, for it was present to an even more remarkable extent in the glittering interiors of the Imperial castle at Karlstein in Bohemia, well into the next century.

Given that this drawing together of the media was under way by the mid-thirteenth century, it is disconcerting to find Stothard casting doubt on the authenticity of the raised work in the Painted Chamber in stating that 'when these . . . paintings were first executed, it does not appear that this composition was at all used', by which he evidently meant that the embossed substance which comprised the relief areas was a later addition.[201] As Stothard did not specify exactly what features of the murals had led him to this conclusion, the status of his remark is uncertain; but it lends credence to the view that the murals had been tampered with at some point after their initial execution. Which murals is not clear. We cannot now tell for certain whether all the relief work in the murals here attributed to the 1260s was contemporary with the painted surfaces it adorned; as we have just seen, there is no reason in principle why such techniques could not have been open to the Westminster painters by the 1260s. There are few recorded details which cast serious doubt on the view that they could have been done in the late thirteenth, or early fourteenth, centuries. And as relief effects were also found in the Old Testament murals by the end of the century, a more important question may be whether earlier gilt or embossed surfaces were the subject of decorative revision, updating, or even completion in the course of later campaigns of work, rather than whether such effects were inconceivable there in the 1260s. As documents for the 1260s show, gilding did not always take place first anyway, and much of it could have been left incomplete on grounds of cost.[202] Given the vicissitudes of royal finance, the room was by any standards a large one to gild at one attempt, and it would hardly be surprising if a scheme of this size, in a domestic context, revealed some signs of decorative inconsistency as a result. Stothard himself seems to have thought as much in noting of the murals that in being repaired for the last time 'the gilder was more employed in exerting his skill than the painter. The additions were partial.'[203] Some inconsistencies can be spotted in the copied evidence. For example, the borders of *Largesce*'s mantle (pl. VI*a*) are decorated in the fashion of the Westminster Retable. Along the bottom hemline is a gilt pattern of roundels enclosing lions and eagles, the interstices filled with three-pronged leaves. This pattern is inconsistent with the hem pattern by the arm of the figure, which comprises a simple foliage scroll like those found on the Retable, and which logically should have continued all along the hem to the bottom. This could be a sign of a repair, for a very similar pattern of roundels to that on *Largesce*'s lower hem is to be found imprinted on the canopy shafts of the tomb of Aveline in Westminster Abbey (pl. L*b*), erected and painted in the 1290s.[204] It is also to be found on an early fourteenth-century embroidered panel of Christ in Majesty in the Victoria and Albert Museum.[205] Similarly, the rows of delicate quatrefoils on the neck and arm openings of *Debonereté*'s surcoat (pl. VI*b*) look like fourteenth-century work.[206] Again, the shafts of *Vérité*'s canopy and the posts of the canopy over the Coronation as copied by Crocker are shown with tiny quatrefoil stamps, each with a central hub (pl. VII), identical to those on the fillets used to separate the scenes from the story of Job executed after 1350 in St Stephen's Chapel in the palace, and so more typical of fourteenth-century work, or at least unlikely before the last years of the thirteenth century.[207] These examples tend to support Stothard's observation that decorative revisions to the gilt surfaces had taken place. Inevitably, however, the use of purely decorative patterns as a criterion of date is difficult since we have little idea at present as to when such patterns were first employed or how long they persisted in use. The first truly substantial evidence we have for the use of relief patterning or paintwork with a modulated surface texture is provided by the tombs of Aveline and Crouchback in Westminster Abbey, both dated after *c.* 1290. It may be significant that the ovoid medallions running along the canopy shafts of *Largesce* and *Debonereté*, and applied horizontally in strips beneath the two-light windows in the spandrels of their canopies, resemble the textured border patterns on the internal faces of the canopy cusps of Crouchback's tomb (pl. LI). But the possibility that this sort of patterning was already in use at Westminster in the years around 1270 is equally suggested by the treatment of some of the shafts on the Westminster Retable and by the use of incised patterning on the gilt borders on page 90 of the Douce Apocalypse. Such a date would be by no means inappropriate for the designs of the crowns of the Virtues or for the Lincoln-like tracery rosettes in their canopies.[208] In short, the evidence that we have for decorative revisions is ambiguous, and, more importantly, is not of itself strong enough to support the wider case that because some alterations took place, earlier painted surfaces were also the subject of drastic revision. These murals were characterized by a mixture of techniques, and so by a complex and perhaps even unstable artificiality, that could have required frequent maintenance in order to avoid tawdriness. The regularity of repairs to the paintings, in the 1270s (conceivably owing to the effects of damp),[209] the late 1280s and the 1290s, is therefore suggestive. Is it impossible that the lavish ornamental adjuncts of these paintings proved difficult to maintain, time-consuming and costly to repair, and that these features of the paintings were the principal subject of later emendations? Something of their vulnerability can be judged from the one surviving product of this workshop, the Westminster Retable. We cannot know how long such bogus decorative displays were expected to last, whether they were considered permanent or disposable. But the evidence is broadly compatible with Stothard's first-hand opinion that the paintings were the subject of piecemeal repair rather than total reworkings as the thirteenth century drew to a close.

Henry III's murals evidently survived the drastic redecoration of the king's chamber undertaken by Edward I in the 1290s. However fragile, they were treated with due respect by a workshop that, under Walter of Durham, executed the Old Testament scenes there; scenes which advanced beyond Henry's work in style and iconography and which, in their splendour, transformed the *magna camera Regis* into the *camera depicta*.

III. THE OLD TESTAMENT SCENES IN THE PAINTED CHAMBER AND THE PATRONAGE OF EDWARD I

When new and fresh, the effect of the Old Testament scenes in the Painted Chamber must have been astonishing. Brilliantly coloured and gilded, the stories ran around the room in registers, completely draping the walls above the dado as far as the ceiling, and amounting to several hundred feet of narrative (fig. 4, p. 83). Lively incident was crammed into every available space; at the top were expansive bands of illustrations from the Maccabees, and beneath were sundry other events, smaller in scale but detailed and elegant in handling. The intervening bands of text, in French, were crowded with lettering, the whole providing ample scope for courtly distraction. It is not surprising that Symon Semeonis and Hugo Illuminator considered these paintings to have been the most remarkable feature of the Palace of Westminster. Their extent and quality made them one of the wonders of the metropolis, and earned their inclusion amongst the spectacles of early fourteenth-century Europe. Here indeed was the Gothic, painted, equivalent of the hangings that adorned the secular palaces of the earlier Middle Ages, such as those in the rich hall of Heorot in the Anglo-Saxon poem *Beowulf*, where

> The wall hangings shone . . .
> Embroidered with gold with many a sight of wonder
> For those that delight to gaze on them.[1]

Entertaining narrative was, of course, an established part of medieval secular decoration. The Old Testament scenes at Westminster are all the more precious for being a well-documented instance of such decorations from a time when no others survive in England, and few on the Continent. But, as members of a distinguished decorative tradition, they had certain obvious peculiarities. Why was a major palace room of this order filled exclusively with Old Testament illustrations, and moreover, illustrations which were seldom, if ever, part of the normal repertoire of English medieval biblical iconography? Why was the Painted Chamber not decorated with more straightforward material, such as stories of Alexander, or the crusades, or romances, or indeed the Old and New Testaments combined, of the sort we find in the documents from the reign of Henry III?[2] The only explanation that has been offered has suggested that this extraordinary programme was the product of the whim of Henry III; that Henry suddenly chose in the 1260s to adopt new features of French Old Testament iconography hitherto unknown in England, which may have had some impact on the decorations of the French royal palaces.[3] Correspondingly, the Old Testament scenes have been attributed in stylistic terms to the same phase of patronage as that which produced the king's chamber murals, the Douce Apocalypse and the Westminster Retable considered in the last chapter.[4] But in fact, the evidence of the copies and the documents casts serious doubt on the theory that these paintings could have been conceived under Henry III. Stylistically, they make little sense in the context of the works surveyed so far, and have many features compatible with a date in the last years of the thirteenth century. Iconographically, they do not fit in with what is known about Henry's tastes. On balance, it appears that by attributing them to Edward I we can best explain their salient features and their peculiar iconographic concerns.

In Part I it was shown that, after the death of Henry III in 1272, wall-painting activity in the Palace of Westminster diminished significantly in importance. Some work certainly took place in the mid 1270s, of the routine sort we tend to find at the beginning of a new reign when the household is adapting its surroundings to new requirements.[5] Nothing substantial happened until the late 1280s, when Edward's interest in the palace revived. At this time repairs in the king's chamber occurred, in all probability to the murals executed under Henry III. But we still have to explain the big campaign of work that took place in the king's chamber and other rooms in the years 1292–7 at the same time as the reconstruction of the new palace chapel.

This documented phase of work was extensive enough to support the idea that the Old Testament scenes could have been undertaken in these years. The great physical extent of these murals, and the richness of their execution, should have made an impact on the documentation of work in the palace rooms of the sort so notable in the 1290s. Because more than one room may have been decorated in this period, it is impossible to establish the total cost of the work being done in the Painted Chamber in these years; but the narratives could well have been the main concern of the six campaigns of work occurring in the years 1292–5, with activity going on until 1297. By 1296 the work in the king's chambers was being pressed urgently on, exempted like the works in Wales from mounting financial constraints. The accounts of particulars give no exact indication as to the nature of the work being done. But one small point may be suggestive. In the case of a vertically extensive series of murals such as the Old Testament scenes—which covered the wall surfaces to a height of 8·54 m. above the dado line—it would be normal for work to start at the top and progress downwards.[6] The fact that the first accounts for the 1292–7 phase of work open in April 1292 with the provision of scaffolding for the painters shows that the first work planned there was indeed some height from the ground.[7] From this point onwards we can observe the activity of Master Walter's workshop as it was slowly occupied by filling up the walls of the king's chamber with imagery for as long as royal finances permitted.

The style of the Old Testament scenes

The stylistic evidence for attributing these scenes to the 1290s is strong. The fashions of dress shown in the paintings, especially of armour, could belong to any time in the late thirteenth century; the armour is sometimes marked by archaisms, such as the use of nasals on helmets (pls. X, XXVa), but is otherwise typical of the period.[8] The outstanding feature of the scenes for dating purposes is their use of a network of small buildings to contain and articulate the stories. Over the style of these buildings, which attain a degree of decorative dominance unusual in the history of English wall painting of these years, the copyists seem to have been in agreement. It is not surprising that they have been used as a reliable indicator of date. For Tristram and Tudor-Craig, their style suggested a date in the middle years of the century under Henry III's patronage.[9] More recently, Bony has briefly drawn attention to the similarity of these buildings to features of the 'new court style' of the 1290s.[10] Bony's theory is undoubtedly correct, and can be extended with respect both to the motifs used by the painters, and to their distinctive contribution to the composition of the stories as a whole.

In his study of English Decorated architecture, Bony has stated that: 'It was part of the refinements of Court art to translate forms from one material into another and to enlarge or reduce them in size, specially in the freer context of the English artistic tradition.'[11] We can take the miniature architectural constructions in the Painted Chamber as just such an instance of the growing taste at court in the late thirteenth century for micro-architectural forms. For Bony, the 'stage-like mansions' containing figures in the Old Testament scenes (pl. XIII) suggested a stimulus from woodwork construction, perhaps from 'the type of temporary tribune built for the king and his entourage on such occasions of display as tournaments or other Court ceremonies'. Most of the woodwork analogies for this style are, of course, lost.[12] But many of the motifs used in the Old Testament scenes are based firmly in the architectural language used by court masons in the 1290s. The Temple of Jerusalem from one of the scenes from II Kings (pls. XVIII, XIX) is evidently closely related to a composition such as the tomb of Edmund Crouchback (d. 1296) in Westminster Abbey (pl. LII). The Crouchback tomb possesses a repertoire of buttress shafts, pinnacles, panels of tracery and steep gables (pl. LII*a*) strongly reminiscent of French portal compositions such as the south transept of Notre-Dame in Paris, or the north transept of Rouen Cathedral.[13] We find the Temple adopting these forms to provide a miniature portal surmounted by an exotic-looking tiled dome. Beneath the arcade of weepers on the Crouchback tomb is painted a row of quatrefoils (pl. LX*a*) like those used to separate the stages of the Temple's towers, very much in the manner of contemporary stained glass aedicules.[14] The tracery painted on the shafts of the tomb is identical to that found on the buttress shafts in the Captivity sequences in the Painted Chamber (pls. LII*c*, XVII). Towards the top of the shafts of the tomb are small crenellated parapets, corbelled out with rows of foils, and painted with tiny arrow slits (pl. LII*b*). This format is cleverly adapted by the Westminster painters to form the stage sets for the stories of Elisha and Naaman (pl. XIII). The very common motif in the Painted Chamber of the row of foils combined with neat crenellations, singled out by Bony as evidence of similarity to woodwork construction (pls. X*a*, XII*a*), is a standard form of the court masons of the 1290s, found on the Eleanor Crosses and in the Westminster-related work in the chapter house at Canterbury executed *c*. 1300 under Prior Eastry.[15] The arcading of the chapter house (pl. LIII*a*) is pertinent for the Old Testament scenes in using not only the same type of crenellations on the cornice, but also some archaizing arch and capital forms. The Prior's throne has a triple gabled canopy canted forward; canting of this order is used by some of the castellated buildings in the Painted Chamber scenes from II Kings and Judges (pls. XV*a*, XX).[16] Other forms in the narratives show close acquaintance with court designs; we might cite the use of square-topped pinnacles in many of the scenes (pl. XII*a*), or the use of a square shaft turned on its axis to show two faces capped by gablets in one of the Isaiah stories (pl. XV*b*), which appears in the arcading of the tomb of Eleanor of Castile designed in the early 1290s, in Westminster Abbey.[17]

All the evidence of the architecture painted in the Old Testament scenes makes admirable sense in the context of the 'new court style' of the 1290s, the development and sources of which have been demonstrated by Bony and others.[18] It looks very much as if Master Walter's *atelier*, formed in the spring of 1292, had direct access to designs emanating from a court mason's lodge, such as that established at Westminster at exactly the same time for the rebuilding of St Stephen's Chapel in the palace.[19] This access may have been obtained in the form of architectural drawings, or even through some measure of intervention by the masons themselves, employed under Michael of Canterbury. So much is suggested by the design of the Coronation Chair in Westminster Abbey, made in 1300–1 by Master Walter (pl. LIII*b*). The Chair, the cage-like structure of which derives from a redaction of Rayonnant ideas, was counterfeited in painted wood after the example (*ad exemplar*) of a bronze prototype, cast bronze being one of the fashionable materials of the 1290s used for the effigies of Eleanor of Castile and Henry III.[20] The bronze model was abandoned in 1297, doubtless for the same reasons that brought a halt to work on the Painted Chamber and St Stephen's Chapel, the latter being relevant for the design language of the Chair.[21] Master Walter had cooperated with court carpenters in Westminster Abbey in the 1290s, and the Chair's design can reasonably be attributed to him or to a carpenter in his charge (witness the strong form 'cathedra de ligno *facta per Magistrum Walterum pictorem regis*').[22] There is therefore evidence that Walter's shop was responsive to current design ideas, used on such pieces of equipment for court ceremonial as the Chair, located by the shrine and high altar of Westminster Abbey.[23] This responsiveness is in turn reflected in the Painted Chamber stages, and by extension sheds further light on the genesis of forms on the Westminster Retable, again conceivably derived from a metalwork model, but in a substantially more archaic mode.[24]

Aside from its motifs, the Painted Chamber is marked out by its use of architecture to representational ends. The decorative application of Rayonnant devices was becoming increasingly widespread in this period.[25] But in the Painted Chamber architecture attains crucial iconographic importance: the copied narratives make little use of simple landscaping to shape the narratives, and the architecture is in effect the landscape. The use of pretty castles, such as Thebez from the story of King Abimelech, with its friendly scale and delicate tracery openings (pl. XX), connects the decorations to new pictorial genres such as the allegorical siege, the Castle of Love, where a neat little castle is surrounded and inhabited by lively figures (pl. LIV).[26] This iconography derived from actual enactments of the allegorical siege in court circles in the thirteenth century, for which fantastic castles were constructed by way of decor.[27] Something similar is also suggested by the popularity of toy castles made for the children at the Edwardian court, such as Prince Alfonso, who was given one in 1279, and Edward of Caernarvon, whose castle was displayed in the Great Hall at Westminster at a royal marriage in 1290.[28] The Painted Chamber buildings are a small but typical expression of the military culture of Edward I's court, reproducing in places the polygonal forms and turrets used by Edward's masons at Caernarvon Castle itself (pl. XX).[29] Their showy and somewhat flimsy appearance fully justifies Bony's analogy of the temporary tribune made of wood and adorned, perhaps, with painted canvas, conceived in such a way as to permit an endless variety of formal combinations improbable in real architecture. The effect is theatrical; the bland blue ground colour and the cool whites, greys and golds of the aedicules seem to have been calculated to show off the gaily coloured figures above and below (col. pls. III–V). Indeed, we can see in these raised constructions a reflection of the visual ideas implicit in the tournament as presented in contemporary Arthurian literature, where the narrative jumps from the tourney enacted in front of the scaffolds, to their inhabitants above, so yielding the double layer of action found, say, in the II Kings stories about Elisha in the Painted Chamber.[30]

In English terms, the genesis of this use of architecture in narrative pictures is hard to trace; there are few signs that English wall painting was developing this format in the years before *c.* 1290, and exact analogies are generally hard to find in English art. Indeed, we have to turn to much earlier, Romanesque, pictorial sequences like the Bayeux Tapestry to find the relentless and inventive use of architecture found in the Painted Chamber.[31] Implied polygonal forms had already made an appearance in early twelfth-century English wall painting (notably in the so-called 'Lewes group'), and in related cycles of miniature painting.[32] Whether or not such displays of architecture in narrative were essentially typical of monumental art is hard to say. The accomplished murals of the 1250s or 1260s in the refectory of the priory of Horsham St Faith in Norfolk, depicting the story of the priory's foundation (pl. LV), have rows of buildings punctuating the narrative in the manner of the Painted Chamber, although the forms themselves (those legible under much later retouchings) are clearly mid-century in nature, and lack the distinctive upper stages of the Westminster examples.[33] The technique is similar to the use of architecture in a bold sequence of pictures such as those in the great Trinity College Apocalypse (Cambridge, Trinity College MS R.16.2). In assessing the use made of micro-architecture at Westminster, we cannot fail to take into account the application of Rayonnant motifs in French miniature painting of the second half of the century. Similar forms occur in Parisian painting of the 1280s or 1290s. The aedicules over *Force* and *Justice* on fol. 91^v of the *Somme le Roi* in London noted in the last chapter (pl. LVI*a*) have comparable shafts, gables and shallow roofs to the canopies in some of the II Kings scenes in the Painted Chamber. The characteristic habit of lining up a row of buildings, each formed from a free, but precise combination of motifs, can be matched in a late copy of the *Psychomachia* executed in Paris in 1289 (BN MS lat. 15158), which portrays architecture rather in the manner of architectural drawing (pl. LVI*b*), and indeed architecture at substantially the same stage of development as that in the Painted Chamber.[34] This feature of French miniature painting almost certainly stemmed from the use of Rayonnant forms to frame pictures—rather than articulate the stories themselves—in the St Louis Psalter, and developed in elaboration in such works as the north French Psalter and Hours of Yolande of Soissons (New York, Pierpont Morgan Library MS M 729) of the 1280s, and the Nuremberg Hours, made in Paris *c.* 1290 for an English patron.[35] It is possible that, as with the Westminster Retable, some of the prototypes for the Westminster buildings were French, and that forms derived from French micro-architecture of the 1280s and 1290s were naturally suggestive of new pictorial applications, applications fostered by the English court's taste for elaborate architectural forms. It only took the 'freer context of the English artistic tradition', and the mediating practices of the court masons, to transform such ideas into something at once novel and charming.

These considerations must rule out the possibility that the Old Testament scenes were initially a creation of the 1260s, superficially updated in the 1290s by the addition of new motifs. It is unlikely that such wholesale repaintings would have occurred in campaigns only some two decades apart, as if the compositions and the architectural forms which defined them were not in some way mutually dependent.[36] Works like the Douce Apocalypse, produced *c.* 1270 in the court context, are certainly notable for a free and imaginative use of English mid-century architectural forms, some allied to seal-design of the period, others to contemporary architectural practices.[37] As already noted, the architecture in Douce is reminiscent of its more French counterpart, the Retable, in its literal transcription of motifs and in the vigour of their handling. The best analogies to the architecture of Douce in the Painted Chamber are provided by the kinked tracery lines of the canopies over the window-splay figures, like the strange, proto-ogival arch of the Church of Pergamum on page 6 of Douce (pl. LVII).[38] But a considerable discrepancy exists between Douce's buildings and those in the Old Testament scenes. The forms in Douce are far more archaic, and are used to quite different pictorial ends.[39] The thin and light members of the Old Testament aedicules cannot be found in Douce; the only significant point of contact between the two is the use of cheerful zig-zag tiling on roofs. Douce, like all the important narrative Apocalypses and saints' lives of the third quarter of the century, and unlike the Old Testament scenes, has predominantly figural rather than architectural compositions. It anticipates the Painted Chamber only in its first ten pages, illustrating the Seven Churches at the opening of Revelation, as instances of a grand kind of architectural heraldry, detailed, exotic and yet manifestly plausible in form, impressed against the bulky figures of St John writing.[40] The architecture is as muscular and earth-bound as its figures. But its narratives, although constrained by the weight of the iconographic models known to them, are relatively free of this sort of conceptual architecture; throughout its pictures, it is only in the case of the prefatory Churches, with their half-length angels set inside complicated openings, peering out like the figures set into the aedicules of some elaborately wrought seal, that we find the first suggestion of the potential of architecture to form a proscenium in the manner of the Old Testament scenes. The decorative milieu of the Rayonnant style, which was becoming of increasing importance in the arts towards the end of the thirteenth century, has had no impact on Douce; it and its more cosmopolitan cousin the Retable are only magnificent ancestors of the later displays in the Painted Chamber.

Changes were also at work in the figure style of the Painted Chamber. Although the copies are not at their strongest here, they nevertheless agree sufficiently in showing what happened to the idiom established by Master Walter's *atelier* in the king's chamber in the 1260s. The copies of Stothard and Crocker indicate that the overall palette of the Old Testament scenes (col. pls. III–V), was rather paler and brighter than that used earlier in the king's chamber, which, as on the Westminster Retable, was marked by subdued and saturated colours. In contrast to the Coronation and splay paintings, the narratives used prettier shades of pinks and lilacs, with very pale blue grounds, flat reds and greens in the garments, and white and grey aedicules. Stothard's copies of some of the figures, such as King Antiochus (pl. XXII*a*), suggest also that gold was glazed over garment colours in the manner of some late thirteenth-century manuscript painting, such as the illustrated roll in the Bodleian Library (MS Bodley Rolls 3) of *c.* 1300.[41] This transition towards paler, more pastel shades conforms generally with shifts in coloration that occurred in Parisian glass and manuscript painting in the second half of the thirteenth century.[42]

Of fundamental importance are the compositional features agreed upon by the copyists. The Old Testament scenes retained the broad-fold elements of the earlier styles; garments are shown with straight hems and angular pockets throughout. But they have lost the mannerist traits associated with the first broad-fold period in England. In the Douce Apocalypse, the Westminster Retable and their stylistic relatives such as the Metropolitan Psalter in New York, there is a quite unmistakable preference for highly contrived gestures and postures, odd stances, back-turned heads and muscular anatomies. None of these features is apparent in the Old Testament scenes. In contrast to the elegant posing of the earlier style, we find figures of slim, modest proportions, with relatively larger heads, making circumspect and economical gestures. Outlines of figures are simple and straight. Douce and the Retable revel in complex figure groupings and subtle rhythms of gesture. But in the Old Testament scenes the relative number of figures in each group is reduced. A sort of decorative shorthand is used to depict crowds of soldiers or civilians, by multiplying basic units of bodies and heads. The vivid, and at times claustrophobic, individualism of the style of Douce is replaced by an idiom which relies more on cumulative patterns of figures, where the cheerful effects of colour and heraldry predominate. The effect becomes sparser and flatter, more bland and less sombre than the earlier Westminster styles. This transformation was effected by stylistic change and the natural requirements of extended narrative painting. The designers of the narratives had to cope with a big, irregular fabric of some height, which obliged them to keep compositions simple and legible within the expanding width of the registers towards the ceiling. Their style had to withstand radical telescoping of scale, the bands growing from 0·76 m. wide above the dado, to 1·75 m. at the top. Their solution was an ingenious *tour de force* which hemmed in the sober, monumental work of Henry III on all sides. Within the limits of the registers, the activity of the figures was reduced to the pattern of the architectural decorations. As a result the compositions were quietened, and their spatial conception made different from antecedent court painting. In the Douce Apocalypse the picture-spaces suggest a sense of depth and recession from the bottom to the top. These spaces are often defined horizontally by a grassy undulating ground, and the figures are disposed either in front or behind it.[43] The volumetric conception of the medallion scenes on the Retable is similar to Douce in this respect. But the compositions of the Old Testament scenes are shallow and rigidly planar. The polygonal forms used in some of the buildings are reduced to a two-dimensional pattern; the buildings are on the whole frontal, and do not recede in depth in the rudimentary manner of the gabled roof in the scene on the Retable of the Raising of Jairus' Daughter (pl. XLVIa). The figures adhere to the base-line provided by the register, and the groups do not mount and swell in space as they do in Douce and the Retable. Instead, spatial relations consist of two planes of figures which slide in front of one another, and changes of level are attained via architecture, not landscape; the arrangement is thus that of a frieze unravelling from left to right, the gestures of the figures aimed at assisting the steady procession of the narrative.

It is hard to gauge the specific details of the figure-style of the narratives from the copies. The figures are in general less active and contorted than those of Douce and the Retable. A few features nevertheless demonstrate the persistence of some of the decorative qualities of the Retable and the king's chamber style of the 1260s. Crocker's copies of the scenes of Elijah and Ahaziah, Elijah and Elisha, and Antiochus and the Maccabean Martyrs (pls. XIIb, XXIIb) show that many of the hems of the garments were trimmed with the same sort of gilt geometric patterns as those of the Retable and the earlier murals. Stothard's version of the group of bound captives from the II Kings sequence of the Captivity (pl. XVIII) indicates that heads were designed with the softly convoluted hair, drooping mouths and rounded beards found on the Retable; these were by now standard conventions—compare the head of St Thomas in the south transept of Westminster Abbey (pl. LXIV).[44] The garments also appear to have resembled those on the Retable more closely than the increasingly sinuous drapery types found on the sculptures of the Crouchback tomb (pl. LXa) or the painting of St Faith in Westminster Abbey (pl. LXII). The elaborate hem style of the sedilia paintings in the abbey (pl. LXIII) appears not to have been in use in the palace in the 1290s. The Old Testament murals therefore show that Master Walter's *atelier* was employing established conventions of figure style as well as some older architectural motifs, but putting them to new compositional uses.

Because of the almost total destruction of court-related painting of this quality from the years *c.* 1300, the style of the Old Testament programme is isolated. Indeed, there is a marked dearth of suitable comparative material from London or Westminster painting of any form in these years. The Old Testament scenes are but distantly related to court manuscript painting of the sort in the Alfonso Psalter or the Ashridge College *Petrus Comestor* (BL Royal MS 3 D.VI),[45] or London products such as the Windmill Psalter or the 'Merton' *Flores Historiarum* at Eton.[46] The only late thirteenth-century painting which is undoubtedly in the style of the Old Testament scenes is the faint mural on the basement of the tomb of Eleanor of Castile in Westminster Abbey (pls. LVIII, LIX), executed by Master Walter during his work on the tomb in 1293 and so contemporary with the first campaigns on the palace murals.[47] This painting originally comprised the figure of Sir Otho de Grandison kneeling, to the right, before the Virgin and Child; but now only the group of four hooded figures to the left of the basement is legible.[48] Like the Old Testament scenes, the painting has a pale blue, or blue-green, ground, the frame being done in a translucent apple green. Its figures, set in a long rectangular space, have short compact frames, matter-of-fact gestures, large heads and garments falling in crisp straight pleats. These features compare very well with many of the figures in the Old Testament scenes, and argue for a common workshop origin; we might compare the hooded figures from the story from II Kings of Elisha, Naaman and Gehazi (pl. XIII). This style finds a sculptural counterpart in the dumpy little weepers sculpted in the early 1290s on Aveline's tomb-chest in the abbey, and was presumably representative of Walter's work for the royal burials at Blackfriars in the same period.[49]

The relative isolation of the Old Testament scenes ends, however, if we take into account developments in Westminster-related painting of the early fourteenth century. The narratives anticipate some of the more distinctive features of the so-called 'Madonna Master' style in the distinguished Psalter of Robert de Lisle (BL Arundel MS 83 part ii).[50] The origins of this style have not been fully explored. It occurs on a monumental scale in the panel paintings on the sedilia in the abbey (pl. LXIII), which can with reasonable confidence be dated to *c.* 1307–8.[51] But some of its elements had appeared before *c.* 1300. The design of the canopy shafts of the Madonna on fol. 131ᵛ of the Psalter is intimately related to the weeper arcade on the tomb of Edmund Crouchback, and so to the designs of court masons—probably Michael of Canterbury—of the 1290s (pl. LX). The same holds true for the figure style of the 'Madonna Master' miniatures, which has detailed analogies in the weeper sculptures on the tomb; the book also shares the same painted details as those used on the tomb—notably the painted tracery of the Madonna's throne on fol. 131ᵛ, which is extremely similar to the tracery painted on the shafts of Crouchback's canopy (pls. LIIc, LXb).[52] The Gospel narratives in the Psalter are unusual in being located either in cusped medallions or under delicate arcades. They reproduce strikingly the shallow spatial conception of the palatine wall paintings as well as their tendency to reduce the number of figures in any one section of action. The Painted Chamber story of King Abimelech consists of four short sequences, of which the left-hand one is framed by a cinquefoiled arch in a frame (pl. XX). The scenes on fols. 132–3 of the De Lisle Psalter employ similar framed arches over correspondingly economical groups of figures (pl. LXI). The scale of the figures in the Abimelech story relates to the architecture in a way comparable to the Entry into Jerusalem miniature on fol. 124ᵛ of De Lisle. The gestures of the captive royal figures in the story of Jehoiachin in the Painted Chamber resemble those of the onlookers at the Raising of Lazarus on the same page of the Psalter. The polygonal buildings guarding the Tower of Wisdom on fol. 135 of De Lisle compare well with some of those in the Painted Chamber.[53] The use of alternating red and blue grounds in some of the Old Testament narratives, such as that of King Abimelech and Jotham (col. pl. V), is also reminiscent of the constant changes in ground coloration and pattern in the De Lisle Gospel sequences such as those on fol. 132ᵛ.

Although the 'Madonna Master' style has been described as having originated in the London area around the beginning of the fourteenth century,[54] it seems more likely that it developed from monumental court painting and sculpture of the 1290s. The Old Testament scenes in the Painted Chamber have not been taken into account as a possible prototype for the clarity and decorative precision of this style. We could go so far as to say that the Old Testament scenes bridge the gap between earlier Westminster styles such as that of the Westminster Retable, and those represented by the sedilia– 'Madonna Master' idiom. This would also provide a better context for the murals of St Thomas, St Christopher and St Faith in Westminster Abbey (pls. LXIV, LXII), which also show that the 'Madonna Master' style had mural connections. These works are commonly regarded as belonging in the immediate orbit of the Westminster Retable, and so well within the thirteenth century.[55] There is much truth in the view that these murals reproduce some features of the Retable, especially its coloration, facial types and proportions. That the Retable had its imitators is hardly surprising; and there is no reason to doubt that in these paintings we have a style that is consequent upon, rather than antecedent to, the Retable itself. Indeed, on close inspection, these paintings betray qualitative and stylistic discrepancies with the Retable, and can be seen to share detailed affinities with the 'Madonna Master' style which have to be taken into account in assessing their date (the murals are undated in all but stylistic terms).[56] With respect to the Retable the style of these murals is looser and in a sense milder. The fold forms of their garments—notably St Faith—are either more rounded or more complex and sensual than those on the Retable or in the Painted Chamber; they are much more closely allied to the meandering hem types so common from the late thirteenth century and typical of the 'Madonna Master' and the sedilia (pls. LXII, LXIII). The Painted Chamber Virtues (pl. VI), which give some idea of how the style of the Retable would expand to monumental dimensions, are stiff and angular in comparison with St Faith. The hemlines of the south transept figures do not have the geometric patterns we would expect of works in the circle of the Retable, but instead have the same pair of thin black lines as the loin-cloth of Christ on fol. 132 of De Lisle. The murals all share the taste—far more typical of the late thirteenth or early fourteenth centuries—for repeat heraldic ground patterns (notably fleurs-de-lis) of the sort on the sedilia or in the De Lisle Crucifixion. Nor are the head types out of key with the 'Madonna Master' style. The posture of the Christ-Child on fol. 131^v of De Lisle simply reverses that of the Child held by St Christopher in the Abbey. Is it therefore inconceivable that in these paintings we have an idiom more suited to the later 1290s or early 1300s?[57] The saintly images in the transept make perfectly good sense as part of the same series of images as the Annunciation and Sts Edward and John on the back of the sedilia facing into the transept, a programme of monumental devotional illustrations akin to those becoming popular in contemporary Psalters and Hours.[58] In purely formal terms, far from representing the Parisian style 'carried abroad', these murals mark a significant step towards types of painting produced in England well into the first quarter of the fourteenth century.[59]

Conclusions

The Old Testament murals in the Painted Chamber add a valuable new element to our understanding of the complex developments taking place in the figurative arts in England in the last decades of the thirteenth century. At Westminster alone, we see in the 1290s the peaceful coexistence of several styles. In the palace were murals dominated by a novel use of architectural motifs, which created compositional formats more typical of the fourteenth century. In the abbey are monumental paintings intimately tied to the new suave figure styles of the Eleanor Cross sculptures and those on the Crouchback tomb, and also to painting styles of the period *c.* 1300 of the sort in the Bodleian Roll in Oxford and the magnificent Peterborough Psalter in Brussels (Bibliothèque Royale MSS 9961–2).[60] At the same time, the bronze effigies of Henry III and Eleanor of Castile, made in the early 1290s, are in a different, more sensitive and austere style, suggesting that the court metalworkers were resisting, for reasons technical or aesthetic, the tendency to elaboration of drapery forms on the Eleanor Crosses.[61] This eclecticism in court products in the 1290s parallels the rapid rise of the new Edwardian court styles in architecture, reacting as they did in various ways to the norms of French Rayonnant architecture.[62]

The stature of the court styles at Westminster is best assessed in the light of the few other major monumental artistic enterprises undertaken in these years. In the 1290s, the chapel of Merton College, Oxford, was magnificently glazed with donor figures and florid, ogival architectural forms, at least as advanced as the cooler, harder style of the Painted Chamber aedicules.[63] The programme of works at York Minster included glazing of comparable quality, and also the decoration of the chapter house with murals and vault paintings; some of the vault paintings, executed *c.* 1290, survive, and include figures such as St Edmund (pl. LXV) and Synagogue with relaxed poses, broad modelled garments, bleached faces and features articulated with black brush strokes, close in style to north French painting such as that in the Psalter and Hours of Yolande of Soissons, or the illustrated *Lancelot* of after *c.* 1300 in New York (Pierpont Morgan Library MS M805).[64] This urbane and cosmopolitan style, which reminds us that early fourteenth-century York diocese manuscripts such as the Tickhill Psalter (New York, Public Library MS Spencer 26) had stylistic and iconographic links with contemporary French painting,[65] deserves comparison with the contemporary Westminster styles. Indeed, the vault paintings are certainly the finest surviving instances of high-quality, monumental panel painting from the years immediately prior to the execution of the sedilia figures in Westminster Abbey.

The architectural history of the period confirms that collegiate or episcopal patronage was capable of emulating the court in the standing of its projects; yet remarkably little survives from the 1290s from the sphere of the figurative arts.[66] Some forms of monastic patronage were clearly orientated towards court ideas. Evidence that court styles may even have spread from Westminster to some monastic centres is provided by the documentation of 1307–8 for the Painted Chamber, stating that Thomas of Westminster was summoned from Peterborough to head the palace *atelier*.[67] Neither the object of Thomas's work, nor his patron, is known for certain, although the patron clearly paid well, because Thomas was able to dictate his terms of employment at Westminster.[68] A candidate could be Abbot Geoffrey of Crowland, a court favourite whose ownership of the Peterborough Psalter argues for some familiarity with tastes akin to those of the court in the years *c.* 1300.[69] Conceivably, Thomas of Westminster exported the style of the glamorous Old Testament scenes, on which he had worked under his father in the 1290s, to East Anglia at a time when royal finances could no longer stretch to the employment of a large force of wall painters after 1297.

While it is likely that such court styles were not the sole preserve of the court, the Old Testament scenes still emerge as an outstanding product of their time, stamped with the vitality of a great royal patron. They show that the court was important not simply because it acted as a focus of diverse stylistic ideas, but also because it resonated as a source of new imagery, particularly the new, secular, imagery of romance and chivalry. Edward's work in the Painted Chamber was the outstanding and unique reflection of the court's prevalent romantic culture; outstanding in its scale, and unique in combining elements hitherto unknown in medieval secular art. This, as much as Edward's grand work as a patron of architecture, reveals the international standing of his patronage.

The iconography of the Old Testament scenes (Cat. nos. 10–27)

The Old Testament scenes decorated all but the west wall of the Painted Chamber (fig. 4). The north wall had up to four registers, the lowest of which passed over the representation of the Coronation of St Edward. Of these, the three top bands passed from the north wall, on to the east wall above the windows, and thence on to the south wall, progressing westwards to stop over the west door. The textual evidence of the inscriptions copied by Crocker shows that the narratives began at the top of the west end of the north wall and ended at the west end on the opposite side of the room. The south wall had six registers, of which the lowest two did not follow from corresponding levels on the east and north walls, but rather ran along the south wall above the level of the dado.[70] Both the bands and the intervening layers of inscription widened towards the top of the room.[71]

The choice of registers had significant visual consequences for the overall appearance of the room and the pictorial construction of the narratives. Although the fabric was irregular, the painters tried to maintain a regular band layout; this demonstrates a consistent decorative approach, and rules out the possibility that the scenes were gradually built up over the years in an *ad hoc* fashion. The coherence of their subject-matter supports this. In theory the ordered, sequential nature of the bands permits some tentative reconstruction of the scenes on the basis of the copied texts and pictures. But only one substantial event, together with all the inscriptions, was copied from the north wall. The east and south walls were marred by highly strategic losses of imagery, and given that the losses seem to have occurred just at the moments when increasingly unusual imagery was employed, the task of reconstruction can only be partially successful.

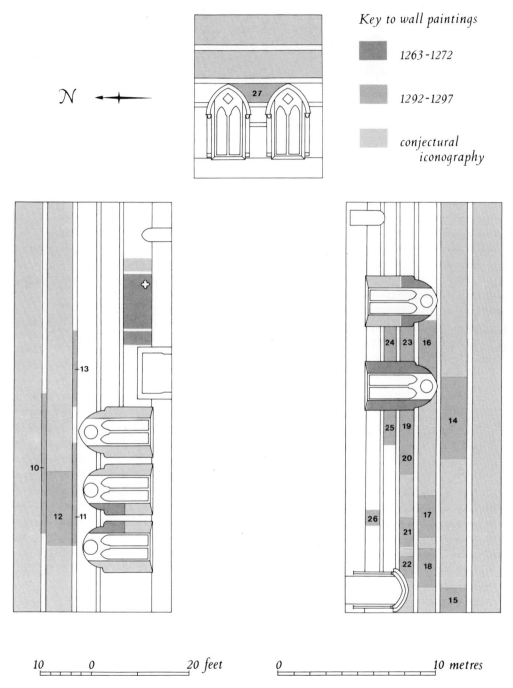

Key to wall paintings

▮ 1263-1272

▮ 1292-1297

▯ *conjectural iconography*

𝒩 ⟵

10   0   20 *feet*

0   10 *metres*

FIG. 4. The Painted Chamber: the scheme as extended by Edward I, showing the layout of the Old Testament scenes and inscriptions (Cat. nos. 10–27) (east wall at top of page)

We have already seen that the shape of the narratives was frieze-like. The scenes were not isolated from each other by frames, creating the possibility of emphatic visual climaxes, but were instead unrhetorical and steady in emphasis, being shaped from within by architecture and changes of ground coloration. Their tendency to dispose events in, or in front of, rows of self-contained mansions reminds us strongly of the scenic principle of medieval theatre, that of *décor simultané*, whereby all the sets needed for the drama were visible on stage at once.[72] In addition to the commentary in the inscription bands, the scenes were further clarified by exclamatory texts within the pictures, labelling places (the Temple of Jerusalem) or people (Judas Maccabeus). But, perhaps for reasons of scale and clarity, this type of textual material cannot compare in volume with that used in the pictures of the Douce Apocalypse (pl. XL), where the main text was supplemented by inscriptions in Latin or French of some detail.[73] In the Painted Chamber, the subsidiary writing has more to do with simple identification than glossing further the main body of commentary held beneath in the inscription bands. Also, the narrative registers were self-contained, providing (to judge from the copied evidence) no suggestions as to alternative pathways of reading other than the horizontal ones, entailing a visual leap from scene to scene across a text band to reveal a new meaning by a new juxtaposition of images. This is not to say that such interpretations were not originally an integral part of the way the scenes were read and conceived; indeed, as we shall see, some cross-references can be sensed. It is rather that the pictorial format did not of itself invite such interpretation. The epic flow of the narratives would not have surprised a Northern audience; but it contrasts with some of the more novel techniques being employed in the most advanced contemporary Italian narrative cycles.[74]

A full description of the picture-cycle is found in the Catalogue.[75] The fragmentary French texts and the pictures from the top two bands (pls. IX–XI) show that these registers were occupied by a remarkably full account of the events in the first Book of Maccabees, running from Antiochus' war with King Ptolemy in Egypt, in 1 Macc. i, 16–19, and the events immediately before, through to the circumstances concerning the death and burial of Judas Maccabeus in 1 Macc. ix. The Painted Chamber devoted some 114 m. of continuous illustration to the first nine chapters of 1 Maccabees alone. This sequence was conceived on a grand scale, embracing the top 4 m. of the painted surfaces of the room, and suggesting that a high degree of completeness was required in the illustration of the text. The narrative was dominated by events directly concerning Judas Maccabeus. He is picked out by name in the *mêlées*, and the pace of the narrative was governed by the consideration that his death should fall towards the end of the second major register on the north wall, bringing the story to a halt. Brilliant war scenes prevailed at these levels (col. pl. III).

Below the Maccabees registers the band widths contracted and the scale of the accounts changed. Their relationships also became more complicated. The third register down passed straight through the level of the window arches; some 1 m. wide, its text band passed along just above the level of the window springers. It started at the west end of the north wall and ran around the room for 39 m. before copied pictures again started 6·7 m. along the south wall from

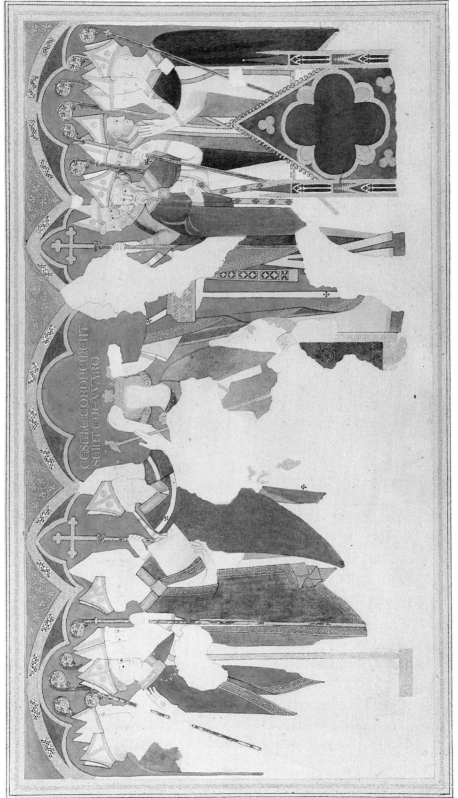

Photograph: Society of Antiquaries

The Painted Chamber: Coronation of St Edward (Cat. no. 1), copy by Stothard

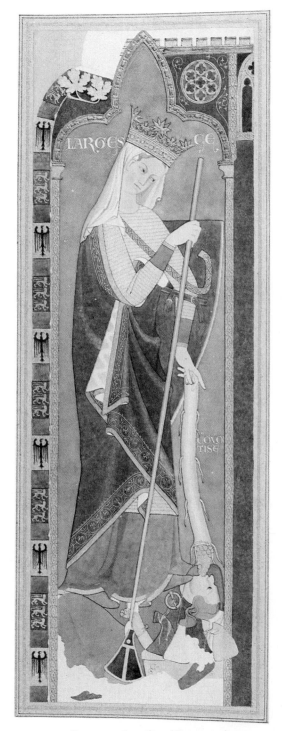 

a. Largesce-Covoitise (Cat. no. 5)   *b. Debonereté-Ira* (Cat. no. 6)

The Painted Chamber, copies by Stothard

Photographs: Society of Antiquaries

COLOUR PLATE III

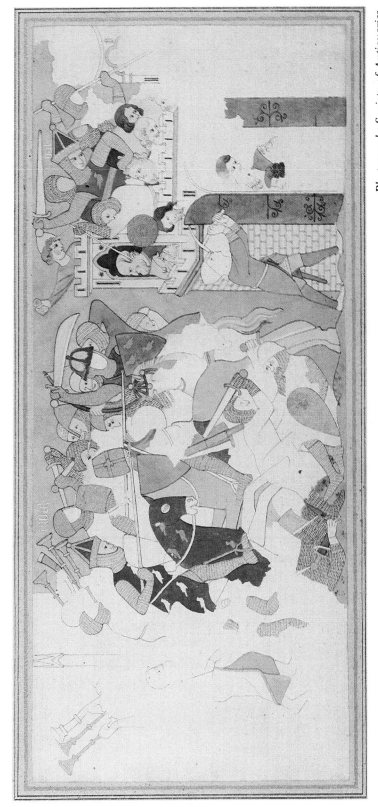

Photograph: Society of Antiquaries

The Painted Chamber: Judas Maccabeus attacks Alema and Dathema (Cat. no. 12), copy by Stothard

The Painted Chamber: Miracles of Elisha (Cat. no. 17), copy by Stothard

Photograph: Society of Antiquaries

The Painted Chamber: Story of King Abimelech (Cat. no. 23), copy by Stothard

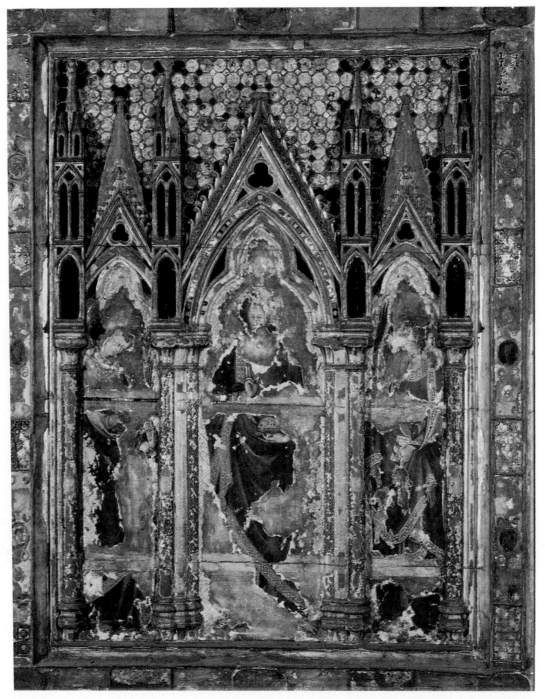

Photograph: RCHM (England)

The Westminster Retable: central section with Virgin, Christ and St John

the east end. Here illustrations from II Kings, i, began between the windows on the south wall and progressed to the west end above the door (pls. XII–XIV). The third band down was the last to embrace all three walls, and presented the first serious *lacunae* on the north and east sides, where neither pictures nor texts were copied. What preceded the II Kings pictures on the north and east walls is therefore very uncertain. From this point, the bulk of the pictorial evidence came from the south wall. Quite clearly, not all the accounts were expected to run all the way around the room, and from here the remaining illustrations were pressed into shorter bands, so abandoning the simple spiralling motion started by the top registers. Thus, at the end of the third row down, the II Kings pictures did not jump across onto the north wall, where band space started again beyond the north windows at the east end, but instead snapped back to the fourth row down on the south wall to the west of the windows (pls. XV–XIX). Between the windows at this level, prior to the continuation of the II Kings pictures, were episodes drawn from the Book of Judges (pl. XX). This had the consequence that the II Kings illustrations formed a solid block on the south wall above further material drawn from II Maccabees on the fifth row down (pls. XXII–XXIII), which one might have expected to be contiguous with the I Maccabees illustrations at the top of the room. Reading downwards on the south wall were, therefore, illustrations from II Kings, i–vii, over 18·3 m.; illustrations from Judges, ix, between the windows; further material from II Kings, xviii–xxv, for 12·2 m.; illustrations from II Maccabees, ix, starting between the window beneath Judges, and one picture from the lowest register from II Sam. iii (pl. XXIV). On the east wall between the windows was a fragmentary war scene (pl. XXV*a*).

In all, the iconography of I Maccabees and II Kings occupied about 145 m. of narrative space in the bands, out of a total of about 244 m.[76] The remaining scenes copied in 1819 occupied a further 7·6 m., so enabling us to identify the general contents of 152·6 m. out of the 244 m. or so originally illustrated. Statistically, this is not an unreasonable basis for a reconstruction of the original contents of the room. Little, however, can be done with the north wall. Conceivably, this continued with yet more pictures from the Maccabees, but we must take into account the fact that the uniform movement of the registers around the room was increasingly dislocated from this level downwards. Also, the general pattern of other Maccabees illustrations tends to favour the idea that the Maccabees pictures stopped with the death of Judas Maccabeus, and started with new events from II Maccabees lower down. The painters were obliged to some extent to shuffle material around on the lower parts of the walls because the adherence to bands was complicated by the frequent interruption of the sequence of the registers by door, and particularly window, openings at these levels.

This had one advantage in that the nature of the wall space itself allowed two forms of narrative exposition: at the top, continuous illustration from I Maccabees unrolling on areas of blank wall space; below, the inclusion of more compact and intense narratives drawn from other areas of the Old Testament, that did not require quite such extensive treatment. That continuous narrative was not a uniform aim in the programme is shown by the complete visual separation of events in I and II Maccabees by quite separate biblical material.

This implies that the episodes on the lower wall areas were seen as being logically separate, and so open to different interpretation, from those above. We might, for example, argue that the iconography of Judas Maccabeus was being formulated independently of that of his disreputable antagonist Antiochus, whose humiliation is the prime concern of the lower, II Maccabees register (pl. XXIII).

If this idiosyncratic arrangement were true also of the blank north registers, then these could well have included themes from any of the more warlike books of the Old Testament, such as Joshua, Judges, Samuel and Kings. The one scene recorded on the east wall obviously came from some such military sequence, and it is perhaps significant that the Judges story of King Abimelech on the south wall brings to a halt a phase of Judges narrative (including the stories of Eglon and Ehud, Jael, Sisera, Barak and Gideon) that is highly warlike in content. That such a selection may originally have been made is suggested by the statement of the Irish friars that the room contained all the warlike scenes of the whole Bible explained by inscriptions in French. They were certainly correct as to the language of the texts, and their account is intriguing as it shows that the Painted Chamber was known more for its stories than for the themes conceived earlier under Henry III. However, their accounts of well-known works are also marked by a certain vague hyperbole; they describe the Sainte-Chapelle in Paris, *illa pulcherrima atque famosa capella*, as being *biblicis historiis mirabiliter ornata*; an unimpeachable account, but of little value in helping us to visualize the astonishing wealth of this building's iconography, let alone its medium.[77] The Painted Chamber did not strictly amount to an encyclopedia of biblical warfare. Many of the events, such as those pertaining to Elijah and Elisha from II Kings on the south wall (pls. XII–XIV), are hardly martial in character. It is not impossible that the popular view of the room's decorations derived largely from the fact that the Maccabees scenes, rich in chivalric incident, were visually the most dominant through being placed on the big, continuous upper bands. If so, then this one contemporary account cannot be used as an absolutely reliable guide as to the original contents of the programme. The physical constraints of the room alone must have led to preferential treatment of some warlike areas of the Bible at the expense of others, for after the remarkably complete I Maccabees series, appropriate material concerning Joshua, Judges, David and Solomon would have had to jostle for space. Indeed, can such imagery be conceived in terms of the sources open to the Westminster painters in the 1290s?

The problem of sources

The incompleteness of the cycle as recorded, and the probability that it did not originally possess straightforward themes, are both obstacles to the search for pictorial sources for the programme. No single known Old Testament cycle from the years before 1300 shares the scope and emphases of the Painted Chamber scenes. Some of the scenes had conventional elements that entitle us to search for pictorial sources for the programme; but inevitably there remains the possibility that some of its iconography was a first-hand creation direct from the text. The Maccabees texts suggest that the formulator of the cycle had, at some point, access to a French translation or close paraphrase of parts or all of the Old Testament, which might indicate the general orientation of the sources (pl. IX). But it will be recalled that, because the texts show signs of being palimpsest, three lines of text having replaced two, the texts we know may not have been originally associated with the pictorial source.[78]

Nevertheless, the Painted Chamber possessed two clear instances of iconography anticipated in earlier French thirteenth-century manuscript illustrations of the Old Testament. The story of King Abimelech from Judges occurs in the Moralized Bibles in Oxford (Bodleian Library MS Bodley 270b) and Vienna (Österreichische Nationalbibliothek Cod. 2554),[79] in the Maciejowski Bible (New York, Pierpont Morgan Library MS M638),[80] and in the glass of the Sainte-Chapelle,[81] as part of a distinct cycle of Judges iconography originating in Paris in the first half of the thirteenth century. The Oxford Moralized Bible provides medallions (fols. 111^v–112) for the murder by Abimelech of his brothers, Jotham's parable of the trees choosing their king, and for Abimelech's death at Thebez (pls. LXVI–LXVII). Maciejowski illustrates (fols. 13^v–14) the murder of the brothers and Abimelech's death, but omits the parable of Jotham (pl. LXVIII). The Painted Chamber example (col. pl. V, pl. XX) has close contacts with both. The scope and rhythm of its scenes is close to the Oxford Moralized Bible in including, and indeed positively stressing by means of a red ground (col. pl. V), the parable of Jotham and the trees. Its version of Abimelech's unfortunate death is closer to Maciejowski in showing Abimelech being dispatched by his squire as well as being hit on the head by a millstone.[82] At Westminster, Jotham is actually present, gesticulating before the trees, whereas in the Moralized Bibles the parable does not include the figure of Jotham and the trees are anthropomorphized by the sprouting of small human heads.[83] Despite these differences, the Painted Chamber Judges scenes are close to the French ones in content and spirit, and they surpass them in fulness, for they include the burning of Shechem, for which authority exists only in much earlier Judges illustrations.[84] Taking the Moralized Bibles and Maciejowski together, we can identify a probable origin for this iconography in thirteenth-century France, an origin which can explain the full treatment of episodes such as Jotham's parable of kingship and the Maciejowski expanded type of Abimelech's death.

Similar sources could account for the episode from II Samuel of David and the murder of Abner by Joab (pl. XXIV). This scene was isolated on the lowest band on the south wall, but was probably part of a sequence of pictures. The illustration of Abner's murder was used in the twelfth century as a type for the Betrayal of Christ,[85] but is absent from the Moralized Bibles and a cycle of David scenes in a north French Psalter and Hours of Arras Use from the mid-thirteenth century.[86] A strikingly similar sequence occurs in the Maciejowski Bible, however, as part of a David cycle of encyclopedic scale (pl. LXIX). It shows (fols. 37–37^v) Michal brought to David, David feasting Abner, Abner leaving David and his murder by Joab.[87] The same sequence of events is found in the Painted Chamber, with a fragment of Michal and Ishbosheth above, and below what appear to be seated figures, possibly David feasting Abner. Lacking its text, the next scene is ambiguous, as it could represent either the departure of Abner from David in II Sam. iii, 21, or the arrival of

Joab's raiding party in II Sam. iii, 23; but the murder resembles in outline the Maciejowski version, given that at Westminster Joab and Abner are shown armed and, for no apparent reason, crowned. The close relationship again enjoyed with Maciejowski proves that the Painted Chamber was open to sequences included only in the fullest known David cycles.

The possibility that some areas of the Painted Chamber were shaped by access to a French thirteenth-century Old Testament picture-cycle of course has implications for the programme as a whole. It has been proposed elsewhere that the Westminster scenes were directly stimulated by works such as the Maciejowski Bible, the Moralized Bibles, the Sainte-Chapelle glass and the St Louis Psalter, and even possibly a related series of murals in one of the Parisian royal palaces.[88] According to this theory, which assumed that Henry III was the author of the Westminster cycle, Henry was keeping up with the latest French royal fashions in introducing the iconography of Old Testament warfare at Westminster, the *locus classicus* of which is the Maciejowski Bible. At a number of points the martial iconography of Maciejowski is very like that of the Painted Chamber; for example, the scene on the east wall of the flight of warriors is reminiscent of the trouncing of the Moabites from Judges, iii, on fol. 12 of Maciejowski.[89] The genre is broadly the same. Indeed, if this connection proved generally true for the Painted Chamber, there would be every reason for supposing that the Abimelech story on the south wall was preceded on the north and east walls by Judges pictures of the sort in Maciejowski. Access to such a model would have obliged much more Davidic illustration too; in these terms, the Joab–Abner sequence on the south wall could have been preceded by the suicide of Saul as on fol. 34[v] of Maciejowski, perhaps falling in the region of the thematically related death of Abimelech in the register above.[90]

The idea that Westminster court art saw a wholesale influx of such French iconography under Henry III raises some difficulties, however. French biblical iconography was undoubtedly known outside France in the mid-thirteenth century, as Buchthal has shown with respect to the Arsenal Bible (Paris, Bibliothèque de l'Arsenal MS 5211) produced in the Latin Kingdom of Jerusalem.[91] Henry III may have been aware in a general sense of contemporary Parisian developments, for in 1250–3, prior to his visit to Paris in 1254, he ordered paintings of the Apostles and Old Testament scenes for St Stephen's Chapel at Westminster, highly suggestive of the recently formed programme in the Sainte-Chapelle of the 1240s, which Henry is believed to have admired.[92] Yet the documented evidence for Henry's interest in biblical narratives implies that he was primarily acquainted with a perfectly standard form of iconography available in England in Bible picture books and especially psalters.[93] Knowledge of a psalter would explain the addition of a Tree of Jesse to the mantelpiece of the king's chamber in 1259.[94] In the month following the marriage of Henry's sister Eleanor to Simon de Montfort in the small chapel by the king's bed in the room, in 1238, Henry ordered that the chapel should be paved, and painted with the story of Joseph 'a tergo ultra sedem regis'.[95] In 1250 the same subject was painted in the king's new chapel at Winchester, and in 1253 the story of King Nebuchadnezzar, presumably drawn from the Book of Daniel, was painted in St Stephen's Chapel at Westminster.[96] While this last choice could have been prompted by the Daniel glass in the Sainte-Chapelle,

Henry's images could equally well have come from earlier English illustrations such as those in the Munich Psalter (Munich, Bayerische Staatsbibliothek Clm. 835), of the early thirteenth century, which include an unusual number of pictures about Joseph and Nebuchadnezzar from Genesis and Daniel respectively (fols. 13ᵛ–16ᵛ, 105ᵛ–107).[97] Henry's orders for 'stories' from the Old and New Testaments to be painted at Winchester in 1237 and 1241, and at Windsor in 1242, also suggest access to the normal run of narrative material found from the twelfth century onwards in English psalters.[98] As these works are all destroyed, we cannot be sure how they would have compared with the big cycles recorded or surviving at Bury St Edmunds, Canterbury and Winchester.[99] But the general flavour of one of these court programmes, that painted in the chapel at Windsor 'in summitate' in 1242, can be judged from the explicit instruction that it was to be like the paintings at Wolvesey; in other words it was to follow an earlier Winchester model of the sort probably known to Henry in his youth at Winchester.[100] There is a strong likelihood that a Winchester model would produce narrative (rather than typological)[101] pictures of the sort in the Munich Psalter, the earlier Winchester Psalter (BL Cotton MS Nero C.IV), the St John's College Psalter noted in the last chapter, and the narrative sculptures from Genesis in the chapter house at Salisbury.[102]

In turn, these English cycles were demonstrably influential on the Continent. The great cycles of Old Testament illustration in the Arsenal Bible, the Moralized Bibles and the Maciejowski Bible betray clear signs of knowledge of older English models used in the Munich Psalter, the Leiden Psalter (Leiden, Bibliotheek der Rijksuniversiteit MS lat. 76A), and the De Brailes leaves (Baltimore, Walters Art Gallery MS 106), as well as the ancient iconography preserved in the Aelfric Pentateuch and Book of Joshua (BL Cotton MS Claudius B.IV) and the Egerton Genesis (BL Egerton MS 1894).[103] This formidable, and widely influential, array of authoritative English Bible iconography has to be borne in mind in assessing the likelihood of a massive influx of French imagery into England in the middle years of the century.

Henry III's court at Westminster must have used the same Old Testament sources as those known at other royal centres in this period. But there is absolutely no evidence for an interest under Henry in material from Judges, Kings and Maccabees which characterizes the Painted Chamber and implies at first sight access to French, rather than English, imagery. This radical change of interest should have occurred at a time when there is more general evidence for the importation of French iconography. And it is significant, for the purposes of the dating of the Westminster murals to the 1290s proposed here, that just this sort of change started to become widespread in England shortly after *c.* 1300. A number of early fourteenth-century English works attest to particularly strong French influence in the formation of their style and iconography.

The most glamorous of these is the Queen Mary Psalter (BL Royal MS 2 B.VII), executed *c.* 1310–20.[104] Queen Mary has an Old Testament cycle which closely resembles French examples such as the Maciejowski Bible. It stresses very much the same narrative themes, and includes a good deal of refined Old Testament warfare. It illustrates the tale of King Abimelech.[105] Although omitting the Jotham parable, the Queen Mary version (pl. LXX*a*) is a conflated instance of the Maciejowski type (pl. LXVIII), for it shows the millstone twice—in the hands of the woman on the ramparts of Thebez and also hitting Abimelech's head—as in Maciejowski, but combines the blow and the dispatch in one. The Queen Mary Psalter has an entire series of contacts of this order with Maciejowski and the St Louis Psalter.[106] It, and the Tickhill Psalter of around the same time, illustrate the story of Joab and Abner found at Westminster (pl. LXX*b*).[107] The very extensive scenes of the life of David in the Tickhill Psalter, whose style, like that of the Queen Mary Psalter, is obviously French-influenced, are related to those in Maciejowski and Morgan MS M730, as indeed are those in the Isabella Psalter in Munich (Staatsbibliothek Cod. gall. 16).[108] The scenes added to the back of the Guthlac Roll (BL MS Harley Rolls Y.6) in the early fourteenth century copy literally events in I Sam. as depicted in Maciejowski and the St Louis Psalter.[109]

Together with the Painted Chamber, these works show that a big French illustrated Old Testament suddenly became known and influential from *c.* 1290 in England, and that knowledge of it spread to various centres. In these terms the Painted Chamber may well have started the fashion of interest in older French cycles of this very comprehensive type; this would be one of the signs of the resonance of the court circle with newly adopted themes. Of course, the fourteenth century in England was also marked by a concern with older English biblical illustration, often of a strikingly conservative order; witness the typological imagery of the Peterborough Psalter and the scenes in the fourteenth-century Egerton Genesis, as well as aspects of the Queen Mary Psalter.[110] French biblical iconography, while making its principal impact in England from around 1300, by no means transformed the contents of English Bible iconography, even if its influence can still be sensed in the choice of scenes for the murals in St Stephen's Chapel after 1350.[111] Indeed, the significant areas of the Painted Chamber programme drawn from II Kings and Maccabees cannot be explained by any of the French cycles known to us. The Painted Chamber illustrated II Kings, i–vii and xviii–xxv, omitting chapters viii–xvii, and concentrating on the miracles of Elijah and Elisha, the fate of Sennacherib and the downfall of Jerusalem after the time of King Hezekiah (pls. XII–XIX). This unusual pattern of interest is alien to the French models under discussion. The principal French II Kings iconography occurs in the Moralized Bibles, the Arsenal Bible and the glass of the Sainte-Chapelle. The Oxford Moralized Bible resembles the Painted Chamber in illustrating the first seven chapters of II Kings, concerning Ahaziah and the miracles of Elijah and Elisha.[112] This may suggest the outlines of the missing iconography on the appropriate register of the south wall of the Painted Chamber, between II Kings, ii, 8, and iv, 38. The Moralized Bible omits chapter iii, but includes events from the story of Elisha in chapter ii, 23–5 (the boys mauled by the she-bears), iv, 2–7 (Elisha and the flask of oil), and iv, 8–37 (Elisha raises the Shunammite woman's child), which could have fitted in before Elisha's sweetening of the potage in II Kings, iv, 38, at Westminster. The Painted Chamber also included space, at the start of the II Kings sequence over the left-hand window arch on the south wall, for the fall of Ahaziah in II Kings, i, 2 (pl. XII*a*); the space was compositionally appropriate, for the fall of Ahaziah as represented as a type for Pride in the contemporary *Somme le Roi* manuscripts shows the king plunging forwards and downwards, suggesting that Ahaziah could have tumbled along the descending line of the window arch.[113] But the Moralized Bibles, the Arsenal Bible and the Sainte-Chapelle cycle cannot account for the especially full treatment of the stories about Hezekiah, Isaiah and the Captivity in the Painted Chamber. The Moralized Bibles in fact contract rapidly at this point, where the Painted Chamber expands; the Arsenal Bible only has the opening sequences from II Kings, and the Sainte-Chapelle, while showing the destruction of the Temple, does not include the detailed Hezekiah and Isaiah stories in the Painted Chamber.[114] The corresponding cycles in the Maciejowski Bible, Morgan MS M730 and their successor in Queen Mary, go as far as I Kings and the story of King Solomon, but break off before II Kings.[115] The same was presumably true of the St Louis Psalter, for it appears that the flagging of interest in II Kings material in these French cycles can be accounted for by a corresponding contraction in one of the major models used by them, the eastern Vatican Kings manuscript (Vatican, Cod. Gr. 333).[116]

The Painted Chamber II Kings selection is both thorough and specialized. Certain basic elements of the narrative, such as the ascent of Elijah from II Kings, ii, 11, are omitted, in this case perhaps because the ascent, although established in English iconography in works like the Winchester Bible,[117] could not have been accommodated effectively within the horizontal framework of the scenes. Quite particular narrative interests may explain the breaking-off of the narrative after II Kings, vii; the stories of Jezebel and the death of Elisha evidently held no appeal for the Westminster audience. The product of this is a sequence of pictures which has little or no contact with known II Kings illustration produced in north-western Europe in the Middle Ages. Such pointed episodes as Elisha's miracle of the floating axe, II Kings, vi, 6, found in Prudentius' *Dittochaeon* and the typological cycle of Prüfening, or the cleansing of Naaman, found on twelfth-century typological plaques, tend usually to constitute *exempla* rather than parts of a larger narrative.[118]

To find convincing parallels for the II Kings sequence we have to turn to more exotic sources. The events concerning the angel smiting the Assyrian army in its camp, and Sennacherib being murdered by his sons while worshipping in the Temple of Nisroch in II Kings, xix, 35–7, find an impressive counterpart in one of a pair of miniature fragments formerly in a private collection in Basle, attributed by Buchthal to a Sicilian scriptorium and dated to the end of the thirteenth century.[119] In this miniature the narrative runs in the opposite direction to that in the Painted Chamber, and includes an extra scene of the flight of the mounted Sennacherib to Nineveh (pls. XV*b*, LXXI). But the image of the armed angel floating over the Assyrian camp, the formation of the tents with their opened fronts, and the corpses of the troops below, are nearly identical. The angel at Westminster has simply been turned slightly to fit into the horizontal register, but still kicks his heels up behind. To the left of the miniature, Adrammelech and Sharezer are seen sticking their spears into the back of Sennacherib as he kneels before the idol under an almost Pompeian aedicule, a formula simply reversed and Gothicized at Westminster. The Sicilian miniature provides extremely strong evidence for believing that this part of the Painted Chamber was derived from an ultimately Byzantine source, a belief also borne out by the occurrence of substantially this iconography in the

prescriptions of Dionysius of Fourna's 'Painter's Manual'.[120] Buchthal con-
cludes that this pair of miniatures in fact illustrated the major and minor
prophets, for the II Kings story is reproduced in Isaiah, xxxvii, 36–8, and the
other miniature illustrates the vision of the prophet Zechariah.[121] But quite
clearly this image could be adapted for use in a II Kings sequence, for a similar
iconography is found in the German Romanesque Gumpert's Bible (Erlangen,
Universitätsbibliothek Cod. 121) along with other II Kings episodes.[122]

Further important parallels are to be found in earlier Spanish works.
Particularly notable in this context is the cycle of II Kings illustrations found in
the Pamplona Bibles: the Picture-Bible of King Sancho el Fuerte of Navarre
(Amiens, Bibliothèque Communale MS lat. 108) and its sister manuscript in
the Harburg Oettingen-Wallerstein Collection MS 1, 2, lat. 4°, 15, both
produced in the early thirteenth century.[123] The programme of illustrations
found in the Amiens–Harburg manuscripts deals in detail with the events from
the fall of Ahaziah, through the miracles of Elisha, to Nebuchadnezzar's taking
of Jerusalem and the blinding of Zedekiah; the story of Hezekiah is fully
treated in illustration of Isaiah.[124] Certain details suggest that the Painted
Chamber cycle was distantly connected to that in the Pamplona Bibles. As in
the Painted Chamber, the Amiens–Harburg manuscripts have separate illustrations of the consuming by fire of Ahaziah's company of fifty men, and the
seated Elijah sparing the last, kneeling company.[125] On fols. 126ᵛ–128ᵛ of
Amiens we also find Elisha's sweetening of the potage, the healing of the naked
Naaman in the Jordan, Gehazi together with Naaman and his chariot, as well
as Gehazi in supplication before the angry Elisha.[126] The inclusion in Amiens
of the trampling of the faithless lieutenant, Nebuchadnezzar taking away the
treasures of the temple and the blinding of Zedekiah is also like Westminster in
extending the narrative with the same stories through to the end of II Kings.[127]
The Pamplona Isaiah pictures are also relevant (pls. LXXII–LXXIIIa). As at
Westminster (pl. XV), Sennacherib's captain Rabshakeh is seen challenging
Hezekiah's servants; Hezekiah is then seen similarly going beneath into the
temple; a scene is devoted to Isaiah addressing Eliakim and Shebna; Hezekiah
goes down again into the temple; the Lord appears to Isaiah from a cloud; and
finally the Assyrian camp is destroyed by the angel.[128] The choice and layout of
scenes in the Pamplona cycle is thus fundamentally similar to the later
Westminster cycle. Aside from the Pamplona Bibles, two other manuscripts
demonstrate the existence in Spain of particularly thorough II Kings illustrations. The first is the Bible of San Millán de la Cogolla (Real Academia de la
Historia, Madrid) executed *c.* 1200–20, which includes amongst its II Kings
illustrations events from Elijah and Elisha by the Jordan to Hezekiah's prayer
(fols. 207–220ᵛ);[129] the second is the earlier Ripoll Bible (Vatican MS lat.
5729), which includes material concerning Hezekiah and Nebuchadnezzar
rather less closely related to that at Westminster.[130]

It is apparent from these parallels, as well as from some isolated German
examples (notably the Kings illustrations in the Mainz Evangeliary (Aschaffen-
burg, Schlossbibliothek MS 13) of *c.* 1260 and the fourteenth-century *Concordantia Caritatis* of Ulrich of Lilienfeld (Lilienfeld, Liberstiftsbibliothek MS
151)),[131] that the Painted Chamber had access to a repertoire of II Kings
iconography not reflected in any of the more classical, Paris-based, Old

Testament cycles of the mid-thirteenth century. As the Sicilian miniature suggests, this repertoire could well have comprised in part older Byzantine formulas preserving a tradition of extensive II Kings illustrations going back to the ninth-century *Sacra Parallela* and beyond, but persisting in some quarters well into the thirteenth century.[132] The connections with independent Byzantine and Spanish Kings illustrations imply that more than one type of source was available at Westminster; there is certainly no evidence apart from the Painted Chamber that a single big II Kings cycle was known in England. But quite how these sources were gathered together is a matter of conjecture. Edward I may have gained access to imagery preserved in the Sicilian miniature as a result of his sojourn in Sicily in the winter of 1270–1.[133] Similar diplomatic links, of course, existed in the case of Navarre; but it is conceivable that in this case intermediary illustrations were brought into play. Bucher notes that the King Sancho Bible probably passed into French hands on his death in 1234.[134] That this cycle was known and admired in France in the late thirteenth century is proved by the fact that the Amiens–Harburg illustrations influenced a French *Bible historiée* executed in the early fourteenth century (New York, Public Library MS Spencer 22).[135] The contacts between Westminster and the earlier Pamplona group may have arisen indirectly through knowledge of a similar French exemplar based on the Pamplona cycle and of late thirteenth-century date. In any event, however we envisage the sources used at Westminster, we can see that the Painted Chamber catered for a more widespread, and increasingly voracious, appetite for detailed and dramatic biblical iconography typical of the late thirteenth and fourteenth centuries in north-western Europe.

Similar considerations apply to the even more remarkable Maccabees programme in the Painted Chamber. The extended illustration of I Maccabees, i–ix, which filled the two top registers of the Painted Chamber is unmatched in known biblical illustration, and appears to be unique in monumental art. The use of French texts has prompted the speculation that the Maccabees pictures were based upon a lost French illustrated translation of the Maccabees of mid-century date; conceivably, such a translation could have provided the basis for other elements in the Painted Chamber cycle.[136] However, it is difficult to square this theory with the relative poverty of surviving French biblical Maccabees illustrations of the thirteenth century. The Painted Chamber cycle enjoys only a passing resemblance to the Maccabees pictures in the Moralized Bibles in London (BL Harleian MS 1526 and Add. MS 18719), and the Arsenal Bible.[137] Indeed, Maccabees sequences are far better represented in earlier, Romanesque picture-cycles. Maccabees pictures of varying density are found in the ninth-century St Paul's Bible in Rome,[138] in the Roda Bible (BN MS lat. 6) and Ripoll Bible from Catalonia,[139] in the St Gall Maccabees codex in Leiden (Leiden, Bibliotheek der Rijksuniversiteit Cod. Perizoni 17),[140] in Gumpert's Bible,[141] in the Bible of Stephen Harding (Dijon, Bibliothèque Publique MSS 12–15),[142] and in the Winchester Bible.[143] While none of these cycles approaches the Painted Chamber in completeness, they present cumulative similarities which suggest that big biblical narratives of this sort were most familiar in pre-thirteenth-century form.[144] England may have had her own corpus of Maccabees illustration. This is suggested by the general similarities between the Maccabees pictures in the Bible of the English Stephen Harding and those in the later Winchester Bible, and also by the record in a Latin versification noted by M. R. James (Cambridge, Clare College MS Kk.5.6) of a series of *tituli* 'super picturam Machabeorum', which James suggested were of Worcester origin.[145] The Stephen Harding and Winchester Bibles include illustrations of events found in the Painted Chamber, such as the fate of Nicanor and the death of Judas Maccabeus. The Cambridge verses harmonize I and II Maccabees to form a narrative in a manner alien to the Painted Chamber, where the books are treated separately; but the verses still stress the defeat of Nicanor, the death and burial of Judas and the attack of Jonathan on the Jambrites (found also in Gumpert's Bible),[146] as at Westminster. It may be significant that these selections agree with what is known of the Painted Chamber cycle in taking the narrative no further than the death of Judas and the story of Jonathan immediately afterwards. Again, the Cambridge verses also imply that some sort of tradition of monumental Maccabees illustration was known in the Romanesque period in England.

The character and extent of the Westminster Maccabees is akin to these earlier cycles, and implies a similar desire for dense pictorial coverage. But in the case of these murals we can also point to developments of a typically thirteenth-century nature, occurring outside the realm of biblical illustration proper, which might have stimulated this revival of older standards of thoroughness. By the end of the thirteenth century, and so towards the time that the Westminster murals were conceived, the biblical text of the Maccabees had been transformed into a secular romance. The roots of this gradual secularization of the Old Testament went back into the twelfth century, when there is evidence that some of the warlike books of the Bible, such as Judges, were translated into the vernacular.[147] Doubtless the chivalric interpretation of the Old Testament present in the Maciejowski Bible arose from the new literary uses of the Bible, catering for the demands of a new class of secular patron, and throwing into relief its more knightly features.[148] Not unnaturally, the Maccabees text, along with Judges and Kings, was an obvious focus for this form of interest. Thus, reference is made to a tradition of Maccabees romances in a north French *prose poétique* version of the Bible of *c.* 1275 (BN MS fr. 6447), which suggestively also includes translations of Genesis, Judges and Kings.[149] The central element in such romances, picking up the chivalric potential in the Bible, is a stress on the deeds of Judas Maccabeus. This was to some extent already present in Romanesque Maccabees pictures like those in Gumpert's Bible, where, as at Westminster, Judas is explicitly named within the action. Such mid-thirteenth-century verses as those of Gautier de Belle-perche, based on I Maccabees, i–xiii, remind us of an older tradition of celebrating the deeds of heroic biblical personalities, of the type found in the earlier thirteenth-century Munich Psalter's unusual interest in the Old Testament heroines Ruth, Judith and Esther.[150] But they also reflect the climate of romance literature, for Judas Maccabeus, like Lancelot, Yvain or Alexander, is expected to accomplish heroic feats.[151] By the 1280s, these romances had become sufficiently canonical and popular to attract pictures. A Picard text on I Maccabees related to that of Pierre du Ries, entitled *La noble chevalerie de Judas Macabé et de ses nobles frères*, of shortly after 1285 (BN MS fr. 15104), is accompanied by 128 small and mass-produced scenes (pl. LXXIII*b*) spread throughout the text.[152] The text acknowledges its derivation from the Bible, and gives a full account of Judas' adventures up to his death (fol. 72), ending with the supplication that (perhaps in contrast to King Antiochus) all should follow his example of courage and just government.[153] Judas Maccabeus is now a type for romantic and strong kingship.

The emergence of such illustrated Maccabees romances in north France by the 1280s is of relevance for the Painted Chamber of the 1290s. The new orientation of interest in the Maccabees was typical of its time in being romantic rather than strictly biblical. Indeed, by its nature, the Maccabees text lay towards the periphery of sacred history. From this time onwards, the Maccabees were regarded primarily as a legitimate part of the wider spectrum of romance literature. It was exactly in this period that Judas Maccabeus was plucked from his biblical context and classed with other heroes of sacred and profane history. He was associated with Roland, David and Alexander in the *Auberon*, regarded as a successor of Alexander in the *Miroir Historial*, and, especially, included in the Nine Worthies of the *Vœux du Paon* composed by Jacques de Longuyon of Liège in 1312.[154] The Maccabees became a facet of the prevailing Arthurian climate in England, north France and the Low Countries. Significantly, the picture-cycles based on the romance texts were successful primarily in monumental form. The vogue for Maccabees miniatures was short-lived.[155] Instead, the Maccabees text was influential indirectly through the immense popularity of the Nine Worthies (pl. LXXIV) as a subject of decorative display throughout Europe,[156] and directly as a romance subject, for Julius von Schlosser noted several instances of tapestries decorated with the tale of Judas and Antiochus being ordered well into the later Middle Ages.[157]

The Painted Chamber lies right at the start of the tradition of using the Maccabees for large-scale secular display; the arms attributed to Judas in the Painted Chamber are essentially those of his later romantic persona in the Nine Worthies.[158] At Westminster, partly as a result of its iconographic priority in this decorative tradition, the details of the account are still strictly biblical, in keeping with the identity of the programme as a whole. The romances may well have stimulated a new interest in the biblical text, but their particular features were not, at this stage, taken over, largely because they were not associated with highly developed picture-cycles. Older, fuller, biblical sources proved pictorially more attractive than the perfunctory miniatures. The text of a work like *La noble chevalerie* required and got no more than a type of pictorial coding for the eight or so standard situations arising in the course of the narrative. Scenes of war, potentially so spectacular, were reduced to a standard, tourney-like, confrontation of two knights.[159] In the Painted Chamber the conventions of medieval warfare are thrust forward much more richly. A great prevalence of this type of military imagery inevitably tended to be somewhat non-literal; not only because accounts of battles tend to be generally similar, but also because it was characteristic of thirteenth-century, and indeed earlier, pictorial thinking to transfer battle scenes of the elaborate *mêlée* type from saints' lives, to Apocalypses, to biblical illustrations, without unduly sacrificing authenticity to text.[160] But what separates the Painted Chamber from the romances, and evinces its vitality, is its literalness. The Maccabees scenes are like the others in the room in including striking, text-bound, images which enable their identification, such as the blowing of trumpets at Dathema in I Macc. v, 31 (col. pl. III), or Nicanor mocking the priests in I Macc. vii, 33–8 (pl. X*a*). These qualities show that the Westminster cycle was the product of an authoritative pictorial source based intelligently on the biblical text itself.

The broad picture offered by the sources known directly or indirectly at Westminster is relatively incoherent. Some of the peripheral elements in the Painted Chamber were undoubtedly derived from a slightly earlier and more or less conventional French illustrated Old Testament sequence. The pictorial traditions lying behind the II Kings illustrations may have been more exotic, and the exact mode of their transference to the Painted Chamber is obscure. English biblical Maccabees illustrations may have been drawn upon; but here, as with the Pamplona Bible cycle, contacts with developments in France, if not Paris, cannot be ruled out by the available evidence. It is tempting to suggest that this odd and diverse concoction of material may have been brought together deliberately to suit the idiosyncratic requirements of the royal patron. We must now turn to some of the considerations that may have occasioned this unique choice of material. The structure and contents of the scenes pose as many problems as the tracing of sources. A broad division of interest was created in the Painted Chamber by filling up the top registers with straight and continuous narratives from I Maccabees, and squeezing in underneath pictures of a different form. The episodes from II Kings, Judges, II Maccabees and Samuel were grouped together on the south wall independently of the I Maccabees pictures, nearer spectator eye-level. Their content changes subtly from the war scenes above. The concern is now focused on the deeds of tyrannical kings, their subjugation of peoples, and their eventual downfall. A prophetic element creeps in. Elijah prophesies the death of Ahaziah; Jotham curses Abimelech; Isaiah curses Sennacherib; the Maccabean Martyrs foretell the fate of Antiochus as they go to their deaths; perhaps, originally, the death of Saul was included, predicted by the ghostly Samuel in I Sam. xxviii, 15–19. For all these royal reprobates, the Wheel of Fortune turns a half-circle. They are all humiliated in death. Ahaziah, the type for Pride in the *Somme le Roi*, falls from a window; Abimelech is mortally wounded by a woman; Antiochus falls from his chariot; Sennacherib is the victim of the treachery of his sons. What notions might have led to this extraordinary choice of scenes for a king's chamber?

The Old Testament scenes and the patronage of Edward I

Just as the pictorial traditions reflected in the Painted Chamber appear to have been diverse and unusual, so the cycle viewed as a whole presents us with a number of interpretative possibilities. Here we have to balance two competing forms of interpretation which have equal claims to our attention; on the one hand, we can place the scenes in the context of distinct literary and pictorial genres, and on the other, we can attempt to understand them as having a certain topicality, as responding to and commenting on prevailing concerns of the Edwardian court of the 1290s. What may be called the formal and the topical elements in the cycle could well have interacted subtly. Such interaction is demonstrated by the major Maccabees illustrations. Of all the imagery in the

Painted Chamber as recast in the 1290s, that drawn from 1 Maccabees is probably the most easy to account for in terms of the known interests of Edward I. In Judas Maccabeus, Edward found an heroic example of knightly biblical behaviour comparable to King David or Joshua. The two Irish friars who described the Painted Chamber in 1323 in the very same passage present Edward to us as the most Maccabean king of the English—'machabeissimi Anglorum regis'.[161] This association of the two figures in this descriptive context must be significant. The analogy between Judas and King Edward was a natural extension of the Edwardian cult of King Arthur, whose various manifestations have been amply described elsewhere.[162] Judas Maccabeus is associated with Arthurian figures in contemporary works such as the *Chronique* of Jan van Heelu, composed c. 1291–2 for Edward's daughter Margaret, and with Edward and Arthur in *Le Rossignos*, written by John of Howden, a clerk in the royal household.[163] Edward is identified with Arthur in the *Siege of Caerlaverock* of c. 1300.[164] The Painted Chamber now provides us with evidence for thinking that the manuscripts circulating at court included not only Arthurian works—Eleanor of Castile possessed romance manuscripts, a 'romanz de Isembart' written and illustrated in France c. 1281, and was the dedicatee of Girard d'Amiens's Arthurian *Escanor*[165]—but also illustrated Maccabees romances. In origin these were probably Picard; north France and the Low Countries had an especially prominent role in the development of Arthurian romance literature and illustration, and both were part of a network of exchanges with the English court.[166] Eleanor's association with the *Escanor* seems to have arisen as a result of her visit, with Edward, to Amiens in 1279.[167] They are likely to have acquired an illustrated Maccabees at this time, conceivably from one of the workshops responsible for producing Arthurian manuscripts.

The Maccabean imagery in the Painted Chamber cannot therefore be viewed separately from the court's chivalric culture and from the associated range of literature that may have been known to it.[168] Viewed topically, the Maccabean emphasis may also be seen in the light of Edward's crusading activities celebrated so notably in *Le Rossignos*, for Edward was still planning to go on crusade in 1293 after the disastrous fall of Acre in 1291.[169] Lethaby argued convincingly that the iconography of the painting on the basement of Eleanor of Castile's tomb, which we have already seen was an offshoot of the palace campaign of the 1290s (pls. LVIII–LIX), was similarly responsive to current events in portraying Sir Otho de Grandison in his capacity as a crusader praying for the queen's soul at the holy sites.[170] In this sense, Edward in the Painted Chamber could be seen taking on the persona of Judas Maccabeus as liberator. Alternatively, there might be some general allusion to Edward's military prowess in Scotland, or more probably Wales; the content of the murals was presumably outlined in or before 1292, and so is more likely to have reflected the ventures of the 1270s and 1280s, rather than the newer Scottish problem of the 1290s. In Judas Maccabeus and Antiochus, we could have types for Edward and Llywelyn; an ironic reversal of the roles of these figures as liberator and oppressor in their biblical context, but one fully consonant with the Edwardian policy of appropriating historical personages such as Arthur, Magnus Maximus, father of Constantine, and Brutus, in support of royal territorial claims.[171] It is, inevitably, somewhat hazardous to place too much emphasis on the possibility of such references; nothing concrete is known about the intentions lying behind the choice of scenes in the Painted Chamber. But an allusive use of the Old Testament would make sense, not only in the light of the absorption of the Bible into the broad pattern of historical writing in the late thirteenth and early fourteenth centuries (notably in the *Historia Scholastica* and its translations), but also, more specifically, in terms of contemporary Westminster historical writing. Thus pointed biblical allusions are found in the 'Merton' *Flores Historiarum* attributed to John of London and already associated with the Painted Chamber through its coronation iconography.[172] In the *Flores*, images from the Psalms, from the story of Balaam's Ass, from Kings and the story of Elijah and Ahaziah's companies, are woven into present-day narrative; during the siege of Stirling in 1304, Edward's troops are held to have reproved the king for going too near the walls unarmed, and to have reminded him of the fate of Abimelech at Thebez, already gorgeously represented at Westminster (col. pl. V).[173] Such *exempla* are common in the romance historiography of the day. John of London's panegyric, the *Commendatio Lamentabilis*, is full of romantic and biblical reference in celebration of the life of Edward I: the barons compare Edward to Solomon; the bishops invoke the conquests of David and his hammering of the Moabites, Ammonites and Philistines; the knights call up Alexander, Brutus, Arthur and Richard I; the priests tell of Edward's superiority to Saul.[174] This is essentially the world-view of the Painted Chamber. The involvement with it of someone like John of London, a contemporary Westminster monk close to the court,[175] and associated with literary uses of the Bible, cannot be ruled out; Edward presumably had his advisers. On the other hand, the critical, even homiletic, streak in the murals leads us also to suppose that, however we may choose to assess their pictorial roots and topical connotations, an element in their final shaping probably derived from a popular, instructive, use of the Bible associated as much with the propagation of exemplary Bible literature within the laity, as with more specialized historical writing.

The imagery drawn from Samuel, II Maccabees, Judges and II Kings is not, however, the normal stuff of contemporary biblical *exempla*, and until more is known of the literary climate of Edward I's court, and the various manifestations of its ideology of kingship, the significance of these narratives will remain a matter of informed conjecture.[176] It is true that these scenes probably had some moralizing importance which went beyond the celebration of knightly heroism in Judas Maccabeus. In this sense, these pictures stand together as illustrations of good and bad kings and the prophets. At this point, Edward's scheme may have been extending a theme already implicit in the virtuous iconography of Henry III's murals, now interpreted in terms of the salutary experience of bad kings. Precedents existed for the use of Old Testament figures as types for certain Virtues and Vices in medieval art. We find such associations in the eleventh-century Bamberg Apocalypse, in the *Speculum Virginum*, in a twelfth-century manuscript from Ratisbon, and in the later thirteenth-century *Somme le Roi*.[177] But this should not be taken as evidence that the Virtues in the room were actually conceived by Edward to point up the significance of the narratives. The physical and iconographic relationship between *Largesce* and *Deboneneté* and the neighbouring biblical stories is too dislocated for this to have been true; the relationship is really fortuitous. For example, the Virtues do not gesticulate meaningfully, in exhortation, to the narratives, in the way that St Peter points moralistically across to the scenes of the Ministry of Christ on the Westminster Retable. There is no evidence that the Old Testament scenes on the north wall, also joined by Virtues, contained any moralizing imagery. In works like the *Somme le Roi*, the linking of biblical characters to certain Virtues and Vices is quite overt and didactically clear, whereas in the Painted Chamber it is no more than *ad hoc*. Again, the south wall registers were so crowded with images that any reference made from window splay to narrative band on either side can at best only have been incoherent; a wasted opportunity if any more direct gloss was intended.[178] The Virtues, as was suggested in the last chapter, belonged to a separate frame of reference from the narratives. Correspondingly, the exemplary nature of the south wall stories seems to have been self-contained, presenting us with more than a grossly inflated *Somme le Roi*, and certainly comprising more unconventional subject-matter. Indeed, it is exactly this independent-minded and idiosyncratic quality in the Painted Chamber that prompts us to look elsewhere for guidance as to its meaning.

We can, first, see these problematic episodes as illustrating a form of antithesis between good and bad kingship; the exploits of Judas Maccabeus are elevated above those of the tyrant Antiochus at the bottom of the wall, and the good prince Hezekiah, the destroyer of idols, is contrasted with the idolatrous Sennacherib murdered in the Temple of Nisroch, Antiochus the worshipper of Zeus, the fratricidal Abimelech, and Nebuchadnezzar. This is moralized Bible history of a sort. More particularly, it is biblical history read in terms of sterile and tyrannical kingship, with a very pointed view of the end of such kingship. As a pictorial theme, these ideas are uncommon, and few artistic analogies spring to mind. We might cite the depictions of the 'thorny' Emperors Julian the Apostate and Maurice Tiberius in the earlier stained glass at Canterbury, as an instance of the form of influence exerted on monastic conceptions of kingship by the theories in John of Salisbury's *Policraticus*, with its accounts of the deeds of the Roman emperors.[179] For our purposes, such theories are not irrelevant, because they carried with them a view of the consequences of tyranny. While, in the Painted Chamber, Hezekiah and Namaan acquit themselves well in the eyes of the prophets, in the cases of Ahaziah, Sennacherib, Abimelech, Antiochus and also conceivably Saul (whose black presence is implied by the Joab–Abner sequence), the narratives seem to have been especially constructed to balance tyrannous behaviour and its consequences, namely humiliating downfall. This view of kingship had a conventional literary element. Its persistence in late thirteenth-century England is well illustrated by the inclusion of Sennacherib and Nebuchadnezzar, along with Pharaoh and the emperors, in a treatise falling under the influence of the *Policraticus*, the *Liber de tyrannis et morte cesaris et aliorum principum et tyrannorum* preserved in a manuscript in Cambridge.[180] Here, the distinctions between prince and tyrant, legitimate and illegitimate ruler, are defined, and, more importantly, the ultimately classical theme of the violent deaths of tyrants especially emphasized.[181] The influence of this *topos* on biblical history can be sensed in the Painted Chamber. It is intriguing to find Edward I absorbing and

appropriating ideas more normally associated with critiques of English kingship. Equally suggestive is the possibility that the Painted Chamber provides us
with a metaphysical gloss on such political theories. Writings such as the *Liber
de tyrannis* employ a religious as well as a secular form of political appraisal.[182]
According to this, rulers were identified with certain metaphysical forces which
decided whether they were to be classed as limbs of Satan, persecutors,
apostates, voluptuaries or heretics. A further striking feature of the Old
Testament scenes is their inclusion of figures who were outstanding types of
Antichrist in medieval exegesis and art. In view of Edward I's patronage of
Apocalyptic material,[183] it is not inconceivable that a strong stimulus at work in
the Painted Chamber could have derived from a reading of Revelation.

The most notorious types of Antichrist in the Painted Chamber are King
Abimelech and Antiochus. Rhabanus Maurus interpreted Abimelech as a type
of Antichrist in his *Commentaria in Librum Judicum*, while taking Jotham's
parable of the trees choosing their king (a miniature sermon on political
legitimacy) as foreshadowing the preaching of Elias, one of the Witnesses in
Revelation, xi.[184] The appropriateness of this gloss for thirteenth-century
audiences can be assessed by its use in the Judges illustrations in the Moralized
Bibles which anticipate the Painted Chamber account iconographically. In MS
Bodley 270b, the stories of Gideon and Abimelech are moralized with
Antichrist imagery in the corresponding medallions (pls. LXVI–LXVII).[185] The
Vienna Moralized Bible presents Jotham's preaching as a type for that of Enoch
and Elias against Antichrist.[186] Such an interpretation would explain the
narrative emphases of the Painted Chamber Judges pictures, in particular their
stress on Jotham's parable, not shared in the related Maciejowski Bible or
Queen Mary Psalter (col. pl. V). In Jotham's parable, Judges, ix, the fig, olive,
vine and thorn enact an allegory of kingship. The thorn tyrannizes the other,
fruit-bearing trees, and threatens them with the sterilizing power of fire. The
notion is strikingly like that of the text referring to the Emperor Maurice at
Canterbury, with its allusion to the thorny ones who bear no fruit, but
nevertheless live a life of luxury.[187] The thorn at Westminster of course stands
for Abimelech, who bears goatish arms and takes fire to Shechem and Thebez,
and is destroyed like Antichrist. The use of tree-imagery also brings to mind
the account in Revelation, xi, 4, where the Witnesses are likened to two olive
trees. The extended account of the miraculous powers of Elijah and Elisha can
be seen in the light of the corresponding powers of the Witnesses described in
Revelation, xi, 5–6.[188] Elijah's action of bringing fire down upon Ahaziah's
men sent to apprehend him (pl. XIIa) can be read as an adumbration of the
Witnesses from whose mouths fire will pour forth to devour their enemies.
Elijah's capacity to bring down fire thus neatly counterbalances the actions of
Abimelech, the bringer of fire, in the register immediately beneath, and was
presumably to have been seen in tandem with it.

The other outstanding instance of parallelism with Antichrist is provided by
the deeds of Antiochus placed on the lowest stratum but one on the south wall
(pls. XXII–XXIII). This interpretation must explain the separate formulation
of I and II Maccabees, found widely parted by intervening registers. Antiochus
is located beneath the contemptible Abimelech, whereas Judas Maccabeus is
raised up. Rhabanus Maurus considered Antiochus to be a type of Antichrist in

his *Commentaria in Libros Machabaeorum*,[189] and this gloss was more generally accepted, particularly in exegesis of the life of Alexander.[190] Antiochus, whose deeds were prophesied by Daniel, is the *radix peccati*, the last tyrant of Joachim da Fiore's Old Dispensation.[191] This interpretation is, again, employed in the Moralized Bibles, for it occurs in BL Harleian MS 1526; Antiochus' torture of the Maccabean Martyrs is likened to Antichrist's persecution of the Christians, and the story of Eleazar, an uncommon subject notably included in the Painted Chamber, is taken to prefigure Enoch.[192] Antiochus is seen presiding over the torture with his bauble-clutching fool at his feet, and so in the guise of the evil kings with their dwarfish jesters in the Lambeth Apocalypse group of manuscripts.[193] The general shape and contents of the scene are reminiscent of representations of Domitian ordering St John to be boiled in a cauldron heated by a fire blown by bellows, such as that on fol. 2 of the Paris Apocalypse (BN MS fr. 403).[194] In the jaunty grimness of this depiction we recognize something of the visual world of the thirteenth-century English Apocalypses.

The notion that the Old Testament scenes were influenced by such popular and distinct literary or pictorial forms, which enabled a recasting of what might otherwise have been a more commonplace iconography, need not surprise us, as there is no reason to doubt that the late thirteenth-century English court had access to a variety of genres and a rich and inventive iconographic milieu. Of course, the exact nature of this milieu has yet to be defined, for at present little is known about Edward I's possession of manuscripts, his reading habits, his literacy or his suggestibility (when books are mentioned in the royal circle they are more usually connected with the queen than the king).[195] This consideration of itself lends importance to the Painted Chamber, because it is through the idiosyncracies of its selection from and presentation of the Bible that we are provided with evidence for processes of thought that is otherwise lacking. But the Painted Chamber scenes are also baffling precisely because they amounted to more than the sum of the conventions which informed them. One of the most important questions they pose is whether the narratives seen as a whole were intended to amount to a single, logically coherent statement about kingship and chivalry seen in biblical terms, or rather whether they represented an instance of secular story-telling, admittedly of unusual quality and extent, held together not so much by rigour of conception as by a jocular, flexible enthusiasm for pungent narrative within a system of reference which is now hard for us to understand. What, in short, did the scheme amount to? A substantial difficulty arises when we come to assess the significance of the division of material between the upper and lower parts of the south wall. We have, first, 1 Maccabees employed at the top as a continuous narrative emphasizing the heroic deeds of Judas Maccabeus as a model of chivalry for any good king; and, second, on the lower parts of the wall, shorter narratives accommodated within the constraints of the door and window openings while at the same time maintaining the decorative regularity of the bands, whose close layering created the possibility of visual cross-reference, and whose subject-matter concerned prophets and bad kings. This division of material certainly implies, at first sight, a systematic confrontation of chivalric values and their diametric opposite, each accorded about half the available wall space. Viewed in this way there seems little doubt as to which kind of biblical kingship Edward I chose to identify himself with. But at the same time this may be to gloss over the contemporary significance of some of the lower wall stories. The choice of purely Old Testament imagery for the Painted Chamber—itself hard to parallel in the history of secular decoration—inevitably brought with it a certain view of the achievements, trials and tribulations of the Jewish people, who produced leaders who were models of chivalry as well as despicable tyrants, and who suffered from alien oppression. All these aspects are presented to us in the Painted Chamber: leadership in the form of Judas Maccabeus; tyranny in the forms of Ahaziah and Abimelech; foreign oppression in the forms of Sennacherib, Nebuzaradan, Nebuchadnezzar and Antiochus. As we have seen, the sequences from II Kings began with the Apocalyptic imagery of fire and miracles, but ended with an unusually extended and detailed account of the fall of Jerusalem after the time of Hezekiah, climaxing with the Captivity (pls. XVI*b*–XIX). We have here a sign of a very particular narrative interest which is hard to understand in terms of conventional Old Testament picture-cycles, but which takes on a distinct connotation in the context of the 1290s in England. In July 1290—just under two years before the inception of the redecoration of the Painted Chamber—an act of the king in his Council decreed that all Jews should leave England.[196] This action was the culmination of decades of royally sanctioned anti-Jewish feeling, which had brought upon the Jews manifold disasters of arrest, imprisonment and execution, which placed them under direct royal authority, and which ended with the first general expulsion of its sort in the medieval period.[197] Having noted that Edward I may have identified, as a warrior-ruler, with Judas Maccabeus, we have also to countenance the possibility that Edward, with sublime irony, was able to construct other pictorial narratives whose similarity to contemporary events can scarcely have gone unnoticed, and so to identify with the very figures who so far have appeared to be archetypal tyrants and oppressors. In this sense, the Painted Chamber, far from presenting us with a conventional antithesis of good and bad rule, can be seen openly to celebrate the wanton cruelty of its patron, recounting and mocking Jewish history with a blunt self-confidence.

The allusive potential of the Old Testament programme does much to create the impression that it was formed within rather specific circumstances, and that whatever pictorial or literary conventions shaped its imagery were masked by more immediate story-telling concerns. This raises a further question: was the scheme as ordained in the 1290s intended to have been of more than comparatively short-term significance? It is hard to believe nowadays that such rare, costly and cleverly conceived interior decorations may originally have been thought of as no more than entertaining, but disposable whimsies. But in comparison with the odd *mélange* of images in the Painted Chamber, more durable historical forms existed, most notably dynastic or biographic picture-cycles whose meaning would have persisted so long as the dynasty survived.[198] The fact that the Painted Chamber was retained in substantially its original form well into the fourteenth century is not of itself evidence that it was intended to be permanent. Indeed, an unforeseen consequence of its retention may have been that its pictures were gradually understood in terms of different expectations from those that shaped them in the first place. Subsequent references to the programme may inform us indirectly of the nature of its original significance. In 1307–8 the pictures are referred to in the accounts of particulars pertaining to their repair as comprising merely *diversae historiae*, terms which convey, if anything, an informality of conception, a lack of any prevailing theme (it is, of course, hazardous to base too much on the terse references so common in such administrative records). But, in 1323, the Painted Chamber is presented to us, in the unambiguous words of Symon Semeonis and Hugo Illuminator, as containing 'all the warlike stories of the whole Bible', a description which, as we have already seen, is not only governed by the hyperbole of the travelogue, but which also fundamentally misrepresents the contents of the scheme and underestimates its narrative richness. Although the scheme is, by its very inclusion in this account, acknowledged to be something singular, it is nevertheless portrayed in undeservedly commonplace terms: as little more than a history of biblical warfare or chivalry, and so as a member of an uncomplicated iconographic category. The banality of this portrayal may be significant. It might tell us something about the expectations of early fourteenth-century Irish mendicants acquainted, conceivably, with the type of imagery in works like the Maciejowski Bible or the Queen Mary Psalter, or other secular invocations of the deeds of the Jewish wars,[199] or indeed about what they thought appropriate for a major state apartment. These assumptions are of themselves instructive. But equally, it could be a sign that within a few years of its completion the allusive subtlety of the scheme was already lost on Westminster audiences; that its meaning was quickly decaying, and that it defied anything more than descriptive platitudes.

In conclusion, the importance of the Old Testament scenes for an understanding of the art of the period is twofold. First, they demonstrate that secular art retained a significant role in formulating ideas that lay strictly on the margins of conventional medieval imagery. Monumental secular art, of course, possessed characteristic and indeed commonplace genres of its own; historical, military, romantic and sacred imagery figures largely from the earliest times.[200] As narratives, the Old Testament scenes conform to this long-established tradition; but they also adapt it in a novel and striking way, revealing allegiance to these conventions while also reflecting on them critically. In the Painted Chamber we have an energetic, perhaps somewhat *ad hoc*, fusion of notions that can have had few precursors, and seems to have had no true successor. At most we have an anticipation of more systematized later medieval iconographies such as the Nine Worthies, but realized with a wit that attests to the continuing inventiveness of English iconography; an inventiveness which produced, in the realm of fourteenth-century domestic decoration, the quite different combination of didactic, scientific and encyclopedic imagery at Longthorpe Tower.[201] Second, we can be left with no doubt that without a record of the appearance and contents of these extraordinary murals, our view of the culture of Edward I's court would certainly be poorer. As it is, the Painted Chamber emerges as an outstanding reflection of the diversity and vitality of English court art at the end of the thirteenth century, bearing witness to the neglected importance of Edward I as a patron of the figurative arts.

CONCLUSION

This study has served as much to complicate as deepen our understanding of court art at Westminster in the thirteenth and early fourteenth centuries. It has been concerned with the monumental art of a great room, in a palace of central importance; and so, in a sense, with the public face of the English kings, turned towards the court circle and anyone admitted to it. To judge from some scholarship on the subject of court art, we might have expected this face to wear a fixed expression, and so to find royal ideology invested with certain eternal preoccupations, fundamental to the notion of 'courtliness'. In principle, it is at Westminster that the most stringent expressions of the 'court style' should be sought, for Westminster was both the heart of the court and also a major focus of the royal works.[1] Yet all the projects associated with the court at Westminster and elsewhere show, by their very diversity, that the notion of a 'court style' has to be handled with care. The range of material in the Painted Chamber alone is hard to square with a single idea of court art, and forces us to recognize that much depended on the differences of outlook of the kings that dominated the age, Henry III and Edward I. Court art is of importance because of its quality, its richly documented history, and its association with outstanding personalities. The 'court style' has been taken as the defining characteristic of the period, extending from the court by artistic osmosis to all manners of patronage and circumstance.[2] But the more closely we examine the idea of a 'court style', the more diffuse it seems, and the less efficient as a working notion it becomes.

Robert Branner addressed this very notion in his study of manuscript painting under St Louis. He concluded rightly that 'it is unfortunately impossible to demonstrate a direct, causative connection between royal patronage and style, as Vitzthum once thought was the case'.[3] For Branner, royal manuscript painting was eclectic in style; it was not just royal, but Parisian. This does not mean that court styles cannot be identified in one sense. Branner drew attention to the painted medallions in the Sainte-Chapelle in Paris as an example of royal painting closely bound up in some way with the tastes of the court, their style being assured of a wider authority in Paris as a whole by this very association.[4] The Sainte-Chapelle medallions are the nearest French equivalent to the Painted Chamber at Westminster in being linked to a great palace, the Cité, and so arguably to the highest values of the court circle. It is hard to fault the argument that court styles existed because certain styles were associated with the court; but it would be proper to question its value. Would it not be preferable to show that these court products were marked by an aesthetic character that was essentially or causally related to court patronage, rather than just associated with it?

This question could be more fruitfully answered if court art had come down to us as a consistent package of forms and images, backed up by independent evidence for the preferences of royal patrons. But the court styles in painting, and particularly architecture, were not strictly uniform; they moved quickly through successive styles, especially in the eclectic late thirteenth century, and if anything were marked by diversity and freedom of design; witness the repertoire of motifs and designs of the Eleanor Crosses, approved by the queen's executors and so presumably representative of court taste.[5] There is of course no problem in identifying certain design habits with court masons or painters and then tracing their influence elsewhere; this is probably the best working method available at present for dealing with the court styles.[6] The real question is how we account for the taste in the first place; how much initiative we ascribe to the working practices encouraged by the crown in a routine sense, and how much we ascribe to the intervention of the crown at a conscious level. Here we are by and large reliant on what is ascertainable from the works themselves. No systematic description of the 'courtly' aesthetic has yet been provided, although it is often taken for granted. Preferences are, inevitably, difficult to account for when so little independent documentary material survives concerning statements made by kings as to exactly what they were doing. The history of royal painting in the thirteenth century is well documented to the extent that it has a coherent chronology. But the royal administration was not designed to record the more abstract ideas associated with royal intentions. The nearest we get is under Henry III, whose use of the Close and Liberate Rolls means that we now have a body of evidence for the type of language used by the king in making his orders; we find the use of certain epithets such as *decens, pulcher* and *sumptuosus* that must have informed Henry's tastes.[7] Henry's intervention can be sensed often throughout his reign.[8] But this sort of evidence cannot provide a real basis for a critical history of royal taste, as we do not know *why* certain things mattered to Henry, only that they mattered at all. The position is worse under Edward I because he stopped using the administration in the way his father had; instead, the evidence from his reign consists largely of the accounts of particulars concerning the activities of his craftsmen.[9] It is only under Edward II that we find statements that work was undertaken *per proprium preceptum ordina- cionem et divisamentum Regis.*[10] Under these circumstances it is doubtful whether the court aesthetic will ever be reconstructed in terms independent of the works themselves, and indeed whether it remains a profitable line of enquiry at all. Nothing in principle separates the court aesthetic from any other in this period.

A more material problem is the absence of any strict evidence for a formal administered body of craftsmen that might have sustained a coherent court style over a long period. The one notable exception to this is provided, in a sense, by the tradition of employing certain painters over long periods, particularly Walter of Durham, whose career stretched over the reigns of Henry III and Edward I. But this tradition may be accounted for by a form of royal preference that may have extended beyond the recognition of specific artistic capacities. Henry's mandates show that he favoured certain painters in particular, notably Master William, a Westminster monk who was expected to work at more than one royal centre. William was employed not only at

Westminster, where he occupied a *domus* or workshop within the precinct of Westminster Abbey while working in the palace, but also at Windsor and Winchester.[11] The steady employment of such peripatetic craftsmen could be a sign that the king required wall paintings of a similar style at more than one residence, which could best be achieved by employing certain skilled individuals. But the dominance of certain painters may also have been a measure of the fact that they had a particularly close relationship with the domestic side of the court and so with the more intimate preferences of the king. Master William was the king's *beloved* painter who took his instructions in the presence of the king rather than via the keeper of the works.[12] Walter of Durham's curial position is not known exactly, but he held a serjeanty and so a nominal post.[13] The king made sure he was adequately compensated for damages incurred while in the royal service.[14] Both he and William are described as king's painter, and both are likely to have retained their positions because they were each, in a sense, a *familiaris*.[15]

We know less than we should about the organization of the royal painters in this period. There is no evidence that a formal post of king's painter existed in the thirteenth century as it did under later kings.[16] The first really detailed evidence for the organization of the painters at Westminster is supplied by the accounts for the St Stephen's Chapel murals executed from 1350.[17] Other records from this time tell us how the masters were appointed and how they were given warrants to seek their assistants.[18] The accounts of particulars for the chapel give rates of pay for those employed, and outline more explicitly than before the occupational structure of the workshop from the master downwards. The similar accounts surviving for the years 1292–7 and 1307–8 are marginally less precise in recording who did what; the tasks of drawing the paintings out on the walls, colouring and gilding can only be attributed very approximately on the grounds of size of wage. The palace *ateliers* of this period were smaller than that recorded in St Stephen's Chapel from 1350. About forty painters can be traced in the chapel accounts, whereas in the years 1292–7 the total was under thirty, varying from fifteen at any one time, as in late 1292, to as few as three in early 1293.[19] No more than a dozen were employed in the palace in 1307–8.[20] At this time, the master was responsible for the delivery of materials from London to Westminster; but beyond this, and the allocation of trivial tasks, such as the preparation of pigments, to apprentices, little of real distinction can be gleaned about working methods.

One point is, however, clear. Royal painters did not work exclusively for the king. Walter of Durham may have been a royal *familiaris*, but it is difficult to see what he would have done in times, such as the 1280s, when a marked decline in the domestic activity of wall painting occurred at Westminster. Very likely he went elsewhere, working 'by appointment' for periods of intense activity at court, but also moving in the service of other patrons; Walter's career may have been very like that of the French royal painter Evrard d'Orléans, who was later employed in the Palais de la Cité while also being available to patrons of the court circle such as Mahaut d'Artois, with whose houses he was associated.[21] The fluid relationship between the court and its painters is strongly suggested by the form of appointment by *assignation*[22] of Thomas of Westminster as head of the painters in 1307–8. This form of appointment was strictly provisional and ended when the work was complete. Thomas was not a royal *familiaris* like the narrative painter John of St Albans, who was rewarded for dancing on a table before Edward II.[23] In fact the nature of Thomas's appointment is strikingly like that of the masons drawn to Westminster by Edward I in the 1290s. In 1292, Michael of Canterbury formed a lodge of masons with a marked Kentish presence, much as Thomas's team of painters had an East Anglian contingent, for the reconstruction of St Stephen's Chapel.[24] No permanent lodge existed at Westminster in the 1290s, because one had to be specially built for Michael.[25] In 1297, on the collapse of royal finances, none of the masons and few of the painters were retained in the court service. By departing from Westminster they may well have disseminated court designs in the service of other patrons, perhaps in Kent, and certainly in East Anglia.[26]

The notion that court wall painting styles were probably the product of specific favoured individuals, rather than formal or permanent court workshops, is complemented by the absence of firm evidence for the existence of an *atelier* of manuscript painters at court. The idea that such a court 'school' existed is now something of an orthodoxy, and to this entity have been attributed some major works, notably *La Estoire de Seint Aedward*, Douce, the Alfonso Psalter and the Ashridge College *Petrus Comestor*.[27] But as yet no corresponding account has been offered of the nature or location of this workshop, largely because no documentation for it is known; it is improbable that such an institution would have completely escaped mention in the royal administrative records.[28] Moreover, despite the links between the related styles of *La Estoire* and the added drawings in the Westminster Psalter (BL Royal MS 2 A.XXII), and Westminster, and the circumstantial links to the court or Westminster of Douce, the 'Merton' *Flores Historiarum*, the Alfonso Psalter and the *Petrus Comestor*, we are hardly confronted by the development of a single coherent court idiom, let alone evidence for a single workshop, in this period.[29] Indeed, a more important question may be whether these styles had commercial or metropolitan existences independent of Westminster as a centre of patronage. What little is known of court manuscript patronage tends to suggest informality of organization. Although Henry's court had glamorous manuscripts—one of them was on deposit at the London Temple—many of these were simply bought when needed, a consideration at variance with the idea of one workshop answering to all the court's needs.[30] Of the various secular manuscripts owned and carried about by Edward and Eleanor of Castile, at least one was bought in France, and others could have originated in the small *ad hoc* shops of select painters appointed by the court, such as that employed in the queen's itinerant household in the years around 1290.[31] It is significant that Robert Branner's study of thirteenth-century French court manuscripts reveals essentially the same pattern at work, with no signs that formal court workshops existed under St Louis or his successors.[32] Master Honoré's association with the French court seems to have been commercial rather than curial.[33] Indeed, it may be possible to show that English court manuscript patronage was closely bound up with manuscript painting on a commercial scale in London; that it was not so much courtly as metropolitan, and that its history was very much like that of court architecture in the late thirteenth century, when a number of royal masons had close London, as well as Westminster, connections.[34] The court may have relied on what it could buy.

The view that, in general, court patronage may have been informal, metropolitan and eclectic in inspiration, rather than merely official, in no way affects its standing. A display of uniformity was not necessarily a better guarantee of prestige than a display of variety, and the vitality of court art in this period is to be assessed by its capacity to call on a wider range of skills, and so techniques and styles, than other forms of patronage. The impressive range of architectural designs open to the court, the coexistence at Westminster of several sculptural styles on court memorials, and the availability of more than one style of manuscript painting, suggest that strength through variety was the real aim of court patronage. An element in this was the court's encouragement of entirely new techniques. It imported the forms of rich applied polychromy used by the French court in Paris; it imported on a scale unparalleled in northern Europe the mosaic decorations associated with Roman and papal patronage for use on pavements, tombs, and the shrine of St Edward;[35] it adapted these mosaics by setting into them brass lettering, so encouraging the growth of a London-based manufacture of brass memorials;[36] it produced for royal burials the finest, if not quite the first,[37] instances of bronze sculpture while at the same time, in the 1290s, importing an effigy decorated with Limoges enamel;[38] and, in the fourteenth century, was quick to adopt yet another new material for royal effigies, alabaster.[39] The extraordinary and almost irreconcilable range of tastes found at Westminster by 1300 can hardly have been matched at any other single centre in England, and leads us to suppose that the court circle had as many styles as it had members.

The wide curiosity of taste that marked the English court styles, showing an awareness of not only French, but Italian ideas, seems to have prevailed under both Henry III and his son. Yet royal patronage at Westminster also illustrates the quite fundamental differences in the ways that Henry and Edward regarded their roles as patrons, differences which transcended the problems of administering the royal works and the diversity of court styles. Their reigns saw a transformation of Westminster as a royal centre. Henry III sustained the new importance given to Westminster by the Angevin kings of the twelfth century as a centre of royal administration.[40] At first, the Palace of Westminster was but one focus of Henry's patronage of the royal residences, receiving a measure of attention also lavished by Henry on Clarendon, Winchester, Windsor and elsewhere. In fact for Henry, the most important work at Westminster was not the palace at all, but the reconstruction of the abbey church undertaken from 1245. The administration of the royal works was gradually adapted to cope with the dual stresses imposed by the demands of a substantial palace and the rising fabric of Westminster Abbey.[41] From the late 1250s, the increasingly sedentary king spent more time at Westminster each year. It is only by the 1260s that Westminster can be said to have truly dominated the king's attention, not only as a result of the narrowing of his own domestic horizons with age, but also precisely because of the new status of the abbey church. The 1250s and 1260s saw a growing degree of cooperation between the palace and abbey. Royal painters were now employed in both buildings, thereby establishing the close formal links between painting at the two places that lasted into the fourteenth century.[42] Henry worked closely, too, with the Abbots of Westminster, notably Richard of Barking, and especially Richard of Ware, who contributed substantially towards the decorative programme of the royal *Eigenkloster* by his international activity.[43] For Henry, the symbolic importance of the complex of palatine and monastic buildings was expressed in the cult and imagery of St Edward.

The reign of Edward I reveals a significant shift of emphasis. In the first place, Edward inherited a royal palace of established importance; at first, he decided to expend no more on it than was absolutely necessary for the purposes of the new royal household. Edward quickly emerged above all as a patron of military works.[44] It is not always easy to make a clear distinction between purely military and artistic activity; Caernarvon Castle illustrates the complex interaction of military planning and visual symbolism in Edward's Welsh policy.[45] But there can be little doubt that war finance of one sort or another was a major factor in Edward's outlook. It had a demonstrable impact on Westminster in the 1290s, when war with both France and Scotland precipitated a retrenchment of royal finances which, in 1297, brought to an abrupt halt the work on St Stephen's Chapel, the Painted Chamber, and even the Coronation Chair, conceived in bronze before the financial crisis, but finally executed in painted wood.[46] A combination of phenomenal energy and political necessity conspired to keep Edward away from Westminster for periods unknown under his father; as a result the palace was neglected in the 1280s, and the pattern of close cooperation with Westminster Abbey established by Henry broken.[47] The 1270s and 1280s were uncertain decades in the history of royal patronage at the church, and the relationship between crown and monastery ceased to all intents and purposes until well into the next century.[48] Edward's interest turned decisively towards new projects: the Welsh castles, the founding of Vale Royal Abbey, the construction of a new palace chapel at Westminster, and the redecoration of the Painted Chamber.[49]

Except perhaps for the Welsh castles, all these projects demonstrate the spasmodic nature of Edward's patronage. For no apparent reason, Edward abandoned the project at Vale Royal suddenly and finally in 1290.[50] For a relatively short period, between the death of Eleanor of Castile in 1290 and the crisis of 1297, Edward's patronage went through a new and unforeseen phase. Edward experienced a new sense of *pietas* which directed him to translate the body of his father from the former grave of St Edward to the new, Italianate tomb in the abbey in 1290.[51] Once royal initiative at Vale Royal had ended, it was transferred to the provision of the remarkable memorials for Queen Eleanor. By 1292, the Palace of Westminster was the subject of a substantial new project involving its secular rooms and intensive investment in the fabric of St Stephen's Chapel. Yet, by Edward's death in 1307, only the Eleanor Crosses were complete; the Painted Chamber was still in need of attention, and work on St Stephen's had stopped for 10 years, not to restart until the 1320s.[52] All the evidence suggests that Edward suddenly, and inexplicably, chose to revive interest in Westminster as a significant subject of royal patronage for the first time since the early 1270s, and that for financial and political reasons he was unable to realize his new ambitions there. It is precisely the precarious nature of Edward's Westminster project of the 1290s that has to be taken into account in explaining why, for the most part, court art in these years was neither formally nor permanently organized, and why royal patronage cannot of itself have acted as the more universal stimulus that some scholars have assumed it did.[53]

More importantly, Edward's concentration on Westminster at the end of his reign was associated with a new royal ideology. Its emphasis was now that of a secularized court culture, deriving much of its impetus from the understanding that the authority of kingship lay as much in its historical as in its spiritual claims.[54] The principal importance of Westminster now lay in the sense of prestige that attached to its palace rather than its abbey. By 1296 the work on the palace was regarded as the metropolitan counterpart to Edward's mighty Welsh plan. Westminster Abbey saw no important royal intervention in the 1290s beyond the royal burials. Edward now used the abbey church as a repository for the trophies of war and conquest in Wales and Scotland; it was now the home of Arthur's crown, the Cross Neath, and the stone of Scone, rather than the centre of the cult of St Edward.[55] Edward's Arthurian enthusiasm was now focused not in Wales, or Scotland, or at Glastonbury, but in the metropolis.[56] Historical and military imagery took on an importance at court that it had not had under Henry III. The pious Henry's interest in the iconography of Alexander, and especially Richard I and Saladin and the *Gestes of Antioch*, was by its nature capricious, resulting primarily from Henry's having taken up the Cross in 1250.[57] Edward revived the spirit of the crusades and appealed to romantic historical precedent more widely, and with a strong sense of the value of propaganda. In Wales he had Arthur and Magnus Maximus; in Scotland, Brutus; at Westminster, Judas Maccabeus. Edward used Geoffrey of Monmouth's *History of the Kings of Britain* in a letter to Pope Boniface VIII in 1301, in support of his claim to the overlordship of Scotland based on precedents going back to the fall of Troy and the time of the prophets.[58] He rifled northern monastic chronicles as well as the royal archives for historical information to this end.[59] This new, opportunistic interest may explain the production *c.* 1300 of illustrated genealogies of the English kings down to Edward I, accompanied by scenes from the stories of Jason, Troy and Brutus; one such genealogy, produced in roll form (Oxford, Bodleian Library MS Bodley Rolls 3) may even have been executed for the royal circle when attention shifted from Westminster to York in the early 1300s during the Scottish campaign.[60]

What motivated Edward's activity at Westminster is hard to decide. Having been away from the palace for long periods from the late 1270s, and having at last completed his tasks in Wales and Gascony, he may have felt on returning to England in 1289 that he was now sufficiently secure politically to embark on a phase of consolidated and domestic patronage.[61] His reasons for rebuilding the palace chapel have gone unrecorded. Whatever intentions he may have had, the position in the 1290s was complicated by the death of Eleanor in 1290. It is not entirely true to say that after her death Edward developed a distaste for the palace; the interest which he showed in the house of the Archbishop of York at Westminster in these years may have arisen because the extent of the works at the principal palace rendered it uninhabitable.[62] It certainly became useless when the fire of 1298 damaged a number of its rooms, after which

Edward had to move his new queen, Margaret, and her household to chambers specially constructed at the Archbishop's house.[63] Whether or not Edward eventually intended to spend more time at the Palace of Westminster, his initial plan in conceiving the works there may have been to provide a glamorous context for the new marriage he hoped for in the 1290s. His desire to remarry exposed Edward to the types of pressure that favoured investment in impressive works of art such as the Painted Chamber. He had, after all, only to consider what his future brother-in-law Philippe le Bel was undertaking by way of works at the Palais de la Cité in Paris.[64] The Cité was like its Westminster cousin in the informality of its planning, and like it saw a gradual concentration of curial and administrative activities, and a similar definition of the public and private sectors of its topography, as the thirteenth century progressed.[65] Louis IX had greatly beautified the Cité by constructing the Sainte-Chapelle; but in the 1290s, at the same time as Edward's project at Westminster, Philippe le Bel decided greatly to expand the palace by reconstructing numerous chambers, and building the immense Grand' Salle, vying in scale with the huge Great Hall at Westminster.[66] Philippe's intense activity at the Cité, which carried on well into the next century, was essentially similar to Edward's at Westminster. Both kings understood the importance and authority of impressive public displays of the iconography of kingship. Philippe redecorated the Sainte-Chapelle at the time of the translation of the relics of St Louis, and devised for the Grand' Salle a spectacular sculpted genealogy of the French kings from the time of the Merovingians.[67] Simultaneously, Edward was supporting his territorial claims by reference to the ancient British past, while at the same time adapting a recent French court prototype for the Eleanor Crosses.[68]

Whatever its motivation or success, Edward's role in enhancing the prestige of the Palace of Westminster was acknowledged by his otherwise wayward son, Edward II. In 1324, moved by a delayed sense of filial piety, Edward ordered that the Lesser Hall next to the Painted Chamber at Westminster should be painted with 'the life of his father whom God assoil'.[69] The evidence of a life of King Edward formerly painted in the bishop's palace at Lichfield in these years suggests that these paintings were probably martial and heroic in character.[70] Within 20 years of his death, Edward I was elevated to the status of one of the *Preux* of history, his life celebrated in the royal eulogies of the period, and adorning the walls of the new Camelot which he, as *Arthurus redivivus,* had tried to create.

With the scenes of the life of Edward I, the decorations of the Palace of Westminster re-enter the mainstream of public, dynastic art in medieval Europe.[71] The Irish friars who described the Painted Chamber as it stood in 1323 cannot have known that, as they travelled towards Jerusalem, Edward II was reviving the theme of the warrior prince at Westminster. What they, or any other members of the public who now frequented the palace in increasing numbers, would have made of the biography of Edward I is unknown. But how intriguing it is to imagine, for a moment, what thoughts may have entered the minds of those now gathering for Parliament at Westminster, Lords and Commons alike, when confronted by the images in the great rooms of its palace.

CATALOGUE

The catalogue which follows provides the reader with a survey of the known copies of the murals in the Painted Chamber, together with a commentary on those aspects of their iconography not described fully in the main text. The murals are considered in the chronological order proposed in the earlier chapters, starting with those paintings attributable to Henry III.

The catalogue draws on four sources:

1. Twenty-two watercolour copies by Charles Stothard of late 1819, in the Library of the Society of Antiquaries of London (hereafter S).
2. Eighteen watercolour copies by Edward Crocker of late 1819, in the Ashmolean Museum, Oxford (hereafter C I).
3. Twelve incomplete watercolour copies squared for transfer, by Edward Crocker, of late 1819, in the Victoria and Albert Museum, Department of Prints and Drawings 93.E.3, pp. 32–9 (hereafter C II).
4. Sketches by John Buckler dated October 1819 in BL Add. MS 36370, fols. 205–9 (hereafter B).

The Stothard copies have always been in the possession of the Society of Antiquaries, and were first published with a scholarly text by Rokewode (see Rokewode 1885). Rokewode's account contains a useful survey of the details of fashion and armour found in the murals. The Crocker copies in the Ashmolean Museum formed part of the 1834 Douce Bequest, and were formerly deposited in the Bodleian Library. A note by one J. Booth on the back of Inscription II (no. 11) of this set reads as follows:

> drawn etc. by the encouragement of Sir Gregory Page Turner Bart. Inscriptions found on the walls of the Painted Chamber taken by Edward Crocker ^{Junior} [sic] Clerk of the Works—*and is the only copy taken*. Mr Crocker has taken copies also, of the remains of paintings on the walls of the P.C. which accompanies [sic] the inscriptions.

The attribution of the Ashmolean copies is confused somewhat by the fact that three Edward Crockers were employed in various capacities in the Office of Works in the eighteenth and early nineteenth centuries. Edward Crocker I (d. 1779) had been First Clerk in the Office (*KW*, vi, 59). His son, Edward Crocker II (*c.* 1757–1836), was employed in the Office for over 40 years. He was Clerk of the Works at Westminster 1818–29, and was in charge of the alterations made to the Painted Chamber in 1818–19 at the time of the discovery of its wall paintings (*KW*, i, 499; *KW*, vi, 59, 115–16, 676). His son, Edward Crocker III, was a Labourer in Trust in the Westminster district 1812–27 (*KW*, vi, 119, 677). As both Edward Crocker II and III were sometimes accorded the epithet 'junior' it is possible that J. Booth's note could refer to either of them. But it is most unlikely that a Clerk of the Works would be confused with a Labourer in Trust, the latter being no more than a site foreman (*KW*, vi, 118); thus the copies must for the present be attributed to Edward Crocker II. The copies were certainly not done by Thomas Crofton Croker, as suggested by Tudor-Craig (1957, 94). Edward Crocker's patron, Sir Gregory Osborne Page Turner (1785–1843), was a collector of pictures and curiosities, an Oxford graduate, and a suspected lunatic. He is known to have employed artists to make drawings of antiquities in the Home Counties (see his obituary in *Gentleman's Magazine* (1843), pt. ii, 93).

The 'spoilt drawings by Mr Crocker' in the Victoria and Albert Museum, which are his on-site drawings, were acquired by the Museum from B. T. Batsford in 1897. The volume in which they are kept contains a miscellany of brass rubbings, drawings and watercolours formerly in the possession of the eminent architect William Burges. According to Professor J. M. Crook, who has guided me on matters concerning the Crocker copies, Burges was distantly related to the Crocker family and was friendly with one of the Crocker sisters (see J. M. Crook, *William Burges and the High Victorian Dream* (London, 1981), 98).

In the following conspectus, the number by the title of each mural refers to its position on the elevation of the Painted Chamber (figs. 3, 4). The location of the murals was established with the aid of Crocker's admirable plan and elevation of the room in the Ashmolean set (pl. XXXII). In some cases, where Stothard copied paintings not copied by Crocker (e.g. nos. 12, 25, 26, 27, 28), the position and size of the originals cannot be exactly ascertained, as Stothard did not provide his own keyed elevation of the room. Each entry gives the sizes of the copies, the approximate size of the original mural, and any texts in the murals. All measurements are metric.

I. THE IMAGES OF ST EDWARD AND THE TRIUMPHANT VIRTUES (nos. 1–9)
(mainly 1263–72) (fig. 3, p. 37)

1. *The Coronation of St Edward*
S   18·3×33·0 cm. (col. pl. I).
CI   22·0×41·1 cm. (pl. II).
CII   27·0×44·1 cm. (p. 39, D. 649·97 whole sheet) (pl. I).
B fol. 207ᵛ includes a sketch of the quatrefoil opening in the mural.
Size of original: 1·73×3·23 m.
Text: CEST LE CORONEMENT SEINT EDEWARD.

2. *Guardian of Solomon's Bed*
CI   25·3×10·2 cm. (pl. III).
CII   26·8× 9·8 cm. (p. 34, D.635·97 whole sheet).
Size of original: 1·73×0·81 m.
Text: indecipherable.

3. *St John the Pilgrim*
S   18·8×12·8 cm. (pl. IV*a*).
CI   17·4×12·6 cm. (pl. V*a*).
Size of original: approx. 1·40×1·12 m.
Text: *Sire dubie(z) me/donez.por lam(ur)/Deu q(ui) bie(n) amez.*

4. *St Edward with the Ring*
S   18·7×12·7 cm. (pl. IV*b*).
CI   17·4×12·7 cm. (pl. V*b*).
Size of original: approx. 1·40×1·12 m.
Text: *Pelerin p(re)nez cest a(nel)* [etc.].

5. *Largesce–Covoitise*
S   37·0×12·8 cm. (col. pl. II*a*).
CI   41·5×12·9 cm. (shows a further small and unidentifiable scene in a panel beneath
     the Vice not included by Stothard) (pl. VI*a*).
The whole splay composition is illustrated in a representation of the Painted Chamber
of *c.* 1820 by Stephanoff, in Westminster City Library, Box 57 (pl. XXVIII).
Size of original: approx. 3·05×1·12 m.
Texts: LARGESCE   COVOITISE.
Arms in block border: England/The Empire.

6. *Debonereté–Ira*
S   37·0×12·6 cm. (col. pl. II*b*).
CI   43·0×12·8 cm. (shows a further scene of animals, contents uncertain, as in no. 5)
     (pl. VI*b*).
Size of original: approx. 3·05×1·12 m.
Texts: DEBONERETE   IRA.
Arms: *Debonereté*'s shield comprises England differenced by two bars.
Arms in block border: England/St Edmund/St Edward.

7. *Angel bearing a crown over Debonereté* (pl. XLI*b*)
B fol. 208,   labelled 'Painting on ye W side of ye sofit of ye most western arch of ye
window on ye S. side—Painted Chamber Westminster Oct. 5. 1819'. The colour notes
record that the angel's mantle was blue and that its ground was red. The corresponding
angel on the opposite side of the arch is shown in Stephanoff's view of no. 5.

8. *Vérité*
CI   20·2×12·8 cm. (pl. VII).
CII 29·0×17·8 cm. (p. 38, D.645·97 whole sheet).
Size of original: approx. 1·52×1·12 m.
Text: VERITE.
Arms: *Vérité*'s round shield bears the arms argent, a cross gules.

9. *A Virtue (? Fortitude)*
S   18·0×12·3 cm. (pl. VIII*a*).
CI   20·2×12·7 cm. (pl. VIII*b*).
Size of original: approx. 1·52×1·12 m.
Arms: on the shield, vert, a saltire fleuronny between four lions passant gardant or.

II.   The Old Testament Scenes (nos. 10–27) (1292–7, repaired or completed 1307–8)
(fig. 4, p. 83)

The scenes are described by bands from the top downwards

10–15. *Texts and Illustrations from 1 Maccabees, i–ix*
   On discovery in 1819, the Old Testament scenes were in a highly fragmentary state.
Most of the surviving scenes were on the south wall on the lower registers. Only one

scene (no. 12) was copied from the north wall. The topmost register was quite void of pictorial evidence. However, Edward Crocker copied three texts from the top two bands of the north wall, and these, taken in conjunction with the meagre pictorial evidence, enable the general contents of the top two bands to be identified. No texts were copied from the lower registers.

The inscriptions used a bold Gothic *textualis* script which on palaeographic grounds may be dated to the late thirteenth, or preferably the early fourteenth century. The *pentimenti* in Inscription I (no. 10) show that the layout, and possibly the contents, of the texts were revised at some point in this period. An earlier layer of lettering of unknown extent was disposed in two, not three, lines of script within the inscription bands beneath the pictures; but this was evidently replaced by a three-line text in an identical script, suggesting that the revisions or additions (the three-line text implies denser textual coverage) occurred soon after the initial execution. The repair or clarification of texts would have had a high priority in the maintenance of the murals. On balance, the palaeographic evidence supports the contention that these narratives were executed towards the end of the thirteenth century and that repairs or revisions took place shortly afterwards, perhaps in 1307–8.

The textual and linguistic evidence of the inscriptions is slight. As with the earlier murals in the Painted Chamber, the language is French, and what can be gleaned from the texts shows that they consisted of a translation, or more likely a close paraphrase, of the biblical text, with one or two signs (notably in no. 10) of editing and adaptation. I know of no comparable translation of 1 Maccabees in French of this period. On the basis of transcripts of these fragments, the late Dr Ruth Morgan suggested to me that some aspects of the declensions, such as *reis-rei* in no. 10, may indicate that the texts are not in Anglo-Norman; but the dialectal evidence is too slight to be conclusive. The texts are primarily of value in helping to identify the contents of registers where no pictures are copied. The Vulgate text is extracted here for comparison.

10. *Inscription I* (pl. IX and see p. 117, A)
Length of original: 8·56 m.

The account is that in 1 Macc. i, 16–19, where Antiochus decides to rule over Egypt; he invades with a great military force and defeats King Ptolemy; the land is sacked. The first part of the register at the top of the north wall, with which the Maccabees account began, must therefore have illustrated the prior events in 1 Maccabees, with the death of Alexander and the rise of his disreputable successor, Antiochus. The text of Inscription I is illegible after v, 19, although 'Antiochus' and 'les chandelabies' can be made out, doubtless in reference to 1 Macc. i, 20–4, where Antiochus despoils the Temple of Jerusalem and carries off the treasures. At this point there occurs a palimpsest in the inscriptions, with an earlier and larger layer of lettering reading perhaps '(Ieru)salem' (pl. IX). Inscription I shows that over 12·2 m. of this register were devoted to the first 24 or so verses of 1 Macc. i; this is therefore deliberate and thorough illustration. The remainder of the top band, which continued around the east and south walls, was void of more pictorial or textual evidence; but its original contents can be determined by the contents of the second band down.

11. *Inscription II* (see p. 117, B)
Length of original: 6·15 m.

This text began over 4 m. into the second band down on the north wall. Although fragmentary, the material is that in 1 Macc. v, 28–34. Judas Maccabeus plunders and burns the town of Bozrah, and at dawn arrives at Dathema to find it under siege by

... regna sur. i.i. reames | Li reis antiochus entra en egipte agrant ost.de chevachars. & ....
... de oliphans & ala sur | mut de batailes en (con)tre le rei tholome' de egipte. & le ....
.... en servage. | citees garnies. & (m)ist tut ala spee e a gref ....

(ut) regnaret super duo regna et intravit in Aegyptum in multitudine gravi in curribus et elefantis (et equitibus et copiosa navium multitudine) et constituit bellum adversus Ptolomeum regem Aegypti (et veritus est Ptolomeus a facie eius et fugit) et ceciderunt vulnerati multi et conprehendit civitates munitas in terra Aegypti et accepit spolia terrae Aegypti [etc.]

A. Inscription I (no. 10)

...... adthien. | Judas & sa gen(t) leveret . . . le iur aparut.il virec gra(n)t peple en vena(n)t' sur. ....
. destrutes. Et | iudas oi la gra(n)t clam(ur) del peple . . . ciel a tubes q(ui) die(n)t . . ..
.... & arse. | en i.i.i. pacues .... viii. mil ho(mm)es. & timotheus

et accepit omnia spolia eorum et succendit eam igni et surrexerunt inde nocte et ibant usque ad munitionem et factum est diluculo cum adlevassent oculos suos ecce populus multus cuius non erat numerus (portantes scalas et machinas ut conprehenderent munitionem et expugnarent eos) et vidit Iudas quia coepit bellum et clamor belli ascendit in caelum sicut tuba (et clamor magnus de civitate et exercitui dixit pugnate hodie pro fratribus vestris) et venit tribus ordinibus (post eos exclamaverunt tubis et clamaverunt in oratione et cognoverunt castra Timothei quia Macchabeus est et refugerunt a facie eius et percusserunt eos plaga magna et ceciderunt ex eis in illa die fere) octo milia virorum [etc.]

B. Inscription II (no. 11)

Timotheus; advancing in three columns, Judas slaughters eight thousand of Timotheus' army. Inscription II continues

> Judas ret(ur)na . . .
> . . mist le feu & . .
> . . . casbo(r)

from 1 Macc. v, 35–6, relating the occupation of Casphor after the burning of Alema. This is followed shortly by

> Judas ase(m)bla tut les ira (?) . . . .

from 1 Macc. v, 45 ('et congregavit Iudas universos Israhelitas'), where Judas gathers the Israelites in Gilead. One of the illustrations from this part of 1 Macc. v, was copied by Stothard.

12. *Judas Maccabeus attacks Dathema and Alema*
S   14·5×33·9 cm. (col. pl. III).
Size of original: approx. 1·60×3·96 m.
Text: *iudas* (over the head of Judas Maccabeus).

To the left, trumpets are sounded and prayer is offered up, 1 Macc. v, 33–4; Judas battles with Timotheus, v, 34, and sacks Alema, v, 35. No. 12 therefore coordinates with the first part of Inscription II.

13. *Inscription III*
Length of original: 4·60 m.

With Inscription II, this text gives a good idea of the general outlines of the contents of the second band down on the north wall. The text is largely indecipherable but includes

> Gorgias pr(?).v.mil.h(ommes).& mil a cheval.& vi(n)t apavilus iude. .

from 1 Macc. iv, 1–2 ('et adsumpsit Gorgias quinque milia virorum et mille equites electos et moverunt castra nocte ut adplicarent ad castra Iudaeorum'), where Gorgias takes five thousand men and a thousand cavalry to attack the Jewish camp unawares.

The ordering of events in nos. 11 and 13 is therefore not according to the biblical sequence, because material in 1 Macc. v precedes that in 1 Macc. iv. If we assume that the ordering of the texts was not mixed up in the process of copying, it then appears that some shuffling about of the 1 Maccabees events may have taken place. Nevertheless, it can be ascertained from Inscriptions II and III that the lower of the two Maccabees bands on the north wall began with material in chapters iv and v. This inevitably circumscribes the contents of the largely void top band which opened on the north wall with the start of 1 Maccabees. As the lower band began with chapter v, beneath the account from chapter i on the top band, it must follow that the remainder of the top band illustrated events between 1 Macc. i, 24, and chapters iv and v. The top band of the Painted Chamber thus related the narrative in 1 Macc. i–iii, at least. The first part of the lower Maccabees band went as far as 1 Macc. v. It is reasonable to conclude, therefore, that this second band down contained approximately the same amount of narrative, i.e. about four or five chapters, as the top band. Thus, the two top bands should have depicted about one half of the total of sixteen chapters in 1 Maccabees.

This is proved by the contents of the two copied scenes from the lower of the two top bands on the south wall, to the west of the windows.

14. *The Warfare of Judas Maccabeus and Nicanor*
S   14·8×42·1 cm. (pl. X*a*).
CI   19·7×64·2 cm. (pl. X*b*).
Size of original: 1·60×5·0 m.
Texts: *iudas* (shown once in S, twice in CI).

An elaborate picture showing two scenes of conflict punctuated by three edifices containing groups of figures. The iconography can be identified as that in I Macc. vii, 29–50, relating the fate of Nicanor at the hands of Judas Maccabeus. First, Judas is seen at the battle of Capharsalama, I Macc. vii, 32. At the centre, Nicanor goes up to Mount Zion, represented by a two-tiered building, and mocks the priests, holding a sword in his right hand; below, the priests go into the Temple and curse Nicanor, I Macc. vii, 33–8. Nicanor then falls at the battle of Adasa, I Macc. vii, 43, and Judas is seen at Gazara, vii, 45.

No. 14 shows that all but the last 9 m. or so of the second band down took the narrative as far as I Macc. vii, as was anticipated in discussion of nos. 11 and 13. It is now possible to describe the overall scope of the I Maccabees events in the Painted Chamber. Chapter viii includes material incidental to the deeds of Judas Maccabeus that have so far formed a central element in the story, and at the start of chapter ix there occurs the dramatic climax of the account, the death of Judas at the hands of Bacchides, vv. 3–22. There is no reason to doubt that the death and burial of Judas Maccabeus brought the narrative almost to a halt at the end of the second band down on the south wall.

15. *The Ambush of the Jambrites' Wedding*
S   15·2×12·1 cm. (pl. XI*a*).
CI   19·3×14·8 cm. (pl. XI*b*).
CII   16·1×17·4 cm. (p. 32, D.628.97 whole sheet).
Size of original: 1·60×1.17 m.

Above, a group of armed figures are concealed behind bushes. To the right, a civilian is assaulted by a mailed figure armed with a pick. Below, an armed and helmeted figure bearing a sword is being addressed urgently by a man. The imagery is that in I Macc. ix, 38–43. Jonathan, seeking revenge, ambushes the wedding-party of the Jambrites; below, Bacchides is informed of the event. The iconography cannot be that suggested by Rokewode (1885, 33) concerning events at Modin in chapter ii. Instead, the scene indicates that the second band down ended with the events immediately after the death and burial of Judas Maccabeus.

16–22. *Illustrations from II Kings*
The illustrations from II Kings started between the windows on the third row down on the south side. What preceded these episodes on the northern and eastern sections of this register is unknown. The first episodes recorded began after King Ahaziah's fall from a window, with Ahaziah's captain and his fifty men being sent to take Elijah.

16. *Elijah and Ahaziah*
S   14·7×45·2 cm. (pl. XII*a*).
CI   14·7×46·4 cm. (pl. XII*b*).
CII   15·6×46·9 cm. (p. 37, D.641.97 whole sheet).
Size of original: 1·12×3·96 m.
Texts: *eli* (over Elijah in each case).

An unidentifiable figure can be seen standing under a canopy with shafts to the left. One of the companies of Ahaziah is destroyed by fire at Elijah's command; the soldiers are seen tumbling down before the figure of the seated prophet, II Kings, i, 9–10. The third company is spared, and kneels in supplication before Elijah, who turns to the angel of the Lord descending with a scroll, II Kings, i, 13–15. The narrative then divides. Over the curve of the window arch, Elijah is seen standing over and condemning King Ahaziah as he lies in bed within an elaborate architectural surround, in illustration of II Kings, i, 16. Below, to the left of the window, Elijah divides the waters of the Jordan with his mantle, in the presence of Elisha, II Kings, ii, 7–8.

17. *The Miracles of Elisha*
S   15·0×32·0 cm. (col. pl. IV).
CI   14·0×28·9 cm. (pl. XIII).
CII   16·5×29·9 cm. (p. 36, D.640.97 whole sheet).
Size of original: 1·12×2·31 m.

To the right of the western window on the south wall some 6·10 m. of the third register down was blank. The next scene from this register relates events from II Kings, iv, 38, to v, 27. The intervening space must therefore have contained illustrations from II Kings, ii, 8, to iv, 38. In no. 17, Elisha is seen seated with an open book in his left hand, instructing a servant to pour meal into a large boiling cauldron heated over a fire, so sweetening the potage, II Kings, iv, 38–41. In a large enclosure above, bread is handed out to the starving people of Gilgal, II Kings, iv, 42–4. The following scenes are similarly disposed in front of and within small raised stages supported on masonry substructures. Naaman, above, brings ten talents of silver, and the letter from the King of Aram, to the King of Israel, who rends his clothes, II Kings, v, 5–7. Below, Naaman, on the instructions of Elisha, bathes in the Jordan to cure his leprosy, II Kings, v, 14. The next building was substantially damaged. Above, Naaman, cured of his leprosy, is seen before Elisha, who accepts no reward for the cure, II Kings, v, 15–19. Below, a figure is seen approaching a gaily adorned horse-drawn cart; the drivers look back. Gehazi, Elisha's servant, has stopped Naaman to obtain a reward against Elisha's wishes, II Kings, v, 20–2. Immediately, in the next building above, Elisha curses Gehazi with Naaman's leprosy, II Kings, v, 25–7.

18. *The Famine in Samaria*
S   14·9×34·6 cm. (pl. XIV*a*).
CI   14·2×30·4 cm. (pl. XIV*b*).
Size of original: 1·12×2·44 m.

This scene followed within a few cm. of no. 17. Its top half was obliterated. The narrative picks up with II Kings, vi. To the left, the blinded host of soldiers turns back to Elisha, who directs them to Samaria, II Kings, vi, 19. Next, within an aedicule, the troops are seen feasting at a table, II Kings, vi, 23. In the next compartment, a dismembered body is lying on a table, in illustration of II Kings, vi, 26–30, where a woman cooks and eats her child during the famine. Finally, the Aramaean camp is plundered and the faithless lieutenant is trampled underfoot, II Kings, vii, 16–20.

19. *King Hezekiah and Sennacherib*
S   14·9×36·4 cm. (pl. XV*a*).
CI   10·6×48·6 cm. (combined with no. 20) (pl. XVI*a*).
CII   13·0×27·2 cm. (p. 36, D.639.97 whole sheet).
Size of original (with no. 20): 0·91×3·90 m.
Texts: *arabians* (over Sennacherib's men) *(e)lye kim* (over Eliakim) *ysai* (over Isaiah).

After II Kings, vii, 20, the narrative from II Kings broke back to the fourth row down on the south wall, immediately to the west of the western window, preceded on this level between the windows by no. 23. The events begin with material in II Kings, xviii; thus chapters viii–xvii were left out. Hezekiah is seen breaking down the Brazen Serpent and idols, II Kings, xviii, 4. Then Sennacherib's commander Rabshakeh is seen with his troop of *arabians* addressing Hezekiah's officials, who look over the ramparts of Jerusalem, II Kings, xviii, 17–35. The next composition is defined by an elaborate two-tiered building. Above, Eliakim, Shebna and Joah are seen before Hezekiah, reporting the words of Rabshakeh; Hezekiah rends his garments, II Kings, xviii, 37–xix, 1. Below, beneath an elaborate triple-gabled arch, the copyists show the bare outline of a kneeling figure, presumably Hezekiah at prayer in the Temple, II Kings, xix, 2. Next, Eliakim (*elyekim*) and Shebna are seen before Isaiah (*ysai*) beneath a fine cinquefoil arch, Isaiah holding a scroll, II Kings, xix, 2–7. Isaiah here curses Sennacherib.

20. *The Destruction of Sennacherib*
S   14·8×34·3 cm. (pl. XV*b*).
CI   (see no. 19) (pl. XVI*a*).
CII   11·9×24·0 cm. (p. 38, D.646.97 whole sheet).
Size of original: see no. 19.
Texts: *adremelec* (over Adrammelech) *serasar* (over Sharezer).

   The scene which followed Isaiah's curse was damaged, but shows a two-tiered building with figures above and below. Above, a crowned figure, presumably King Hezekiah, is addressed by a man; the scene must be the confrontation of Hezekiah by Sennacherib's messenger, II Kings, xix, 9–13. Below, Hezekiah is seen kneeling before an altar with a chalice on it, praying to the Lord, II Kings, xix, 14–19. Next, the Lord with a cross nimbus descends and speaks to the kneeling Isaiah, II Kings, xix, 20–34. There follows immediately the destruction of the camp of Sennacherib by an angel bearing a sword, who floats over the tents, II Kings, xix, 35. Finally, Sennacherib's sons Adrammelech (*adremelec*) and Sharezer (*serasar*) are seen murdering Sennacherib in the Temple of Nisroch, II Kings, xix, 37.

21. *Nebuchadnezzar and Jehoiachin*
S   14·9×34·2 cm. (pl. XVII).
CI   10·8×24·3 cm. (pl. XVI*b*).
CII   17·4×28·2 cm. (p. 36, D.638.97 whole sheet).
CII   12·0×24·9 cm. (p. 37, D.643.97 whole sheet).
Size of original: 0·91×1·90 m.

   The narrative from II Kings continued on this register after a break of some 2·60 m., towards the west end of the room. No. 21 shows the treasures of the Temple of Jerusalem being carried off on camels; King Jehoiachin is seen on his knees in supplication, and then being taken into captivity by a crowned, sword-bearing figure on a horse, presumably Nebuchadnezzar. Jehoiachin and his queen raise their hands to their faces in distress. The material is drawn from II Kings, xxiv, 10–17.

22. *Zedekiah and the Fall of Jerusalem*
S   15·1×21·4 cm. (pl. XVIII).
CI   11·4×15·9 cm. (pl. XIX).
CII   12·3×16·7 cm. (p. 37, D.642.97 whole sheet).
Size of original: 0·91×1·24 m.
Texts: *le temple de ierl'm   le ge(n)s de ierl'm* (S only).

   To the left is seen a figure with a sword about to strike, probably concerning the slaying of King Zedekiah's sons, II Kings, xxv, 6–7. Next, the Temple of Jerusalem is pillaged by soldiers and the people of the city (*le gens de ierl'm*) are bound and taken off, II Kings, xxv, 8–17.

23. *The Story of King Abimelech*
S   14·7×35·5 cm. (col. pl. V).
CI   10·4×24·5 cm. (pl. XX).
CII   11·9×26·9 cm. (p. 32, D.626.97 whole sheet).
B fol. 207 includes the death of Abimelech with part of no. 24 below (pl. XXI).
Size of original: 0·91×2·10 m.
Texts: *Ioatham* (CI gives *Ioathem*) *Abimelec*.

The area between the windows on the south wall, on the fourth band down, was occupied by an episode from the Book of Judges which must have concluded any preceding Judges illustration at this level to the east of the windows. King Abimelech is seen under a slim arch slaughtering his seventy brothers, Judges, ix, 5. The next two scenes were poorly preserved. Jotham (*Ioatham*) is seen gesticulating towards the trees, whose leaves are differentiated by naturalistic foliage, Judges, ix, 7–15. Of the following scene only some heads and a mailed foot can be made out, together with the pinnacle of a citadel; the scene was probably that of Abimelech setting fire to Shechem, as burning brushwood is seen at the base of the tower, Judges, ix, 49. Then Abimelech (*Abimelec*) is hit on the head by a round millstone dropped from the ramparts of Thebez by a woman; his falchion falls from his right hand. He is promptly dispatched by his squire, Judges, ix, 50–4.

24. *Antiochus and the Maccabean Martyrs*
S   14·7×38·2 cm. (pl. XXII*a*).
CI   9·1×24·3 cm. (pl. XXII*b*).
B fol. 207 includes part of the figure of King Antiochus with no. 23.
Size of original: 0·76×2·10 m.
Texts: *antiocus   la mere.&.vii.filtz.*

This incident was located in the register between the windows immediately under no. 23, and was continued in no. 25. To the left, Eleazar is seen kneeling and bound, being forced to eat pork, II Macc. vi, 18–30. In the centre, beneath a shallow cusped canopy, is a representation of the Maccabean Martyrdom. To the left, figures are seen being boiled in giant cauldrons, heated by a fire blown by bellows. To the right of centre, Antiochus sits with his fool at his feet, the fool holding a bauble. Antiochus is commanding the torture of the seven sons; one is having his tongue torn out to Antiochus' right. To Antiochus' left, the mother is seen encouraging her remaining son, II Macc. vii, 1–40. In a separate compartment, Antiochus is seen kneeling before the idol of Jupiter Olympus, the Abomination of Desolation, in allusion to II Macc. vi, 2.

25. *The Fall of Antiochus*
S   14·9×42·8 cm. (pl. XXIII).
Size of original: approx. 0·76×2·20 m.

The II Maccabees narrative continued at the same level as no. 24, but to the west of the western window on the south wall, in the register beneath the account of King Hezekiah. The bulk of the pictorial evidence from this band was lost. Antiochus is seen retreating in disorder from Persepolis, II Macc. ix, 1–3. Next, beneath a canopy, he hears of the fate of Nicanor and Timotheus, II Macc. ix, 3–4 (events related separately in the upper two registers). Finally, he is seen plunging from his chariot while the exasperated charioteer tears his hair, II Macc. ix, 7–8. The location of the scene is not noted in the elevation in CI.

26. *The Murder of Abner*
S   14·7×17·4 cm. (pl. XXIV).

This scene was noted in *Gentleman's Magazine* (1819), pt. ii, 391–2, as being on the lowest register on the south wall towards the west end. It was badly damaged, but shows first, above, a dialogue between a sword-bearing figure and a crowned female, who raises her hand to her face in distress, and below, seated figures. Next is depicted a group of armed men bearing pennons speaking with a king at a gateway, and last, a man is seen sticking a sword into the belly of another. There is no reason to doubt that the iconography is that suggested by Rokewode (1885, 27): Ishbosheth sends Michal back to King David, II Sam. iii, 14–16, Joab addresses David, II Sam. iii, 24 and then murders Abner, II Sam. iii, 27. The scene was presumably part of a sequence of pictures from II Sam. on the lowest register of the south wall running above the dado.

27. *Warriors in Flight*
S   14·8×20·8 cm. (pl. XXV*a*).

This scene was noted by Rokewode (1885, 35) as being located between the windows on the east wall on the third row down, that is at the same level as the opening II Kings sequence on the south wall. The image, which shows a group of armed warriors on horseback being pursued into a citadel, is commonplace, and its iconography cannot be usefully identified.

28. *Fragment of Decorative Painting*
S   18·9×12·8 cm. (pl. XXV*b*).

This item adorned the arch of one of the blocked windows on the south side, and so presumably pre-dated Henry III's remodelling of the fenestration of the king's chamber. A late twelfth-century date is likely.

Notes

(see also *Abbreviations*, p. xi)

Introduction

[1] Cambridge, Corpus Christi College MS 407: see Esposito 1960, 1–22.

[2] *Ibid.*, 30, 34, 72, 78, 84.

[3] *Ibid.*, 26.

[4] Capon 1835, pl. XLVII, 7; for Capon, see *Gentleman's Magazine* (1828), pt. i, 105.

[5] Smith 1807, 263; *Gentleman's Magazine* (1800), pt. ii, 625 ff.; H. C. Marillier, 'The tapestries of the Painted Chamber', *Burlington Magazine*, xlvi (1925), 35.

[6] Capon 1835, 4–7.

[7] J. M. Hastings, *Parliament House* (London, 1950), 77 ff.

[8] J. Topham, *Some Account of the Collegiate Chapel of Saint Stephen, Westminster* (London, 1795), 13 ff.; Smith 1807, v–ix; *KW*, vi, 515, 525–6.

[9] Smith 1807, vi; for Wyatt see *Gentleman's Magazine* (1789), pt. ii, 873, 1064; A. Dale, *James Wyatt* (Oxford, 1956), 99–125; J. Evans, *A History of the Society of Antiquaries* (Oxford, 1956), 207 ff.; J. Frew, 'The "Destroyer" vindicated?: James Wyatt and the restoration of Henry VII's Chapel, Westminster Abbey', *JBAA*, cxxxiv (1981), 100.

[10] Smith 1807, viii, and cf. Smirke's account in *Gentleman's Magazine* (1803), pt. i, 204.

[11] Evans, *op. cit.* (note 9), 213 n. 2.

[12] *Gentleman's Magazine* (1800), pt. ii, 734, 736, 813, 837.

[13] Capon 1835, 3.

[14] Dale, *op. cit.* (note 9), 119 ff.; *KW*, v, 385 ff.; *KW*, vi, 49, 496 ff.

[15] Topham, *op. cit.* (note 8), pls. I–XIV; Evans, *op. cit.* (note 9), 191, 206.

[16] J. Carter, *The Ancient Architecture of England*, i (London, 1795), 47, pl. LXVI; Capon 1835, 1.

[17] *Gentleman's Magazine* (1807), pt. i, 14, 133, 426; (1814), pt. i, 9; see also N. Pevsner, *Some Architectural Writers of the Nineteenth Century* (Oxford, 1972), 20; Smith 1807, 48.

[18] Capon 1835, 5.

[19] Edward Crocker was Clerk of the Works for Whitehall, Westminster, St James's Palace and the King's Mews, 1818–29: see *KW*, i, 499, and *KW*, vi, 16, 24, 26, 59–60, 71, 75, 115–17, 119–20, 131, 327, 353, 455, 477, 485, 497, 628, 673–7.

[20] *Gentleman's Magazine* (1819), pt. ii, 389, 391.

[21] Stothard 1823, 304–5.

[22] The attribution of the copies is discussed in the Catalogue, pp. 113–14.

[23] Now BL Add. MS 36370, fols. 205–9.

[24] Soane presented a general survey of the Palace in 1817, which reported that the roof of the Painted Chamber was in need of attention. In 1819, a plaster replica was made of the medieval ceiling; see *KW*, vi, 519; also P. M. Rogers, 'Medieval fragments from the Old Palace of Westminster in the Sir John Soane Museum', in *Parliamentary History, Libraries and Records, Essays presented to Maurice Bond*, ed. H. S. Cobb (House of Lords Record Office, 1981), 1 ff.

[25] *Gentleman's Magazine* (1823), pt. ii, 99, 489; drawings were made by Capon, see Westminster City Library, Box 57, and Soane, in PRO Works 29/17–18.

[26] Drawing by Stephanoff, Westminster City Library, Box 57.

[27] For the post-fire damage to the room, see E. W. Brayley and J. Britton, *The History of the Ancient Palace and Late Houses of Parliament at Westminster* (London, 1836), pls. XIV, XV, and for its temporary rehabilitation, *KW*, vi, 573–4, 603, 609, pl. 35b. For the survey, see Rokewode 1885, 1–8. A number of fragments of the fabric passed into the Cottingham collection (see A. Shaw, *Catalogue of the Museum of Mediaeval Art, 43 Waterloo Bridge Road* (London, 1850), 28), but these appear to have been dispersed after Cottingham's death in 1847.

28 For a full description of what was found, see the Catalogue, p. 113.

29 Particularly Lethaby 1905; Wormald 1949, 172–6; Tristram 1950, 89 ff.; Tudor-Craig 1957; *KW*, i, 495–500.

30 See principally Tudor-Craig 1957, 100–5.

31 These notions are explored by A. C. Esmeijer, *Divina Quaternitas* (Assen, 1978), 1–29.

32 Particularly *KW*, i, 130–57, 494–510.

33 Tudor-Craig 1957, 92.

Part I. The Painted Chamber: the Evidence

1 The principal sources used in this discussion are as follows: drawings by John Buckler in BL Add. MS 36370; drawings by Edward Blore in BL Add. MS 42022; drawings by William Capon in Westminster City Library, Box 57; drawings by Sir John Soane in PRO Works 29; a series of drawings in BL Crace Collection I, xi–47, II, xv; drawings by John Carter in BL Add. MS 31153 (cf. also Victoria and Albert Museum Dept. of Prints and Drawings R.2a, T.10). Secondary sources include: J. Carter, *The Ancient Architecture of England*, i (London, 1795), 47, pl. LXVI; Smith 1807; articles, many by John Carter, in *Gentleman's Magazine* (1800), pt. i, 33, 214, 300, 422, 527; (1800), pt. ii, 625, 722, 734, 736, 813, 837; (1806), pt. ii, 1004, 1092, 1127, 1185; (1807), pt. i, 15, 133, 322, 426, 531; (1814), pt. i, 10; (1819), pt. ii, 389; (1823), pt. i, 390; (1823), pt. ii, 99, 489; Stothard 1823, 307–11, 317–28; Capon 1835, pl. XLVII; Rokewode 1885, 1–8, pls. XXVI–XXVII; W. R. Lethaby, 'The Palace of Westminster in the eleventh and twelfth centuries', *Archaeologia*, lx (1906), 131; I. M. Cooper, 'The meeting-places of Parliament in the ancient Palace of Westminster', *JBAA*, iii (1938), 97; Tudor-Craig 1957, 93–4; *KW*, i, 491–510; H. Colvin (ed.), 'Views of the Old Palace of Westminster', *Architectural History*, ix (1966). See also J. M. Hastings, *Parliament House* (London, 1950); L. F. Salzman, *Building in England down to 1540: a Documentary History* (Oxford, 1952); M. E. Wood, *The English Mediaeval House*, 2nd edn. (London, 1981).

2 *KW*, i, 493.

3 *KW*, i, 514.

4 *KW*, i, 120 ff. The same was true, for example, of the Parisian palace of the Cité: see J. Guerout, 'Le Palais de la Cité à Paris des origines à 1417', *Mémoires, Fédération des Sociétés Historiques et Archéologiques de Paris et de l'Île-de-France*, i (1949), 57, 147 ff.

5 Capon 1835, 5 and Rokewode 1885, 7. The wooden floor of the chamber was 23 cm. above a lower, late medieval tiled floor.

6 *KW*, i, 545.

7 O. Demus, 'European wall painting around 1200', in *The Year 1200: a Symposium*, Metropolitan Museum of Art (New York, 1975), 95–9.

8 *CLR* 1233, 219.

9 Rokewode 1885, 8; Tristram 1950, 90.

10 RCHM, *London*, ii: *West London* (London, 1925), pl. 177; *KW*, i, 47. The capitals were included in the 1984 exhibition of English Romanesque art: *English Romanesque Art 1066–1200* (London, 1984), 154 no. 105.

11 For Winchester, *KW*, i, 87; ii, 857; for Westminster, Lethaby, *op. cit.* (note 1), 144–6; *KW*, i, 492–3.

12 The position of one of the twelfth-century windows blocked by Henry III, at the west end of the south wall, is recorded by Crocker in his elevation in the Ashmolean Museum. Although he shows this window as having a pointed arch, it is clear that the window was blocked *c.* 1230 to admit the new doorway in the south wall, at that time; the window must thus be earlier and should have had a round arch. The position of a fourth window in the south wall, also blocked by Henry, is not known for certain, but its existence is attested to by Rokewode (1885, 1–2, 7 n. 2).

13 *KW*, i, 494–5.

14 *KW*, i, 501.

15 *CLR* 1233, 218–19; *KW*, ii, 861, and also *KW*, i, 87.

16 D. Park, 'The wall paintings of the Holy Sepulchre Chapel', in *Medieval Art and Architecture at Winchester Cathedral*, BAA Conference Transactions for the year 1980, vi (1983), 38, 60.

17 But not so forward-looking as to have radically changed the shape of the twelfth-century upper chamber. The presence of thick and early cross-walls on the ground floor has been

taken as evidence that the upper chamber was subdivided at an earlier stage of its development: see Capon 1835, 4–7; Rokewode 1885, 6–8; Cooper, *op. cit.* (note 1), 98–9; and plan, *KW*, i, 493. But the evidence for the subdivision of the room is not, in fact, very strong. When the upper and lower compartments are considered in elevation, the cross-walls coincide on plan with the two easterly windows of the south wall of the chamber above, showing at the very least that the division of the upper chamber must have been abandoned when the system of fenestration known to us was adopted (i.e. in the later twelfth century). The size of the upper chamber would be consonant with its status as the third major domestic room of the palace. Lethaby, *op. cit.* (note 1), 146–8, rejects the idea of subdivision on the grounds that the eastern wall in the lower chamber formed part of a vaulted passage passing north–south beneath the upper chamber. Both the upper and lower chambers may, of course, have been divided by wooden partitions: see P. A. Faulkner, 'Domestic planning from the twelfth to the fourteenth centuries', *Archaeological Journal*, cxv (1958), 150, 162.

18 *KW*, i, 99–101.

19 *KW*, ii, 858–62; Colvin 1971, 90–187, pl. 6; see also M. Portal, *The Great Hall, Winchester Castle* (Winchester, 1899). The paintings are documented as follows: Westminster, *CCR* 1236, 271; *CLR* 1237, 283; *CCR* 1237, 484; Winchester, *CLR* 1233, 218; *CLR* 1237, 305.

20 Henry also remodelled the detailing of the lower chamber: Rokewode 1885, 7, pl. xxvii, N, O.

21 PRO Works 28/18, illustrated *KW*, i, pl. 29, and PRO Works 29/17, see *KW*, i, pl. 30. See also *KW*, i, 125–6 and fig. 20. For Thomas of Waverley, *ibid.*, 501.

22 Nearing completion in 1259: *KW*, i, 141.

23 See, for example, Portal, *op. cit.* (note 19), pl. opp. 45.

24 Compare the windows of the Great Hall at Winchester: *KW*, ii, 860 and fig. 66; or those of the Hall in the Archbishop's Palace at Canterbury: see T. Tatton-Brown, 'The Great Hall of the Archbishop's Palace', in *Medieval Art and Architecture at Canterbury before 1220*, BAA Conference Transactions for the year 1979, v (1982), 112.

25 Compare the doorway to the south-west transept of Lincoln Minster, and the use of unpierced lozenges over lancets on the exterior of the chapter house.

26 For the Westminster chapter-house vestibule, see RCHM, *London*, i: *Westminster Abbey* (London, 1924), pl. 156; for Hereford, J. Bony, *The English Decorated Style* (Oxford, 1979), 4–5, pl. 22.

27 This example of the possible influence of Cistercian ideas on English domestic architecture was drawn to my attention by Dr Christopher Wilson. Compare the tracery of the lavabo of the monastery of Poblet in Spain: see C. N. L. Brooke, *The Monastic World 1000–1300* (London, 1974), 226–7, 261 and pl. 380.

28 In general, see N. Pevsner, *The Leaves of Southwell* (London, 1945); P. Wynn-Reeves, 'English Stiff-Leaf Sculpture', unpublished Ph.D. thesis, University of London (1952); Stone 1972, 138.

29 Westminster City Library, Box 57, dated 1823: *KW*, i, 501; Colvin, *op. cit.* (note 1), figs. 138–42.

30 For Windsor, Lethaby 1925, fig. 52; *KW*, ii, 868; for Westminster, RCHM, *London*, i, *op. cit.* (note 26), 38, pl. 67.

31 *Pace* Tudor-Craig (1957, 99).

32 Thus, in 1236 the text *Ke ne dune ke ne tine ne prent ke desire* was painted 'in magno gabulo . . . juxta hostium': *CCR* 1236, 271.

33 Sketched by Buckler, BL Add. MS 36370, fol. 207ᵛ; Colvin, *op. cit.* (note 1), fig. 119.

34 Capon 1835, 5.

35 *CCR* 1236, 270.

36 *CCR* 1255, 157, and cf. also *CCR* 1263, 316, for the *capella regis retro lectum regis*. The *Chronica Majora* refers to the chapel in 1238 as being *in angulo camerae*: see Matthew Paris, *Chronica Majora*, ed. H. R. Luard, *RS*, 57, iii (London, 1876), 470–1. What may be the springers of the vault of the chapel are shown on the outside of the north wall in the view in Smith 1807, pl. xxvii.

37 In 1244 the chamber was wainscoted and the bed decorated anew (so implying its earlier existence): 'et columpnas circa lectum regis de novo depingi viridi colore vivo et auro estencellari, et curtinas circa lectum illum honestatem regiam decentes que ad placitum apponi et deponi possint, fieri faciat', *CCR* 1244, 169. Matching green linen was also supplied for the bed, *CLR* 1243, 205.

[38] P. Eames, 'Furniture in England, France and the Netherlands from the twelfth to the fifteenth century', *Furniture History*, xiii (1977), 74–5, 91.

[39] Colvin 1971, 248.

[40] P. Eames, 'Documentary evidence concerning the character and use of domestic furnishings in England in the fourteenth and fifteenth centuries', *Furniture History*, vii, (1971), 41, 44.

[41] Eames, *op. cit.* (note 38), 73.

[42] See pp. 17, 18.

[43] Eames, *op. cit.* (note 38), 74–5. See Theophilus, *De Diversis Artibus*, ed. C. R. Dodwell (London, 1961), 130.

[44] *KW*, i, 497–8. Compare also the imitation in paint above the figures on the sedilia in Westminster Abbey of the projecting wooden canopy, and consider also the original decorations of the Coronation Chair in the abbey: see S. Rees-Jones, 'The Coronation Chair', *Studies in Conservation*, i (1954), 103, 109.

[45] The south windows may have been darkened to some extent by the proximity of the new queen's chamber. Many of Henry's mandates illustrate his concern about the location of windows in chambers to enhance points of status, as at Nottingham, Clarendon, Bristol, Fakenham and Winchester: *CLR* (Appendix) 1267–72, 289; *CCR* 1243, 68; *CLR* 1244, 223; *CLR* 1250, 300–1; *KW*, i, 123; and *CLR* 1233, 218–19.

[46] Colvin 1971, 194, 196, 288, 342, 346; also 304, 326, 356, 372, 386.

[47] See *Annales Monastici*, ed. H. R. Luard, *RS*, 36, iii (London, 1866), 220: 'Eodem anno, circa Purificationem Beatae Mariae, rege infirmato apud Westmonasterium, exivit ignis de camino camerae suae, et combussit eandem cum capella Sancti Laurentii; et transiliit ignis usque ad cameram receptae, quam combussit'; see also the *Liber de Antiquis Legibus*, ed. T. Stapleton, Camden Society (1846), 51: 'Anno eodem septimo die Februarii, combusta sunt proprio igne suo parva aula domini regis apud Westmonasterium, camera, et capella, et receptaculum, et alie plures domus officiales'; *KW*, i, 498.

[48] *CLR* 1263, 120, 123; *CCR* 1263, 207, 210–11, 216, 219, 239; painting from *CCR* 1263, 316.

[49] The *paterae* comprised a lobed square set within a lobed square, in alternation on the ceiling with smaller quatrefoil bosses, quite possibly originally set with glass; see Lethaby 1927, 136–7; *KW*, i, 495–6. The *patera* form is probably a metalwork derivative; compare the cover of the book held by Christ on the *trumeau* of the central portal of the south transept of Chartres: see W. Sauerländer, *Gothic Sculpture in France 1140–1270* (London, 1972), pl. 109. Lethaby's comparison with the ornamentation on the Westminster Retable is a fair one; we might note also that the boss at the centre of the round shield held by the Virtue Fortitude (?) from the north side of the room (pl. VIII) exactly reproduces this form.

[50] Stothard 1823, 310; Rokewode 1885, 2. The iconography of painted heads was anticipated in the 1230s at Winchester: *KW*, ii, 859.

[51] Colvin 1971, 422, 426; PRO E101/467/6 (2), E101/467/7 (3).

[52] PRO E101/467/17, 19–20; *KW*, i, 504–5.

[53] See *Flores Historiarum*, ed. H. R. Luard, *RS*, 95, iii (London, 1890), 104: 'Accedente rege Angliae apud Westmonasterium iv.kal. Aprilis, accensoque igne vehementi in minori aula palatii, ac flamma tecturam domus attingente ventoque agitata, abbatiae vicinae aedificia devoravit'. Also *Annales Monastici*, ed. H. R. Luard, *RS*, 36, iv (London, 1869), 536; *KW*, i, 505.

[54] The Painted Chamber underwent several alterations in the later Middle Ages which must have marked the obsolescence of its murals. In the fourteenth century four windows were inserted high in the west wall, and in the fifteenth century, or perhaps the early sixteenth, the fireplace was rebuilt and a window inserted high in the south wall, of three lights, cutting through parts of the Old Testament scenes. A similar window was added on this side in 1819. The eastern window on the south side was half closed and had an aumbry inserted into it. Other windows were blocked with fragments of painted stone, of which Stothard remarked: '. . . I selected from them a complete series of subjects, representing the employments of the Twelve Months of the Year. It had been imagined that these painted stones belonged to the walls of some other room which was destroyed; but as the present chimney-piece in the Painted Chamber, from its architecture, is about the time of Henry VII. I am inclined to believe that the Twelve Months appropriately ornamented the frieze of the original chimney-piece; the form and arrangement of the stones confirm me in this conjecture' (Rokewode 1885, 2). Carved angel brackets were inserted in the east wall, and the small

chapel retiled: *KW* i, 536–7. Details of the new fireplace were drawn by Buckler, BL Add. MS 36370, fol. 207^v; Colvin, *op. cit.* (note 1), fig. 119.

55 *CLR* 1228, 103; *CCR* 1231, 9; *CCR* 1233, 207.

56 *CCR* 1236, 270–1.

57 *CCR* 1236, 239; cf. Clarendon, *CLR* 1246, 63; *CLR* 1251, 362; Windsor, Tristram 1950, 623; Winchester, *CLR* 1233, 219; *CLR* 1237, 205. Capon copied a piece of green curtain from a dado in the queen's apartments in 1823, of very uncertain (post-medieval?) date, Westminster City Library, Box 57; Capon 1835, 7; Colvin, *op. cit.* (note 1), fig. 137.

58 *CLR* 1237, 283.

59 *CCR* 1237, 484; for Odo the Goldsmith, see *KW*, i, 101–2.

60 *CCR* 1238, 26.

61 *CCR* 1239, 162; *CLR* 1239, 364; *CLR* 1239, 376; *CLR* 1239, 389; *CLR* 1239, 399; *CLR* 1239, 404; *CLR* 1240, 442; *CLR* 1240, 444.

62 *CCR* 1243, 19–20.

63 *CCR* 1243, 45.

64 *CCR* 1244, 169.

65 Colvin 1971, 218, 220, 190; *CCR* 1249, 203.

66 *CCR* 1252, 57.

67 *CCR* 1256, 326: 'Rex in presencia magistri Willelmi Pictoris, monachi Westmonasterii, nuper apud Wintoniam ordinavit et providit quandam picturam faciendam apud Westmonasterium in garderoba ubi capud suum lavari consuetum est, de rege qui per canes suos rescussus fuit de sedicionibus ab hominibus suis adversis eundem regem prolocutis [etc.].' The iconography—the story of the King of the Garamantes—was identified by D. J. A. Ross, 'A lost painting in Henry III's palace at Westminster', *JWCI*, xvi (1943), 160.

68 *CCR* 1255, 157; F. Devon, *Issues of the Exchequer* (London, 1837), 43 ff., 53.

69 *CCR* 1263, 316.

70 *CCR* 1264, 366; *CLR* 1268, 10; *CLR* 1265, 156. Colvin 1971, 390, prints an account of 1265 including Walter of Durham and other painters working at Westminster, possibly in both the palace and abbey.

71 *CLR* 1266, 251; Colvin 1971, 418; *KW*, i, 498.

72 *CLR* 1267, 253, 266.

73 Colvin 1971, 422.

74 The riot was caused by a mob of soldiers of the Earl of Gloucester; the *Liber de Antiquis Legibus, op. cit.* (note 47), 92, states that the mob entered Westminster 'et ibi mutilaverunt palatium Domini Regis, frangentes cathedras, fenestras, et hostia, et quicquid potuerunt asportantes . . .'; cf. also *Annales Monastici*, ed. H. R. Luard, *RS*, 36, iv (London, 1869), 199–200, 203, and R. Holinshed, *Chronicles of England, Scotland and Ireland*, ii (London, 1807), 472; Colvin 1971, 422.

75 Colvin 1971, 426.

76 *Ibid.*, 428.

77 *Ibid.*, 430.

78 G. G. Scott, *Gleanings from Westminster Abbey*, 2nd edn. (Oxford and London, 1863), 113; *KW*, i, 500, the account being for the years 1257–69 and so possibly referring to the work done by William on the walls around the chimney of the chamber in 1259; Colvin 1971, 326, 356; also Tristram 1950, 576.

79 Colvin 1971, 434.

80 *KW*, i, 504; see, for example, PRO E403/1230, Devon, *op. cit.* (note 68), 79; Tristram 1950, 576.

81 *KW*, i, 504–5; PRO E101/467/6 (2), mems. 3, 7, 8, 11, 12; Tristram 1950, 99–100, 576.

82 PRO E101/467/7 (3), mem. 3.

83 The unpublished Liberate Roll PRO E403/1230 (1 Edward 1) includes a payment to Master Walter the king's painter ('pictori nostro'), settling his account to the end of 1272. A Walter the Painter is also recorded in PRO E101/467/7 (6), mem. 5. He is not specified as a master: nevertheless, he painted a picture in the queen's chapel and is presumably to be identified with Walter of Durham. PRO E101/467/9, mem. 8, records that Walter the Painter provided two painted wooden dragons' heads for the queen's barge. Both accounts belong to the period 1275–9: see Tristram 1950, 576. *KW*, ii, 1037, notes the presence of a new painter at Westminster, Stephen, king's painter ('pictori nostro'), and suggests that he was later employed by Master James of St George in the Viennois. William of Nottingham, who also

figures in the records from the 1270s, cannot be traced in Henry III's reign and appears to have been a new recruit.

[84] *KW*, i, 504.

[85] Among the last payments are those in E101/467/7 (6), mem. 5.

[86] The exceptions to this were the building of new kitchens and a new gateway, *KW*, i, 505, 547.

[87] H. Gough, *Itinerary of King Edward the First Throughout His Reign* (Paisley, 1900), i, 38–126, 166; ii, 20; *KW*, i, 504–5; F. M. Powicke, *The Thirteenth Century, 1216–1307*, 2nd edn. (Oxford, 1970), 511.

[88] PRO E101/467/16–17.

[89] PRO E101/467/19, E101/468/2, E101/468/4; Tristram 1950, 577.

[90] E101/467/19 includes the purchase of 'tegulis subtilibus' for the paving of the stone chamber.

[91] PRO E101/467/20 includes repairs to the glazing of the king's chamber.

[92] Rokewode 1885, 11, printed from E101/467/19, mem. 3; Tristram 1950, 577.

[93] E101/468/2, mems. 3–10, including repairs to the roof and chimney, and the barring of windows.

[94] E101/467/19, mem. 3, and E101/468/2 mems. 3b, 10b. A Majesty was known in the refectory of Westminster Abbey, and was alluded to in the Ware customary: see *Customary of the Benedictine Monasteries of Saint Augustine, Canterbury and Saint Peter, Westminster*, ed. E. Maunde Thompson, ii (London, 1904), 107, 110, 125, 182.

[95] PRO E101/468/6; *KW*, i, 510 ff. for the chapel.

[96] Rokewode 1885, 11.

[97] Smith 1807, 78–81; E. W. Brayley and J. Britton, *The History of the Ancient Palace and late Houses of Parliament at Westminster* (London, 1836), 88 ff.

[98] E101/468/6, roll 1.

[99] Alder-wood was used for the uprights of a scaffold: see Salzman, *op. cit.* (note 1), 318 ff. This would be normal in the case of a large programme, where the painters would start at the top, and work downwards.

[100] E101/468/6, rolls 1–18, 28–37, 45ii–ix, 90–3, 106–18, 141–2.

[101] *Ibid.*, roll 110.

[102] E101/468/6, rolls 18, 29, identify Thomas. J. Harvey, *The Perpendicular Style 1330–1485* (London, 1978), 50 and 267, erroneously states that Thomas was the son of the master mason of St Stephen's, Michael of Canterbury, and suggests that the *picturae* that Thomas was engaged upon were architectural drawings in the tracing house. He cannot be the Thomas of Canterbury later working at Westminster: *KW*, i, 514.

[103] This work must be distinguished from that in the main palace for the years 1295–7, and is recorded in PRO E405/1/7, E405/1/6 mem. 2; BL Add. MS 8835, fol. 20ᵛ; E101/468/10, mems. 8–10; E101/468/11, mems. 1, 5. See also, PRO E101/547/18, fols. 162, 166, 170, 171, 172; PRO E403/99, mems. 2, 4.

[104] PRO E159/69, quoted *KW*, i, 380 n. 1.

[105] PRO E405/1/11, mem. 8.

[106] *Ibid.*, mem. 9. For the financial crisis of 1297, see M. Prestwich, *War, Politics and Finance under Edward I* (London, 1972), 247 ff.

[107] *KW*, i, 512.

[108] *Ibid.*, 510–13.

[109] *KW*, i, 479 ff.

[110] T. H. Turner, *Manners and Household Expenses*, Roxburghe Club (London, 1841), 95–115.

[111] *Ibid.*, 116 ff., 121 (Hilary term 1293): 'Item, Magistro Waltero de Dunolmia, pictori, pro operibus faciendis circa tumulum Reginae, apud Westmonasterium. i.marc'; 123: 'in partem solutionis pro pictura coopertorii Regis et Reginae. iij.marc.'; 124–5: 'in partem solutionis pro pictura cooperculorum supra imagines Regis et Reginae. xl.s.'

[112] Edward was at the palace until the start of work in the king's chamber in April 1292, which lasted until January 1293. He returned in April and stayed until August. On his departure Walter returned to the palace, Gough, *Itinerary, op. cit.* (note 87), ii, 104–7. Work in the king's absence must have been quite normal and is indeed recorded at King's Langley in this period: 'Et cuidam pictori London' facienti apud Langel' in aula in estate domino absente . . . liiij scuta. iiij milites querentes hastiludium' (*KW*, ii, 972). The king's chamber at Westminster could well have been scaffolded throughout this period, and the extent of its use is unknown.

113 Work restarted after 1319: *KW*, i, 514.

114 *Ibid.*, 512, n. 6.

115 Principally PRO E101/468/21 and BL Add. MS 30263; also PRO E101/468/16 (Rokewode 1885, 12); E101/468/15, repairs at the palace in 1307–11, is printed in *KW*, ii, 1041, and cf. also E101/468/21, fols. 119–121ᵛ.

116 Walter's date of death is unknown. His last commission was the Coronation Chair, accounts cited in Tristram 1955, 195–6, in 1300–1; he may have been dead by 1304–5, as he is absent from accounts for works in the house of the Archbishop of York in this period, e.g. PRO E101/468/10–11, which include painters employed by the king.

117 E101/468/21, fol. 72. *KW*, ii, 610, notes that Edward II, as Prince of Wales, was already taking some initiative in choosing wall paintings as early as 1301 at Chester Castle, when a picture of the Martyrdom of St Thomas was painted in the lesser chapel next to the Great Hall.

118 *KW*, i, 507 n. 5, gives 'Burgo' as Bury St Edmunds, but the usual translation would be Peterborough.

119 E101/468/21, fols. 19–19ᵛ, 20ᵛ, 24, 26, 29, 31; E101/468/15, 'De reparacione emendacione & de pictura magne aule contra coronacionem', quoted *KW*, ii, 1043, no. 28.

120 E101/468/21, fols. 34ᵛ, 36ᵛ.

121 E101/468/21, fols. 40, 46, 50; also *KW*, ii, 1043, no. 32.

122 E101/468/21, fol. 54ᵛ.

123 This presumably means the window splays and soffits.

124 E101/468/21, fols. 58–58ᵛ, 60ᵛ, 63ᵛ, 65, 69, 72, 74ᵛ, 81ᵛ, 84ᵛ, 87, 93.

125 E101/468/21, fol. 106ᵛ; Hugh appears earlier with Peter of Malines paving the Painted Chamber and the Marculf Chamber, *ibid.*, fols. 79, 81ᵛ, 85ᵛ, 103ᵛ, 121ᵛ.

126 E101/468/16, quoted Tristram 1955, 206.

127 *KW*, i, 505.

128 J. Harvey ('The origin of the Perpendicular Style', in E. M. Jope, *Studies in Building History* (London, 1961), 134, 142) suggests that the fire damaged the new chapel; cf. also Lethaby 1906, 199. The account in the *Flores Historiarum* (above, note 53) suggests that the fire spread to the abbey to the west rather than north and east to the chapel. Damaged buildings in the Palace of Westminster included the Lesser Hall, the Queen's Hall, the nursery and the Maydenhalle, *KW*, ii, 1041. For the abbey, see R. B. Rackham, 'Building at Westminster Abbey, from the Great Fire (1298) to the Great Plague (1348)', *Archaeological Journal*, lxvii (1910), 259.

129 The term 'painted chamber' of course distinguished rooms at Winchester Castle and Clarendon Palace in the 1230s and 1240s: *CLR* 1233, 219; *CLR* 1241, 60. Tristram 1950, 93, noted a reference to a painted chamber at Westminster in 1243 (*CCR* 1243, 123) to support his general contention that the room was decorated to its full extent at the start of Henry's reign, but this chamber was in the Abbot's House: *KW*, i, 500 n. 6.

130 Tristram (1950, 89–100, 97) states: 'the post-fire scheme almost certainly incorporated the general lines of the previous one, dating from c. 1237–9'. Tristram also argued that the Coronation and Virtues were added in the 1260s *after* the Old Testament scenes, *ibid.*, 98.

131 Tudor-Craig 1957, 96 ff.; cf. Lethaby 1905, 259–60.

132 J. M. Hastings, 'The Court Style', *Architectural Review*, cv (1949), 3; J. H. Harvey, 'St Stephen's Chapel and the origin of the Perpendicular Style', *Burlington Magazine*, lxxxviii (1946), 192; J. M. Hastings, *St Stephen's Chapel and its Place in the Development of Perpendicular Style in England* (Cambridge, 1955); *KW*, i, 479–85, 494–527.

133 Tristram 1950, 113–15, 573–7. Tristram's understanding of the chronology of the building of St Stephen's was no more advanced than that of Smith 1807, 75–81. Smith nevertheless rightly concluded that the extent of the work in the 1290s 'makes it more probable that the paintings were not even heraldical bearings . . . but historical subjects; such as were afterwards painted on the walls [of St Stephen's] when the chapel was rebuilt by Edward III'. Smith was unaware of work on the chapel under Edward II recorded in accounts first printed in Brayley and Britton, *op. cit.* (note 97), 88–90, 120 ff.

134 Stothard 1823, 174.

135 J. Evans, *A History of the Society of Antiquaries* (Oxford, 1956), 225.

136 Stothard 1823, 21 ff.; C. A. Stothard, *The Monumental Effigies of Great Britain* (London, 1817).

137 Richard Smirke executed tracings in St Stephen's Chapel.

[138] Stothard 1823, 29 ff., 124.

[139] *Ibid.*, 218.

[140] *Ibid.*, 289 ff. See *Vetusta Monumenta*, vi (1885), pls. I–XVII, and C. A. Stothard, 'Some observations on the Bayeux Tapestry', *Archaeologia*, xix (1821), 184.

[141] Consider the renditions of the Bayeux Tapestry in Dom B. de Montfaucon, *Les Monuments de la monarchie françoise*, i (Paris, 1729), 371 ff., pls. XXV–XLIX; ii (Paris, 1730), pls. I–IX. The analogy between the narrative art of the Bayeux Tapestry and the Painted Chamber was not lost on Stothard: see Stothard 1823, 309.

[142] Stothard 1823, 85–6.

[143] Stothard, *Monumental Effigies, op. cit.* (note 136), 37 (Aveline, Countess of Lancaster), 40 (Edmund Crouchback, Earl of Lancaster), 46 (Aymer de Valence, Earl of Pembroke).

[144] Stothard 1823, 304.

[145] Rokewode 1885, pls. XXX–XXXIX.

[146] For the work of the Commission, see F. Bercé, *Les Premiers Travaux de la Commission des Monuments Historiques 1837–1848* (Paris, 1979).

[147] R. Branner, 'The painted medallions in the Sainte-Chapelle in Paris', *Transactions of the American Philosophical Society*, ii (1968), 5, 11.

[148] Lethaby 1905, 257.

[149] October, 5th, 1819, BL Add. MS 36370, fol. 208.

[150] As Crocker was on site as Clerk of the Works he may well have begun work before Stothard's arrival; for Buckler's elevation, BL Add. MS 36370, fol. 205.

[151] Victoria and Albert Museum, 93.E.3.

[152] Moreover, both men copied one scene of the Captivity of the Jews which fell off the wall before Stothard could finish his copy (Stothard 1823, 314), ruling out the secondary nature of Crocker's copies (Cat. no. 22).

[153] BL Add. MS 36370. fol. 208.

[154] Notes in the Ashmolean Museum, preserved with the copies.

[155] Stothard 1823, 305, 317.

[156] *Ibid.*, 309–10.

[157] *Ibid.*, 310.

[158] *Ibid.*, 319.

[159] *Ibid.*, 320.

[160] The analogy drawn by Stothard between the Painted Chamber and the Westminster tombs is also made by S. R. Meyrick, *A Critical Enquiry into Antient Armour*, i (London, 1824), 165 ff., particularly as regards ornamental motifs.

[161] Stothard 1823, 321–4.

[162] Stothard alludes to Margaritone of Arezzo's life: see G. Vasari, *Lives*, ed. Mrs J. Foster, i (London, 1850), 88, 91.

[163] H. Walpole, *Anecdotes of Painting in England*, i (Strawberry Hill, 1762), vi–vii, 1–22.

[164] Stothard 1823, 324.

[165] *Ibid.*, 325–6.

[166] Smith 1807, 55 ff., 74 ff.

[167] Stothard 1823, 326.

[168] Walpole, *op. cit.* (note 163), 1–22.

[169] A writ of 1250 printed by Walpole, *ibid.*, 10–11, refers to a loan to the queen of a book of the Gestes of Antioch, a manuscript concerning the crusades correctly identified by Walpole, *ibid.*, 20; Stothard 1823, 327–8, took this to be a reference to King Antiochus and so to the material in the Painted Chamber.

[170] *Gentleman's Magazine* (1819), pt. ii, 392: 'The inscriptions as well as the paintings were renewed in antient times, and it is not difficult to discover the most antient, by the partial mutilation of the most modern workmanship.'

[171] Rokewode 1885, 36, 35, 33.

[172] *Ibid.*, 15.

[173] His observation that the paintings were regilded is entirely plausible. Examples of restoration by repainting are harder to find; one example would be the narrative scenes concerning the foundation of the priory of Horsham St Faith, Norfolk, painted in the refectory of the priory in the mid-thirteenth century and subsequently subjected to piecemeal restoration in the mid-fifteenth century. This example was drawn to my attention by Mr David Park.

[174] Walpole, presumably following Vertue, attributed the shrine of St Edward and the Retable at Westminster, as well as the Eleanor Crosses, to 'Cavalini': see Walpole, *op. cit.* (note 163), 17–19. Vertue's observations on the shrine and the Retable, of which a sketch was included, are in Society of Antiquaries MS 262, fols. 123–7, and were published by Vertue in *Archaeologia*, i (1770), 32. Cf. also Evans, *op. cit.* (note 135), 55, 98.

[175] J. C. Brooke, 'An account of an ancient seal of Robert, Baron Fitz-Walter', *Archaeologia*, v (1779), 211.

[176] T. Kerrich, 'Some observations on the Gothic buildings abroad, particularly those in Italy; and on Gothic architecture in general', *Archaeologia*, xvi (1812), 292; Evans, *op. cit.* (note 135), 206; D. Watkin, *The Rise of Architectural History* (London, 1980), 58.

[177] Stothard 1823, 21, 37.

[178] Such as that in Cottingham's possession: Rokewode 1885, 15.

[179] A. N. L. Munby, *Connoisseurs and Medieval Miniatures 1750–1850* (Oxford, 1972), 35 ff.; Rokewode 1885, 2. Douce was evidently familiar with both Crocker's and Stothard's copies, as a set of Stothard's drawings was coloured by him and exhibited at the Society of Antiquaries in 1835; see Evans, *op. cit.* (note 135), 237 n. 6.

[180] J. Dart, *Westmonasterium, or the History and Antiquities of the Abbey Church of St Peter, Westminster*, ii (London, 1723), 7, 11; R. Gough, *Sepulchral Monuments* (London, 1786–96), i, 69 ff.; Sir Joseph Ayloffe, 'An account of some ancient monuments in Westminster Abbey', *Vetusta Monumenta*, ii (1789) (dated 1780), 10 ff.

[181] See, for example, Walpole, *op. cit.* (note 163), 6; Gov. T. Pownall, 'Observations on ancient painting in England', *Archaeologia*, ix (1789), 141 ff.; Capon 1835, 7; Munby, *op. cit.* (note 179), 33.

[182] For Strutt, see *ibid.*, 28–30; Stothard was a devotee of Scott: see Stothard 1823, 484. Rokewode's description of the Old Testament scenes in the Painted Chamber (Rokewode 1885, 27 ff.) is greatly concerned with their depiction of armour. It should be recalled that Thomas Stothard, Charles's father, was a leading illustrator of historical subjects, a genre for which such works as the *Monumental Effigies* provided material.

[183] Rokewode 1885, 17 ff.

[184] *Ibid.*, pls. XXVIII–XXIX.

[185] *Ibid.*, 1–14

[186] *Ibid.*, 15–16. Faraday 'found little combustible matter in the paint, too little to allow of the notion that the paintings were originally in oil'. Phillips concluded 'I still incline to imagine, from the specimens you left with me, that the paintings of figures in the Painted Chamber were in distemper, oiled or varnished over, and not painted having oil blended with the colour; and one reason is, that the surface of the paint is most exceedingly thin. There are ornamented parts which are covered thick, but even those have a thin coating which appears to me oil varnish.' Rokewode compared the embossed material in the Painted Chamber to that on the tomb of Edmund Crouchback in Westminster Abbey.

[187] *Ibid.*, 26. Rokewode described it as a frontal and attributed it to 'Peter de Hispania'. The discovery of the Retable by Blore is noted in *Gentleman's Magazine* (1827), pt. i, 251. The Society of Antiquaries preserves two early drawings of the Retable by Stephanoff; one in Westminster Abbey Red Portfolio, 18 (which notes that the panel was found before 1821); and a coloured drawing of St Peter, dated 1827.

[188] Watkin, *op. cit.* (note 176), 56 ff.

[189] Munby, *op cit.* (note 179), 57 ff. A list of Rokewode's publications is given in *Gentleman's Magazine* (1842), pt. ii, 659; see especially 'A dissertation on St Æthelwold's Benedictional', *Archaeologia*, xxiv (1832), 1, and 'Remarks on the Louterell Psalter', *Vetusta Monumenta*, vi (1885), pls. XX–XXV; for his library, see Cambridge University Library, Hengrave Hall MS 49, 'Bibliotheca Rokewodiana'.

[190] Munby, *op. cit.* (note 179), 140–5.

[191] See especially Brayley and Britton, *op. cit.* (note 97); Devon, *op. cit* (note 68); Turner, *op. cit.* (note 110); and such surveys as J. Hunter, 'On the death of Eleanor of Castile', *Archaeologia*, xxix (1842), 167.

[192] See D. Robertson, *Sir Charles Eastlake and the Victorian Art World* (Princeton, 1978), 58 ff.

[193] Viollet-le-Duc was inclined to attribute the Westminster Retable to the 'école française', on the grounds of its style and decoration, in his *Dictionnaire raisonné du mobilier français*, i

(Paris, 1858), 234, 236, 382, and pls. IX, XXII, and also in the *Dictionnaire raisonné de l'architecture française*, vii (Paris, 1864), 107 n. 1.

[194] Essays in Scott, *op. cit.* (note 78), 105 ff.; see also J. M. Crook, *William Burges and the High Victorian Dream* (London, 1981), 294, for the general context of Burges's interest in Westminster.

[195] See Lethaby 1905; 1906, 257 ff., 263–4; 'English Primitives', *Burlington Magazine*, xxix (1916), 189, 281, 351; 'English Primitives', *ibid.*, xxxiii (1918), 3, 169; 1925, 204–10, 254–9; 1927, 123.

[196] See especially C. L. Eastlake, *Materials for a History of Oil Painting*, i (London, 1847), 30, 49, 176–7. Eastlake's concern certainly reflected the current controversy over the appropriate medium of decorations in the new Palace of Westminster.

[197] Burges, for example, while deeply influenced by Viollet-le-Duc, argued against his view that the Westminster Retable was French on the grounds of its similarity to the Painted Chamber: see Scott, *op. cit.* (note 78), 105 ff.; and for Viollet's influence, R. D. Middleton, 'Viollet-le-Duc's influence in nineteenth-century England', *Art History*, iv (1981), 203 ff. Viollet presumably saw the Retable in 1850. Lethaby first regarded it as an English work, following Burges: see Lethaby 1906, 263–4. Yet by 1916 he had come to accept Viollet's view and proposed that the Retable was executed 'by the chief of the palace atelier in Paris around 1260'; see Lethaby 1916, *op. cit.* (note 195), 351, 357. He repeated this view in his paper of 1927 and appears to have been drawn to it after seeing Omont's facsimile of the St Louis Psalter of 1905; but there is no doubt that he was also more generally inclined to accept the type of analysis of Gothic architecture proposed by the rationalist Viollet; see H. Omont, *Psautier de Saint Louis* (Paris, 1905), and Watkin, *op. cit.* (note 176), 92.

[198] M. Rickert, *Painting in Britain: the Middle Ages* (Harmondsworth, 1954), 124.

[199] Tristram 1950, 135–7.

[200] P. C. van Geersdaele and L. J. Goldsworthy, 'The restoration of wallpainting fragments from St Stephen's Chapel, Westminster', *The Conservator*, ii (1978), 9, 11–12.

[201] Mr David Park advises me that oil technique may have been more common than is usually thought; Tristram (1955, 70) notes, for example, that the fourteenth-century murals at South Newington (Oxon.) employed oil or an emulsion of oil.

[202] Rokewode 1885, 15: 'The outlines of the subjects seem to have been indicated, sketched, or drawn on the walls, in the several ways following; scratched with a pointed instrument; sketched freely with red chalk; painted firmly and decidedly in reddish brown colour with a hair pencil; painted decidedly with lamp or ivory black; and, with some substance which has perished, leaving a smooth white raised line or ridge on the wall, the plaister on either side having become rough by the action of the air, it would seem, when the colour decayed or was destroyed . . .'

[203] Tristram 1950, 398 ff.

[204] Rokewode 1885, 15–16. Oil is mentioned in painting at Westminster in 1239 (*CLR* 1239, 393); an account of 1265 mentions oil and eggs for use at Westminster (Colvin 1971, 398); these materials were also used in the 1270s (Tristram 1950, 576), while oil and size figure prominently in the Westminster accounts for the 1290s (E101/468/6 *passim*). A valuable study of the combination of oil and tempera techniques in contemporary Norwegian panel painting is to be found in L. E. Plahter, E. Skaug and U. Plahter, *Gothic Painted Altar Frontals from the Church of Tingelstad* (Oslo-Bergen, 1974).

Part II. The Paintings in the Great Chamber of Henry III

[1] Borenius 1943, 40; *KW*, i, 120–30.

[2] *KW*, i, 93–6, 162–3.

[3] *Ibid.*, 151–4, and J. Bony, *The English Decorated Style* (Oxford, 1979), 2–8.

[4] *KW*, i, 127–30.

[5] P. Eames, 'Documentary evidence concerning the character and use of domestic furnishings in England in the fourteenth and fifteenth centuries', *Furniture History*, vii (1971), 41, 53–4.

[6] *KW*, i, 534.

[7] The Westminster household ordinances of 1279 are unhelpful: see T. F. Tout, *Chapters in the Administrative History of Mediaeval England*, ii (Manchester, 1920), 158.

[8] H. G. Richardson, 'The Coronation in medieval England', *Traditio*, xvi (1960), 111, 197.

9 *CCR* 1279, 505. The small chapel by the bed was used by Edward I for semi-official business: see *Registrum Epistolarum Fratris Johannis Peckham*, ed. C. T. Martin, *RS*, 77, iii (London, 1885), 962.

10 'Plebe in sua camera circumstante': see *Flores Historiarum*, ed. H. R. Luard, *RS*, 95, iii (London, 1890), 296. See also I. M. Cooper, 'The meeting-places of Parliament in the ancient Palace of Westminster', *JBAA*, iii (1938), 97, 112. An entry of 1259, *CLR* 1259, 457, stating that John de Crachale was to demolish the fireplace in the king's chamber and to replace it after the Parliament of Easter 1259, has been taken to imply that Parliament may have met in the chamber and interrupted work there. The precise venue of the Parliaments recorded at Westminster between 1244 and 1259 is unknown; see *Handbook of British Chronology*, ed. F. M. Powicke and E. B. Fryde (London, 1961), 499–503.

11 *KW*, i, 506 n. 3; P. Eames, 'Furniture in England, France and the Netherlands from the twelfth to the fifteenth century', *Furniture History*, xiii (1977), 77, 85–6.

12 *KW*, ii, 1042 no. 10; Rokewode 1885, 13; cf. the York household regulations of 1318: T. F. Tout, *The Place of the Reign of Edward II in English History*, 2nd edn. (Manchester, 1976), 241 ff.

13 M. McKisack, *The Fourteenth Century, 1307–1399* (Oxford, 1959), 10.

14 J. R. Maddicott, *Thomas of Lancaster 1307–1322* (Oxford, 1970), 288, specifying the *magna camera*.

15 *Rotuli Parliamentorum*, ed. J. Strachey (London, 1767–83), ii, 107 (4), 127 (8), 135 (3), 136 (8), 237 (7, 8); Cooper, *op. cit.* (note 10), 112 ff.; J. G. Edwards, *The Second Century of the English Parliament* (Oxford, 1979), 3–11.

16 Esposito 1960, 26.

17 *CCR* 1243, 150.

18 H. Johnstone, 'Poor-relief in the royal households of thirteenth-century England', *Speculum*, iv (1929), 149 ff.; cf. the useful account in R. K. Lancaster, 'King Henry III and the Patronage of Religious Art', unpublished Ph.D. thesis, Johns Hopkins University, Baltimore, 1967, 22 ff.; *KW*, i, 157–9.

19 Eames, *op. cit.* (note 5), 47–8, 50 n. 59; a throne was made for Henry at Westminster in 1245, possibly for the Great Hall: see F. Wormald, 'The Throne of Solomon and St Edward's Chair', in *De Artibus Opuscula*, xl: *Essays in Honour of Erwin Panofsky*, ed. M. Meiss (New York, 1961), 532, 537.

20 Eames, *op. cit.* (note 5), 48.

21 Eames, *op. cit.* (note 5), 41 ff.; Eames, *op. cit.* (note 11), 181 ff.

22 *CCR* 1236, 270–1; cf. *CLR* 1240, 3–4, for the occurrence of the same text in Latin at Woodstock.

23 As at Ludgershall, *CLR* 1246, 32, Northampton, *CLR* 1252, 97, and Guildford, *CLR* 1256, 262–3; Borenius 1943, 40–1. Rokewode (1885, 15) suggestively notes that a fragment of a painting comprising 'a dog licking the feet of a beggar, perhaps part of the story of Dives and Lazarus' was 'one of the smaller subjects which served to ornament' parts of the Painted Chamber.

24 Above, p. 17.

25 Above, p. 14; the terminology used here is that of Eames, *op. cit.* (note 5), 57 n. 10; Eames, *op. cit.* (note 11), 74, fig. 16.

26 Eames, *op. cit.* (note 5), 54–5; *CLR* 1243, 205–6; Eames, *op. cit.* (note 11), 76.

27 *CLR* 1251, p. 372.

28 Matthew Paris, *Chronica Majora*, ed. H. R. Luard, *RS*, 57, iii (London, 1876), 337–8; Lethaby 1925, 269.

29 Colvin 1971, 248.

30 *KW*, i, 479, 497–8.

31 Jean de Joinville, *Histoire de saint Louis*, ed. N. de Wailly (Paris, 1868), 20–1, 240.

32 The fundamental study is now S. Hanley, *The Lit de Justice of the Kings of France* (Princeton, 1983), esp. 15 ff.

33 A similar rod was found in Edward I's tomb in 1774: see the drawing in Society of Antiquaries, Westminster Abbey Red Portfolio, 30a, and the observations of Sir Joseph Ayloffe in 'An account of the body of King Edward the First, as it appeared on opening his tomb in the year 1774', *Archaeologia*, iii (1786), 376, 384; see also L. G. Wickham Legg, *English Coronation Records* (Westminster, 1901), lii, and A. Gransden, *Historical Writing in*

England c. 550 to c. 1307 (London, 1974), 458; further remarks on the connotation of the 'mertlot' of St Edward are found in J. J. G. Alexander, 'Painting and manuscript illumination for royal patrons in the later Middle Ages', in *English Court Culture in the Later Middle Ages*, ed. V. J. Scattergood and J. W. Sherborne (London, 1983), 141, 142, n. 5.

[34] For the 'Merton' *Flores*, see Gransden, *op. cit.* (note 33), 456 ff. The evidence of the king's chamber mural lends strong support to Gransden's contention that this manuscript was a Westminster compilation. For the Westminster Abbey copy, see J. A. Robinson and M. R. James, *The Manuscripts of Westminster Abbey* (Cambridge, 1908), 82. The weak and cursory drawing of the 'Merton' scene suggests that it must be a successor of the mural in question.

[35] A. Hollaender, 'The pictorial work in the "Flores Historiarum" of the so-called Matthew of Westminster (Ms Chetham 6712)', *Bulletin of the John Rylands Library*, xxviii (1944), 361, 367; Henderson 1967, 83–4; R. Vaughan, *Matthew Paris*, 2nd edn. (Cambridge, 1979), 92–103.

[36] The mural was damaged in the critical area around the hand of the archbishop to St Edward's left, but as the 'Merton' version is in general so close and does not show the anointing there is no reason to believe it was included in the mural. M. Schapiro ('An illuminated English psalter of the early thirteenth century', in *Late Antique, Early Christian and Mediaeval Art* (London, 1980), 329, 341, figs. 13–14) suggests wrongly that the Westminster scene included the anointing.

[37] Henderson 1967, 71–85.

[38] M. R. James, *La Estoire de Seint Aedward le Rei*, Roxburghe Club (Oxford, 1920); Henderson 1967, 80 ff.; Vaughan, *op. cit.* (note 35), 168 ff.

[39] Henderson 1967, 83–4.

[40] Vaughan, *op. cit.* (note 35), 92.

[41] *Ibid.*, 173–5.

[42] *KW*, i, 147; Lancaster, *op. cit.* (note 18), 185 ff.

[43] *CLR* 1250, 325. The image occurs, for example, in the *Hortus Deliciarum*: see G. Cames, *Allégories et symboles dans l'Hortus Deliciarum* (Leiden, 1971), 74–7, pl. XL.

[44] The very fragmentary text to the guard's right could refer to 'laur(ence)' in allusion to the dedication of the chapel behind the bed to St Lawrence mentioned in the Dunstable Annals, *Annales Monastici*, ed. H. R. Luard, *RS*, 36, iii (London, 1866), 220.

[45] Wormald, *op. cit.* (note 19), 538–9.

[46] *CLR* 1261, 21.

[47] R. Branner, 'The painted medallions in the Sainte-Chapelle in Paris', *Transactions of the American Philosophical Society*, ii (1968), 5, 14.

[48] James, *op. cit.* (note 38), fols. 26–7. The story of St Edward was specified for paintings as early as 1235–6 at Clarendon: *KW*, ii, 915.

[49] L. E. Tanner, 'Some representations of Saint Edward the Confessor in Westminster Abbey and elsewhere', *JBAA*, xv (1952), 1–12; M. Harrison, 'A life of St Edward the Confessor in early fourteenth-century stained glass at Fécamp, in Normandy', *JWCI*, xxvi (1963), 22, 25 ff.

[50] Borenius 1943, 47–50; Henry appears to have had portable images of this sort: see *CLR* 1240, 478.

[51] *KW*, i, 148–9.

[52] Lethaby 1905, 264; R. B. Green, 'Virtues and Vices in the chapter-house vestibule in Salisbury', *JWCI*, xxxi (1968), 148, 158, erroneously states that the room 'probably had no more than six or seven'.

[53] *KW*, i, 500.

[54] *CCR* 1242, 514. The Wise and Foolish Virgins occur on the outer order of the arch over the tympanum of the Judgement porch at Lincoln: Stone 1972, 126, pl. 100a.

[55] Listed in *CPR*, 1266–72, 139; see also *KW*, i, 148, and P. C. Claussen, 'Goldschmiede des Mittelalters', *Zeitschrift des Deutschen Vereins für Kunstwissenschaft*, xxxii, 1–4 (1978), 46, 70, 82–5. The iconography of St Peter and Nero is discussed by G. Henderson, 'The Damnation of Nero, and related themes', in *The Vanishing Past*, ed. A. Borg and A. Martindale, BAR International Series 111 (Oxford, 1981), 39 ff.

[56] By the 1260s splendid heraldic display was an established feature of window decoration in Henry's residences, either in glass or on shutters, as at the Tower in 1240 (*KW*, ii, 714), Rochester in 1247 (*ibid.*, 809), Winchester in 1266 (*ibid.*, 861), and most spectacularly at Havering in 1268 (*ibid.*, 957). For the shields in the choir aisles of Westminster Abbey see RCHM, *London*, i: *Westminster Abbey* (London, 1924), pls. 102–3, 53, 55, and *KW*, i, 144–6.

For heraldic glazing at Westminster Abbey, see Sir C. Peers and L. E. Tanner, 'On some recent discoveries in Westminster Abbey', *Archaeologia*, xciii (1949), 151, 160 ff., pl. XXXIII. Block borders with heraldic motifs appear earlier in the glazing at Chartres in the window with the figures of Ezekiel carrying St John: see Y. Delaporte and E. Houvet, *Les Vitraux de la cathédrale de Chartres*, iii (Chartres, 1926), pl. CC.

[57] Rokewode 1885, 35–6; Tristram (1950, 105–6) attributes the arms *Or, an eagle displayed sable* to Richard Earl of Cornwall 'in his character as King of the Romans', rather than to the Empire. If this is so (and we cannot be certain) these arms would have some dating value, because Richard died in 1272. For *Deboneretē*'s swan badge, see note 206 below.

[58] A. Gardner, *A Handbook of English Medieval Sculpture* (Cambridge, 1937), 87–9, fig. 90; Stone 1972, 89–90; A. Katzenellenbogen, *Allegories of the Virtues and Vices in Mediaeval Art* (Nendeln/Liechtenstein, 1977), 20

[59] See J. Y. T. Winjum, 'The Canterbury Roundels', unpublished Ph.D. thesis, Michigan, 1974, 23 ff.

[60] Lisbon, Museu Calouste Gulbenkian MS L.A.139; BL Add. MS 42555. For the Berengaudus commentary, *PL*, xvii, col. 881 ff. See also Henderson 1968, 137.

[61] At this point the iconography of Abingdon is a decayed form of that in Lisbon, for scrolls are inserted in the hands of the Virtues and not weapons.

[62] M. Evans, 'An illustrated fragment of Peraldus's *Summa* of Vice: Harleian MS 3244', *JWCI*, xlv (1982), 14, 27–9, pl. 3; for the Eadwine Psalter, see M. R. James, *The Canterbury Psalter* (London, 1935).

[63] Green, *op. cit.* (note 52), *passim*.

[64] Katzenellenbogen, *op. cit.* (note 58), 19–20, pl. x, fig. 19.

[65] *Ibid.*, 14–21.

[66] Green, *op. cit.* (note 52), 151, pl. 50a, b.

[67] *Ibid.*, 157 n. 61.

[68] The Abingdon Apocalypse is intimately related to that in Lisbon and contains a medieval inscription recording that it was once in the possession of Bishop Giles Bridport, the great Salisbury patron who died in 1262: see R. E. W. Flower, 'The date of the Abingdon Apocalypse', *British Museum Quarterly*, vi (1931–2), 109; most recently, S. Lewis, 'Giles de Bridport and the Abingdon Apocalypse', in *England in the Thirteenth Century*, Proceedings of the 1984 Harlaxton Symposium, ed. M. W. Ormrod (Harlaxton College, 1985), 107, accepts a date for the manuscript of before 1262 and notes that its iconography subtly reflects certain specifically episcopal interests.

[69] For this text, see *Lives of Edward the Confessor*, ed. H. R. Luard, *RS*, 3 (London, 1858), 50, vv. 872 ff. Edward 'Debonaire ert a ses amis', *ibid.*, 51, v. 911; indeed, 'N'ai oi ki unc fist maire/Simplicité debonaire,/Fors sul Jhesu...', *ibid.*, 55, v. 1052; 'Nel dei pas passer ne taire/Cum il fu duz e debonaire', *ibid.*, 79, v. 1915. Edward's largesse is illustrated by the tale of the thief in the treasury, *ibid.*, 53, v. 980 ff., and later it is stated that Edward 'Ne se laist veintre de avarice,/Mais le tint a mut grant vice', *ibid.*, 79, vv. 1901–2.

[70] As in the case when Edward has a vision at Westminster of the King of Denmark drowning, James, *op. cit.* (note 38), fol. 12, and *Lives of Edward the Confessor, op. cit.* (note 69), 61, v. 1291, 'Surrist cum en transe mis;/Si s'esmerveillent tut du ris'. In 1240 two fair cherubim were to be made for the great cross in the chapel of St Peter ad Vincula in the Tower of London, 'with cheerful and joyous countenances': *CLR* 1240, 15; contrast the figure of Winter to be painted by the fireplace of the queen's chamber at Westminster, to be identified by its 'sad looks and other miserable portrayals of the body': *CLR* 1240, 444.

[71] *Lives of Edward the Confessor, op. cit.* (note 69), 50, v. 872: 'Lors est la terre en bon estat Cunte, e baron, e li prelat, N'est nuls a ki li reis ne pleise.' For the Dublin painting, *CCR* 1243, 23.

[72] *Lives of Edward the Confessor, op. cit.* (note 69), 50, v. 890: 'Ben semble le roi Salamun/De grant fame, de grant renun'; cf. *ibid.*, 64, v. 1373.

[73] Richardson, *op. cit.* (note 8), 136 ff.; Wormald, *op. cit.* (note 19), 537–9.

[74] *CCR* 1252, 290; Tristram 1950, 104–5.

[75] G. Henderson, 'Romance and politics on some medieval English seals', *Art History*, i (1978), 26, 30; cf. Tudor-Craig 1957, 104.

[76] A. Bennett, 'The Windmill Psalter: the historiated letter E of Psalm One', *JWCI*, xliii (1981), 52, 64 ff.

77 Wormald, *op. cit.* (note 19), 532 ff.

78 *Ibid.*, 537, illustrated in F. P. Pickering, *Literature and Art in the Middle Ages* (London, 1970), pl. 3a.

79 See above, p. 17.

80 It should be noted that although the Liberate Rolls for the years 1230–2, 1233–4, and 1235–6 are lost, the Close Rolls are complete. As the fabric was worked on until *c.* 1235, the *magna historia* is unlikely to have been an element in Henry's work in the room before 1237. This seems primarily to have been non-figurative, with large expanses of green painted drapery. For Winchester and Rochester, see *CLR* 1233, 218–19; *KW*, ii, 861; *CLR* 1239, 365.

81 The reference occurs in BL Cotton MS Nero D.V., fol. 1ᵛ: see Vaughan, *op. cit.* (note 35), 247. The image was current in the 1230s, for a *Mappa Mundi* was painted in the Great Hall at Winchester in 1239: *CLR* 1239, 405. The painting of a city ordered for the queen's chamber at Winchester in 1246 (*CLR* 1246, 30) could reflect the cartographic interest in the Matthew Paris itineraries: Vaughan, *op. cit.* (note 35), 242 ff., and see also Tudor-Craig 1957, 100–3.

82 *KW*, ii, 859.

83 *Ibid.*, 915.

84 *Ibid.*, 1012, 736.

85 *Ibid.*, 730.

86 *CLR* 1240, 468–9; *CCR* 1242, 514.

87 *CLR* 1246, 30.

88 *CLR* 1247, 157.

89 *CLR* 1250, 325.

90 *CLR* 1256, 307–8.

91 *CLR* 1259, 486; *CLR* 1261, 21.

92 *KW*, ii, 944.

93 *CCR* 1236, 239.

94 *CCR* 1238, 26.

95 *CCR* 1245, 287.

96 *CLR* 1240, 444.

97 *CCR* 1256, 326. See D. J. A. Ross, 'A lost painting in Henry III's palace at Westminster', *JWCI*, xvi (1953), 160. For earlier uses of Bestiary imagery such as this one, see G. Henderson, 'Giraldus Cambrensis: a note on his account of a painting in the king's chamber at Winchester', *Archaeological Journal*, cxviii (1961), 175.

98 For Winchester, *CLR* 1256, 307–8; for Woodstock, *CLR* 1239, 411; *CLR* 1268, 14; for Ludgershall, *KW*, ii, 730.

99 Borenius 1943, 47–50; *KW*, i, 127 ff.; Lancaster, *op. cit.* (note 18), 141 ff.

100 M. T. Clanchy, 'Did Henry III have a policy?', *History*, liii (1968), 203, 214.

101 A. Gransden, 'The continuation of the *Flores Historiarum* from 1265 to 1327', *Medieval Studies*, xxxvi (1974) 472, 491–2; *KW*, i, 491–2.

102 *KW*, i, 133.

103 Richardson, *op. cit.* (note 8), 136 ff.

104 M. T. Clanchy, *England and its Rulers* (Oxford, 1983), 282–3.

105 Above, p. 18.

106 Wormald 1949, 172–3; Wormald's views have influenced those of Gardner and Klein: see J. Gardner, review of H. Belting's *Die Oberkirche von San Francesco in Assisi*, in *Kunstchronik*, xxxii (1979), i, 63, 82, and P. Klein, *Endzeiterwartung und Ritterideologie* (Graz, 1983), 15–16, 45 n. 208.

107 Above, p. 22.

108 Above, p. 19.

109 Wormald 1949, 173.

110 I would therefore qualify the view of Colvin in *KW*, i, 505, that in the 1290s 'the paintings in the Painted Chamber were undergoing extensive *restoration*' (my italics) and reject the statement of Gardner, *op. cit.* (note 106), 82, that the works in the room can 'aufgrund der Dokumente ebenso plausibel 1290 wie 1260 datiert werden'.

111 Above, pp. 17–21.

112 For the 1265 account, see Colvin 1971, 390; Walter was already entitled *Magister* at this stage. For Walter's employment in the king's chamber, *CLR* 1266, 251. By 1266 he appears to have replaced Master William, the Westminster monk employed in the king's service from

the 1230s: see Tristram 1950, 94, 100, 574–5, 622–3; *CCR* 1239, 158, 185 (appointment as painter for life at St Swithun's Priory, Winchester). William's last certain work in the chamber was that recorded on the Jesse Tree on the new fireplace in 1259, above, p. 17.

[113]   Stothard 1823, 326.

[114]   Tudor-Craig 1957, 98, pl. xx; Klein, *op. cit.* (note 106), 45 ff.

[115]   BL Add. MS 36370, fol. 208; Westminster City Library, Box 57 no. 49. The angels painted on the intrados of an arch in Caesar's Tower at Chester Castle are, in contrast, half-length, more in the manner of the angels carved on the soffits of the north transept of Westminster Abbey, for which see C. J. P. Cave and L. E. Tanner, 'A thirteenth-century choir of angels in the north transept of Westminster Abbey and the adjacent figures of two kings', *Archaeologia*, lxxxiv (1934), 63, pls. x–xii. For Caesar's Tower, see *KW*, ii, 610–11. My attention was drawn to the murals there by Mr David Park.

[116]   Wormald 1949, 172–3.

[117]   *Ibid.*, 167–8.

[118]   Lethaby 1927, 123, 137; above, p. 15.

[119]   Lethaby 1927, 127–8; Wormald 1949, 170–3; Tristram 1950, 103; Tudor-Craig 1957, 97–8; Klein, *op. cit.* (note 106), 34–9.

[120]   See especially Henderson 1967, 91 ff.; Branner, *op. cit.* (note 47), 15 ff.; R. Branner, *Manuscript Painting in Paris during the Reign of Saint Louis* (Berkeley, 1977), 95–141.

[121]   Branner, *op. cit.* (note 120), 139.

[122]   Branner, *op. cit.* (note 47), 15 ff.

[123]   Branner, *op. cit.* (note 120), 62–3.

[124]   For the choir glazing at Amiens of the 1260s, see L. Grodecki, *Vitraux de France du XIe au XVIe siècle*, Musée des Arts Décoratifs (Paris, 1953), 62 no. 24, pl. 17; L. Grodecki *et al.*, *Les Vitraux de Paris, de la région parisienne, de la Picardie et du Nord-Pas-de-Calais*, Corpus Vitrearum Medii Aevi (Paris, 1978), 144, pl. xxva; for the glazing of the choir of Saint-Urbain at Troyes of *c.*1270, see L. Grodecki, 'Les vitraux de Saint-Urbain de Troyes', *Congrès archéologique de France*, cxiii (1955), 123, 126 ff., figs. 1, 2a, 2b; for Beauvais, Grodecki, 1978, *op. cit.* (this note), 144, pl. xxvb.

[125]   W. de G. Birch, *Catalogue of Seals in the Department of Manuscripts in the British Museum*, i (London, 1887), 215 no. 1498, pl. vii.

[126]   For Bridport's tomb and effigy, see M. E. Roberts, 'The tomb of Bishop Giles de Bridport in Salisbury Cathedral', *Art Bulletin*, lxv (1983), 559 ff., which includes a discussion of the Wyle and Lusignan memorials; for Aquablanca's effigy, see E. S. Prior and A. Gardner, *An Account of Medieval Figure-Sculpture in England* (Cambridge, 1912), 605, fig. 678; and for Lincoln, *ibid.*, 265–76, figs. 286–300.

[127]   James, *op. cit.* (note 38), 37; Tristram 1950, 622, pl. 26, supplementary pl. 18; M. Rickert, *Painting in Britain: the Middle Ages* (Harmondsworth, 1954), 123–4, pl. 110b; Tudor-Craig 1957, 102 n. 2; *KW*, ii, 867–9; Henderson 1967, 85.

[128]   See note 115,

[129]   The nave paintings in St Albans Abbey become more advanced stylistically as they progress along the piers of the nave towards the east; in this context, see Tristram 1950, pl. 165, and for the Oxford chapter house, *ibid.*, 586–7, pls. 83–93. The Oxford paintings are related by Brieger (1968, 180–1) to the style of the Oscott Psalter Apostles, but they resemble more closely the transitional style found at the end of the Trinity College Apocalypse (see below). On fol. 31 of this work there appears an unfamiliar artist working over older drawings in the new broad-fold style, but retaining the open-faced, wide-eyed heads of the earlier work in the book. The effect is comparable to the Oxford paintings, whose heads are in a similar, but more emphatic idiom, and whose garments show signs of hardening into more angular shapes.

[130]   For the Trinity College Apocalypse, see Henderson 1967, 117–28, and P. Brieger, *The Trinity College Apocalypse* (London, 1967); for the Lambeth, Lisbon and Abingdon Apocalypses, Henderson 1967, 88 ff.; 1968, 129 ff.; for the Oscott Psalter, D. H. Turner, 'Two rediscovered miniatures of the Oscott Psalter', *British Museum Quarterly*, xxxiv (1969–70), 10; for the Metropolitan Psalter, see *Transformations of the Court Style, Gothic Art in Europe 1270–1330* (Brown University, 1977), 120 no. 44; for MS K.26, Henderson 1968, 145–7.

[131]   Henderson 1967, 92 ff.; 1968, 131–7.

[132]   Henderson 1968, 137–8, 143 n. 50.

[133] The style and iconography of this work are discussed fully in G. Henderson, 'MS. K.26 in the Library of St John's College, Cambridge: a Study of the Style and Iconography of its Thirteenth-Century Illustrations', unpublished Ph.D. thesis, Cambridge, 1959.

[134] Vaughan, *op. cit.* (note 35), 173 ff., argues that *La Estoire* was based upon a St Albans text composed by Matthew Paris in the 1240s, but notes correctly that the illustrations are not by Matthew's hand; Henderson (1967, 83–102) favours Westminster authorship for the pictures. Exactly what 'Westminster' may mean in this context is unclear. Klein, *op. cit.* (note 106), 65–8, attributes an entire succession of manuscripts to the 'court school' at Westminster, including the former Dyson Perrins (now Getty) Apocalypse, BL Add. MS 35166, *La Estoire*, Douce and BN MS lat. 10474. He supposes, p. 46, that the Lambeth Apocalypse group may have originated in a Salisbury or Winchester scriptorium. So far as the 'court school' at Westminster is concerned, I can find no evidence whatsoever for its existence in the documentary records of the day; I put this view forward in my 1983 thesis (Binski 1983, 127–8), and find my scepticism shared by R. K. Lancaster, whose paper 'Henry III, Westminster Abbey, and the Court School of illumination', in *Seven Studies in Medieval English History and other Historical Essays, presented to H. S. Snellgrove*, ed. R. H. Bowers (Jackson, Mississippi, 1983), 85 ff., admirably disposes of too simplistic a view of manuscript painting done for the court in this period.

[135] Henderson (1967, 83–102) proposes a date of *c.* 1245–55: Klein, *op. cit.* (note 106), 52, favours *c.* 1250–60.

[136] See note 68.

[137] Henderson (1967, 102–4) notes that the book was owned by Alionora de Quincy, and proposes that it was made in the lifetime of her husband Roger de Quincy, 2nd Earl of Winchester, who died in 1264. Alionora is unlikely to have displayed the de Quincy arms on fol. 48 after her marriage to Roger de Leybourne in 1267, so we must presume that the book dates at the latest to before 1267; Henderson 1968, 137–45.

[138] Turner, *op. cit.* (note 130), 10 ff.; Henderson 1968, 145–7; Klein, *op. cit.* (note 106), 46–7.

[139] Branner, *op. cit.* (note 120), 116–17, fig. 338, 122 ff., 236, fig. 375, 131–2, 238, fig. 389, 132–7, 238, figs. 395–400; Klein, *op. cit.* (note 106), 51–63.

[140] Henderson (1968, 143–5) adopts the radical solution of placing both Douce and the Retable *c.*1260 and then tracing their impact on manuscripts such as the Abingdon Apocalypse.

[141] Here I part with Klein, *op. cit.* (note 106), 44–6, whose argument relies on a starting-date for the murals of *c.*1265 rather than 1263–4 and who suggests that Douce's style could only have appeared after the completion of the paintings in *c.*1272. Klein also accepts Tristram's date of *c.* 1270 for the large paintings of saints in the south transept, and argues that Douce must post-date their style. I consider this to be the wrong chronological ordering, for in my opinion, expressed in my 1983 thesis (Binski 1983, 108–19), the abbey murals could well date to the end of the thirteenth century or the early fourteenth century, and should substantially post-date the idiom of Douce (see p. 80).

[142] The material is thoroughly summarized by Klein, *op. cit.* (note 106), 3–16, 33–49.

[143] Klein, *op. cit.* (note 106), 38–9. The shield held up by Edward on fol. 1 is damaged, but was described as having a label by Nicholson. The modest, uncrowned figures of Edward and Eleanor would be appropriate before Edward's accession to the throne.

[144] Klein, *op. cit.* (note 106), 38–9; Binski 1983, 94.

[145] This depends on whether we accept the significance of the heraldry introduced in some of the pictures, suggestive of the baronial opposition to the crown in 1264–5: Klein, *op. cit.* (note 106), 42–4.

[146] Thus Klein, *op. cit.* (note 106), 42–9, takes the Edward–Eleanor initial as a *terminus post quem* for the execution of the pictures.

[147] Klein, *op. cit.* (note 106), 39–40, argues for a late start for the pictures on stylistic grounds, for he supposes that the Edward–Eleanor initial is similar to the William of Devon Bible style or works from Branner's *Grusch atelier* in Paris, and so is fitted to the later 1260s. Even if we accept Klein's analogy, the dating which follows from it is too vague to rule out the possibility that the work was started as a whole in the 1260s, albeit the late 1260s. Klein (*ibid.*, 48) states that we are forced to the assumption that the book was ordered around 1270, so placing the pictures later; but this assumption is groundless unless we also assume a late date for the style of the pictures in turn.

[148] Thus the style of the initials in the former Dyson Perrins Apocalypse differs from that of the

pictures; but no one has argued for two campaigns of work on this book: see M. R. James, *The Apocalypse in Latin* (Oxford, 1927).

149 Klein, *op. cit.* (note 106), 51 ff. I take it that Klein is here extending the view of Robert Branner that the Douce Apocalypse and the 'frescoes' in Westminster Abbey represent the 'Parisian Style when it was carried abroad', Branner, *op. cit.* (note 120), 138.

150 G. Henderson, 'An Apocalypse manuscript in Paris: BN MS Lat. 10474', *Art Bulletin*, lii (1970), 22–9; Klein, *op. cit.* (note 106), 57–9. The same applies to the Abingdon Apocalypse, Henderson 1968, 143–5.

151 Lethaby 1927, 127–8; Wormald 1949, 170–1; Tristram 1950, 128–9; Henderson 1968, 128–9; Klein, *op. cit.* (note 106), pls. 4, 6, 10, 11.

152 Henderson, *op. cit.* (note 150), 22 ff.; Klein, *op. cit.* (note 106), 57 ff.

153 The wall painter Peter of Spain provided painted panels for the Chapel of St Mary in Westminster Abbey: *CLR* 1258, 424; *CPR* 1258, 613; Colvin 1971, 210, 230, 238, 252–8, 262–84. For Master Walter's work on painted panels for the royal tombs in the 1290s see above, pp. 20–1.

154 See Binski 1983, 108 ff.; see also p. 80.

155 F. Baron, 'Enlumineurs, peintres et sculpteurs parisiens des XIIIe et XIVe siècles d'après les rôles de la taille', *Bulletin archéologique*, iv (1968), 37, 41–3, 50 no. 9.

156 The literature is extensive; see principally D. G. Vitzthum, *Die Pariser Miniaturmalerei von der Zeit des hl. Ludwig bis zu Philipp von Valois* (Leipzig, 1907), 39 ff., 47 ff., pls. VII, IX; Tristram 1950, 139 n. 2; G. Schmidt, *Die Malerschule von St Florian* (Graz–Cologne, 1962), 113 ff.; Brieger 1968, 212; D. H. Turner, 'The development of Maître Honoré', *British Museum Quarterly*, xxxiii (1968–9), 53; E. Kosmer, 'A Study of the Style and Iconography of a Thirteenth-Century *Somme le Roi* (British Museum Ms. Add. 54180)', unpublished Ph.D. thesis, Yale, 1973; A. Martindale, *Gothic Art* (London, 1974), 135; E. Kosmer, 'Master Honoré: a reconsideration of the documents', *Gesta*, xiv, 1 (1975), 63; the most useful recent discussion is E. Beer, 'Pariser Buchmalerei in der Zeit Ludwigs des Heiligen und im letzten Viertel des 13. Jahrhunderts', *Zeitschrift für Kunstgeschichte*, xliv (1981), 62; Klein, *op. cit.* (note 106), 15–16, 47, 62.

157 Beer, *op. cit.* (note 156), 76 ff., 91.

158 Beer, *op. cit.* (note 156), 83 ff., summarizes the position.

159 Vitzthum, *op. cit.* (note 156), 75, pl. XVI; Brieger 1968, 223; Klein, *op. cit.* (note 106), 47.

160 Bennett, *op. cit.* (note 76), 52–3, 66; see also R. Calkins, *Illuminated Books of the Middle Ages* (Ithaca, 1983), 215, colour pls. 16–19, pls. 118–24, and A. Bennett, 'A late thirteenth-century Psalter Hours from London', in *England in the Thirteenth Century* (see note 68), 15–27, for the occurrence of this style in the Mostyn Psalter Hours as late as the 1290s.

161 The taste for elaborately posed figures is also typical of mid-century Parisian painting, such as the Sainte-Chapelle medallions, the St Louis Psalter (see M. Thomas, *Le Psautier de Saint Louis* (Graz, 1972)) and the related Isabella Psalter (Cambridge, Fitzwilliam Museum MS 300): S. C. Cockerell, *A Psalter and Hours Executed before 1270 for a Lady Connected with St Louis, probably his Sister, Isabella of France* (London, 1905); Branner, *op. cit.* (note 120), 63, 132–40. Some painters employed in the two royal psalters also show a marked liking for strongly modelled garments, lost profiles and back-turned heads.

162 cf. the Vatican Cope: A. G. I. Christie, *English Medieval Embroidery* (Oxford, 1938), pls. XLVI–XLIX.

163 The Retable is constructed from two vertical outer panels and four central horizontal planks; to this base were pegged the spires and gables, the shafts being carved out of the backing timber with the exception of two at the centre.

164 E. E. Viollet-le-Duc, *Dictionnaire raisonné du mobilier français*, i (Paris, 1858), 234: 'Ce retable est de fabrication française . . . il date du milieu du XIIIe siècle'; cf. Lethaby 1927, 128: 'The crocketed gables, capitals with square and octagonal abacuses, and the star-shaped panels, all seem to me of French character.' Contrast Wormald 1949, 169, and Tristram 1950, 132. I am grateful to Dr Christopher Wilson for advice on the general stylistic orientation of the Retable's architecture.

165 Reproduced Lethaby 1925, 67 ff., fig. 23, and shown in this form in Wren's 1719 drawing of the transept: *KW*, i, 141, 144, 151.

166 For the French sources used at Westminster, see R. Branner, 'Westminster Abbey and the

French Court Style', *Journal of the Society of Architectural Historians*, xxiii (1964), 3, and Bony, *op. cit.* (note 3), 3–4. For Reims, H. J. Kunst, 'Der Chor von Westminster Abbey und die Kathedrale von Reims', *Zeitschrift für Kunstgeschichte*, xxxi (1968), 122.

[167] W. Sauerländer, *Gothic Sculpture in France 1140–1270* (London, 1972), pl. 191.

[168] See, in general, R. Branner, *Saint Louis and the Court Style in Gothic Architecture* (London, 1965); Lethaby 1906, 15, and 1925, 264. For the Évreux shrine, executed under Abbot Gilbert 1240–55, see J. Taralon, (ed.), *Les Trésors des églises de France* (Paris, 1965), 111–13, no. 217, pl. 113, and J. Taralon, 'La châsse de Saint-Taurin d'Évreux', *Bulletin monumental*, cxl (1982), 41; for the Sainte-Chapelle reliquary, see G. Souchal, 'Un reliquaire de la Sainte-Chapelle au Musée de Cluny', *Revue des arts*, x (1960), 179, figs. 1, 2, and P. Brieger *et al.*, *Art and the Courts, France and England from 1259 to 1328*, The National Gallery of Canada (Ottawa, 1972), i, 129 no. 40, ii, pl. 58; and for the *châsse*, R. Branner, 'The Grande Châsse of the Sainte-Chapelle', *Gazette des beaux-arts*, lxxvii (1971), 5, fig. 1.

[169] That in the chapel of Saint-Eugène: J. Formigé, *L'Abbaye royale de Saint-Denis* (Paris, 1960), 141–2, figs. 115–16; F. Joubert, 'Les retables du milieu de XIIIe siècle à l'abbatiale de Saint-Denis', *Bulletin monumental*, cxxxi (1973), 17, fig. 4.

[170] e.g. fol. 13ᵛ, Branner, *op. cit.* (note 120), fig. 402; cf. also many of the line-endings.

[171] Lethaby 1927, 128–31.

[172] C. Donnay-Rocmans, 'La châsse de Sainte Gertrude à Nivelles', *Gazette des beaux-arts*, lviii (1961), 185 ff.; J. Lestocquoy, *L'Art de l'Artois* (Arras, 1973), 99 ff.

[173] See p. 75.

[174] Branner notes that the architectural devices found in mid-century works like the Sainte-Chapelle Evangeliary reflect elements present in recent Parisian architecture: see Branner, *op. cit.* (note 120), 128, fig. 365. We might add that the arcading over the scenes in the St Louis Psalter is related to the gables on the inside of the south transept of Notre-Dame in Paris under construction *c.* 1260, and that the use of slim tracery-filled rectangular windows in the related Isabella Psalter follows from the type of window used at the court chapel at Saint-Germain-en-Laye of the 1230s: see Branner 1965, *op. cit.* (note 168), 101, 51–2, pls. 112–13, 60, and *op. cit.* (note 120), figs. 395–400, 400–2.

[175] L. L. Gee, ' "Ciborium" tombs in England 1290–1330', *JBAA*, cxxxii (1979), 29, 33 ff., 36.

[176] See p. 74.

[177] See p. 80. C. Wilson, 'The Neville Screen', in *Medieval Art and Architecture at Durham Cathedral*, BAA Conference Transactions for the year 1977, iii (1980), 90, 93, notes the 'up-to-date Parisian detailing' of St Faith's canopy. An implication of his essay is that this type of altar-figure plus ciborium may have been more typical of thirteenth- rather than fourteenth-century altar fittings, a consideration which still does not rule out the possibility that St Faith's altar was reproducing earlier altar types in the church; its retable undoubtedly harks back to altarpieces like the Westminster Retable itself. One such figure, of the Virgin, adorned the altar over the retable in the Lady Chapel: see the 1304 inventory printed in H. F. Westlake, *Westminster Abbey*, ii (London, 1923), 502.

[178] Bony, *op. cit.* (note 3), 9, pl. 50.

[179] I therefore agree substantially with Turner, *op. cit.* (note 156), 62.

[180] Branner, *op. cit.* (note 120), 97–141.

[181] R. Branner, 'The Johannes Grusch atelier and the Continental origins of the William of Devon Painter', *Art Bulletin*, liv (1972), 24; Branner, *op. cit.* (note 120), 82 ff.; Klein, *op. cit.* (note 106), 39–40.

[182] Branner, *op. cit.* (note 47).

[183] See above, p. 134, note 197.

[184] Marquis de Fayolle, 'Tableau de la Confrérie de Rabastens', *Bulletin archéologique* (1923), 73, pls. x-xii; R. Mesuret, 'Les primitifs du Languedoc', *Gazette des beaux-arts*, lxv (1965), 1, 3, no. 7. I am grateful to Pearson Macek for bringing this to my attention. The vulnerability of this type of painting makes it hard to accept the full force of Erwin Panofsky's statement in *Early Netherlandish Painting* (Cambridge, Mass., 1953), 28, that 'a tradition of panel painting' was 'practically nonexistent in France at the beginning of the fourteenth century' and that in consequence panel painting tended to remain 'somewhat *retardataire*'.

[185] Lethaby 1927, 128–32.

[186] Quoted in Suger's *De Administratione*, in *Abbot Suger on the Abbey Church of St-Denis and*

its Art Treasures, ed. E. Panofsky, 2nd edn. (Princeton, 1979), 62–3.

[187] Tristram 1950, 152 ff.; 1955, 38 ff.

[188] Branner, *op. cit.* (note 47), 5 ff.

[189] See the copies by Steinheil, Duban and Boeswillwald executed 1845–70: Paris, Musée des Monuments Français, Centre de Recherches, dossiers Seine iii. The original glass inlays of such medallions as N 6 (Branner's enumeration) had patterns of eight-pointed stars like the Westminster Retable or the pattern recorded by Lethaby in Notre-Dame at Dijon: Lethaby 1927, fig. 1. Enamels are similarly set into the fabric of Crouchback's tomb, and were employed in the embroidered frontal made in the 1260s for the high altar of Westminster Abbey (G. G. Scott, *Gleanings from Westminster Abbey*, 2nd edn. (Oxford and London, 1863), 113–14) as well as in wall painting: Colvin 1971, 426, 428.

[190] Dossiers Seine iii, copies by Duban and Boeswillwald dated 1845. Branner, 'Grande Châsse', *op. cit.* (note 168), 14, suggests that the relic platform and screen were added after 1254; they were in place by 1267, for Joinville states that in that year St Louis went up to the relics to take down that of the True Cross, Joinville, *Histoire de saint Louis, op. cit.* (note 31), 261.

[191] E. E. Viollet-le-Duc, *Dictionnaire raisonné de l'architecture française*, ii (Paris, 1859), 39; Stone 1972, 141–2.

[192] Rokewode 1885, 16.

[193] Stothard 1823, 321 ff.

[194] BL Add. MS 36370, fol. 207^v.

[195] *Gentleman's Magazine* (1819), pt. ii, 389, 391: 'The chain mail is represented by *stucco*, and likewise some of the principal ornaments, while the features and draperies are painted; a mixture which does not destroy the actual flatness of the latter, but which remarkably aids the substance and nobleness of the former.'

[196] J. Mickelthwaite's note in *Proceedings of the Society of Antiquaries*, viii (1881), 524.

[197] Rickert, *op. cit.* (note 127), pls. 140–1.

[198] See the study by M. S. Frinta, 'The puzzling raised decorations in the paintings of Master Theodoric', *Simiolus*, viii (1975–6), 49, 58, figs. 18–20. For the technique of the paintings see P. C. van Geersdaele and L. J. Goldsworthy, 'The restoration of wallpainting fragments from St Stephen's Chapel, Westminster', *The Conservator*, ii (1978), 9, 11–12.

[199] For Winchester, O. Demus, *Romanesque Mural Painting* (London, 1970), pl. 239; for Assisi, see the valuable new study by P. Mora, L. Mora and P. Philippot, *Conservation of Wall Paintings* (London, 1984), 123. The taste for glass inlays also marked Sienese art of the period: see G. Swarzenski, 'Das Auftreten des Églomisé bei Nicolò Pisano', in *Festschrift zum sechzigsten Geburtstag von Paul Clemen*, ed. W. Worringer *et al.* (Düsseldorf, 1926), 326. Lethaby (1927, 136) claimed that the *paterae* of the Painted Chamber were set with glass.

[200] Demus, *op. cit.* (note 199), 634, pl. 298; Mora *et al, op. cit.* (note 199), pl. 80 and 123; cf. the *Salle des Morts* of Le Puy Cathedral: O. Demus, 'European wall painting around 1200', in *The Year 1200: a Symposium*, Metropolitan Museum of Art (New York, 1975), 95, 98–9.

[201] Stothard 1823, 321.

[202] See *CCR* 1264, 366.

[203] Stothard 1823, 309–10.

[204] Gee, *op. cit.* (note 175), 33.

[205] Tristram 1950, 105; Rickert, *op. cit.* (note 127), pl. 135.

[206] Her swan brooch alluding to patience may thus not be original; for the image see A. R. Wagner, 'The Swan Badge and the Swan Knight', *Archaeologia*, xcvii (1959), 127 ff.; and *Lexicon der christlichen Ikonographie*, ed. E. Kirschbaum *et al.*, iv (Freiburg, 1972), cols. 133–4.

[207] Tristram 1955, pl. 1.

[208] The crown forms resemble that on the effigy of Robert the Pious at Saint-Denis of *c.* 1263–4: Sauerländer, *op. cit.* (note 167), pl. 273. The roundel patterns in the spandrels are identical to the big central oculus filled with circlets in the Lincoln east window, perhaps designed in the 1250s. The tympana of the lateral doors of the south transept of Westminster Abbey were orginally filled with circlets containing cinquefoils: see G. Webb, 'The decorative character of Westminster Abbey', *JWCI*, xii (1949), 16, 18, pl. 14a.

[209] See above, p. 18, for the use of charcoal to dry paintings.

Part III. The Old Testament Scenes in the Painted Chamber and the Patronage of Edward I

[1]   Quoted C. R. Dodwell, 'The Bayeux Tapestry and the French secular epic', *Burlington Magazine*, cviii (1966), 549, 550.

[2]   Borenius 1943, 40–50.

[3]   Tudor-Craig 1957, 103–5.

[4]   Tristram 1950, 89–111; Tudor-Craig 1957, 96–9.

[5]   Above, p. 18.

[6]   This was certainly true of Italian monumental painting of the early Trecento: see J. White, *Art and Architecture in Italy 1250–1400* (Harmondsworth, 1966), 203 ff.; and *Duccio* (London, 1979), 93 ff.

[7]   See above, p. 19.

[8]   The use of armour is described by Rokewode (1885, 27 ff.).

[9]   Tristram 1950, 102; Tudor-Craig 1957, 97.

[10]   J. Bony, *The English Decorated Style* (Oxford, 1979), 19–29.

[11]   *Ibid.*, 22.

[12]   Stagings of this order were constructed for the coronation of Edward II in 1308: *KW*, i, 507.

[13]   R. Branner, *Saint Louis and the Court Style in Gothic Architecture* (London, 1965), 101, pls. 112–13; L. L. Gee, ' "Ciborium" tombs in England 1290–1330', *JBAA*, cxxxii (1979), 29, 35–6; the tracery on the walls flanking the north transept at Rouen has a similar tripartite arrangement to Crouchback, and dates to after 1281: see P. Frankl, *Gothic Architecture* (Harmondsworth, 1962), pl. 91.

[14]   As in the hemicycle of Saint-Père at Chartres *c.* 1295–1300 (see M. P. Lillich, *The Stained Glass of Saint-Père de Chartres* (Connecticut, 1978), pl. 14) or the north nave aisle of York Minster *c.* 1310–20 (see *A History of York Minster*, ed. G. E. Aylmer and R. Cant (Oxford, 1977), pl. 108); Bony, *op. cit.* (note 10), 21.

[15]   See C. Wilson, 'The Origins of the Perpendicular Style and its Development to circa 1360', unpublished Ph.D. thesis, University of London, 1980, 93 ff.; F. Woodman, *The Architectural History of Canterbury Cathedral* (London, 1981), 141, 144–5.

[16]   The throne also relates to current Westminster practices in having elaborate coloured inlays, including glass. Compare also the polygonal podia with embattled cornices to either side of the chapter-house entrance at York: Aylmer and Cant, *op. cit.* (note 14), pl. 33.

[17]   Square-topped pinnacles, which occur frequently in French micro-architecture, notably on the south transept of Notre-Dame in Paris, are also found on the tomb of Bishop de Luda (d. 1298), at Ely, which is directly related to that of Crouchback at Westminster, and also on the tomb of Aymer de Valence (d. 1324). For Queen Eleanor's tomb chest see Wilson, *op. cit.* (note 15), 80 ff. Evidence that court masons were involved in the design of royal tombs is provided by a later reference to payments made to the daughter of William Ramsey for the construction of the tomb of Queen Isabella, in 1359: see F. D. Blackley, 'The tomb of Isabella of France, wife of Edward II of England', *Bulletin of the International Society for the Study of Church Monuments*, viii (1983), 161.

[18]   Bony, *op. cit.* (note 10), 1–29; Wilson, *op. cit.* (note 15), 28 ff.

[19]   *KW*, i, 510: Wilson, *op. cit.* (note 15), 34 ff.

[20]   See G. G. Scott, *Gleanings from Westminster Abbey*, 2nd edn. (Oxford and London, 1863), 122–3. Tristram (1955, 195–6) prints the following account for 1299–1300: 'Compotus Adae aurifabri Regis de jocalibus emptis ad opus Regis. . . . Eidem pro diversis custibus per ipsum factis circa quandam cathedram de cupro quam Rex prius fieri preceperat anno XXV° post reditum suum de Scocia, pro petra super quam Reges Scociae solebant coronari inventa apud Scone anno XXIIII^{to} superponenda juxta altare ante feretrum Sancti Edwardi in Ecclesia Abbathiae Westmonasterii: et nunc eadem petra in quadam cathedra de ligno *facta per Magistrum Walterum pictorem Regis* loco dictae Cathedrae quae prius ordinata fuit de cupro est assessa: videlicet pro una Cathedra de ligno facta *ad exemplar* alterius cathedrae fundendae de cupro—c. sol. . .' (my italics).

[21]   See RCHM, *London*, i: *Westminster Abbey* (London, 1924), pls. 22–3; S. Rees-Jones, 'The Coronation Chair', *Studies in Conservation*, i (1954), 103; J. M. Hastings, *St Stephen's Chapel and its Place in the Development of Perpendicular Style in England* (Cambridge, 1955), 147; Bony, *op. cit.* (note 10), pl. 330; and cf. the use of large quatrefoils set in frames on the base

of the shrine of St Alban, *c.*1305: *ibid.*, pl. 110. Certain details also relate the Chair to the throne at Canterbury.

22 T. H. Turner, *Manners and Household Expenses*, Roxburghe Club (London, 1841), 123–5; *KW*, i, 217, 481. The Chair received two layers of painted decoration, only the first being by Master Walter: see Rees-Jones, *op. cit.* (note 21), 113, and P. Eames, 'Furniture in England, France and the Netherlands from the twelfth to the fifteenth century', *Furniture History*, xiii (1977), 141, 191–2.

23 According to Rishanger, the Chair was also used in the celebration of mass: see W. Rishanger, *Chronica et Annales*, ed. H. T. Riley, *RS*, 28, ii (London, 1865), 163. It may have been placed in a position like that of the abbot's chair by the high altar at Peterborough: see C. Wilson, 'The Neville Screen', in *Medieval Art and Architecture at Durham Cathedral*, BAA Conference Transactions for the year 1977, iii (1980), 90, fig. 1.

24 Above, p. 60.

25 Good comparative material is provided by Scandinavian panel painting: see, for example, H. Fett, *Norges Malerkunst i Middelalderen* (Kristiania, 1917), 131 ff., for works such as the frontals from Dale and Nedstryn; see also H. Bock, 'Zum Tabernakelmotiv des 14. Jahrhunderts in England', in *Der Mensch und die Künste, Festschrift* for H. Lützeler, ed. G. Bandmann *et al.* (Düsseldorf, 1962), 412; R. Becksmann, *Die architektonische Rahmung des hochgotischen Bildfensters* (Berlin, 1967). Rayonnant forms spread to Sienese painting in the early 1300s: Bony, *op. cit.* (note 10), 63, pl. 361; see also G. Schmidt, 'Die Chorschranken-malereien des Kölner Domes und die europäische Malerei', *Kölner Domblatt*, xliv–xlv (1979–80), 293.

26 Popular in manuscripts from *c.* 1300 onwards (see L. F. Sandler, *The Peterborough Psalter in Brussels and other Fenland Manuscripts* (London, 1974), fig. 57), and especially ivories (see *Les Fastes du Gothique—le siècle de Charles V* (Paris, 1981), 172–3 no. 127).

27 R. S. Loomis, 'The allegorical siege in the art of the Middle Ages', *American Journal of Archaeology*, xxiii (1919), 255 ff.

28 A. J. Taylor, 'Military architecture', in *Medieval England*, ed. A. L. Poole, i (Oxford, 1958), 98; *KW*, i, 202.

29 *KW*, i, 370; Bony, *op. cit.* (note 10), 37–8.

30 See J. Vale, *Edward III and Chivalry* (Woodbridge, 1982), 14.

31 *The Bayeux Tapestry*, ed. F. M. Stenton, 2nd edn. (London, 1965), 76 ff.

32 See D. Park, 'The "Lewes Group" of wall paintings in Sussex', in *Anglo-Norman Studies*, vi, Proceedings of the Battle Conference 1983, ed. R. Allen Brown (Woodbridge, 1984), 200 ff., most notably in the case of the representation of heaven on the chancel arch of Clayton Church. Compare also the bow-fronted proscenium of the Pentecost scene in the St Albans Psalter (O. Pächt *et al.*, *The St Albans Psalter (Albani Psalter)* (London, 1960), pl. 33b) and the use of small aedicules in the four detached Bible leaves in London and New York (C. M. Kauffmann, *Romanesque Manuscripts, 1066–1190* (London, 1975), pls. 177–8, 180).

33 I am indebted to Mr David Park for advice on these murals, to date unpublished. The narrative scenes are one of the most outstanding examples in English wall painting of overpainted *secco* murals, various obvious revisions having taken place in the fifteenth century to figures and buildings, without radical changes to the compositions.

34 R. Stettiner, *Die illustrierten Prudentius-Handschriften* (Berlin, 1895), 144–8.

35 M. Thomas, *Psautier de Saint Louis* (Graz, 1972); K. Gould, *The Psalter and Hours of Yolande of Soissons* (Cambridge, Mass., 1978), 26; C. F. Barnes, 'Cross-media design motifs in XIIIth century France: architectural motifs in the Psalter and Hours of Yolande of Soissons and the Cathedral of Notre-Dame at Amiens', *Gesta*, xvii, 2 (1978), 37; Bony, *op. cit.* (note 10), 15–16, pls. 93–4; D. H. Turner, 'The development of Maître Honoré', *British Museum Quarterly*, xxxiii (1968–9), 53, 55 ff. For the role of architectural drawing, see R. Branner, 'Villard de Honnecourt, Reims, and the origin of Gothic architectural drawing', *Gazette des beaux-arts*, lxi (1963), 129, 140–1, and R. Recht, 'Sur le dessin d'architecture gothique', in *Études d'art médiéval offertes à Louis Grodecki*, ed. S. McK. Crosby *et al.* (Paris, 1981), 233 ff.

36 cf. Tudor-Craig 1957, 97, for a date in the 1260s for these forms.

37 Compare the Churches in the opening pages of Douce to some of the more complex seal designs of the mid-thirteenth century, such as that of Southwick Priory: see F. Madden, 'A description of the matrix of the seal of Southwick Priory, in Hampshire', *Archaeologia*, xxiii

(1831), 374, and H. S. Kingsford, 'Some English medieval seal-engravers', *Archaeological Journal*, xcvii (1940), 155, 161, pls. IV, VI. The Church of Sardis on page 8 of Douce has steeply pointed flanking arches of the sort found on the lower stages of the central tower at Lincoln c.1240, or by the clerestory windows of Henry III's nave at Westminster: see G. Webb, *Architecture in Britain: the Middle Ages* (Harmondsworth, 1956), pl. 107; *KW*, i, pl. 6. Diapering is delicately executed in white paint over the arches in accordance with the decorative taste of the interior of the abbey: see G. Webb, 'The decorative character of Westminster Abbey', *JWCI*, xii (1949), 16.

[38] Bony, *op. cit.* (note 10), 25.

[39] cf. Tudor-Craig 1957, 98 and pl. XXI.

[40] Compare Douce's sister manuscript in Paris: G. Henderson, 'An Apocalypse manuscript in Paris: B.N. MS Lat. 10474', *Art Bulletin*, lii (1970), 22, 26; P. Klein, *Endzeiterwartung und Ritterideologie* (Graz, 1983), pls. 42–8.

[41] O. Pächt and J. J. G. Alexander, *Illuminated Manuscripts in the Bodleian Library, Oxford*, iii (Oxford, 1973), 45 no. 483.

[42] R. Branner, 'The painted medallions in the Sainte-Chapelle in Paris', *Transactions of the American Philosophical Society*, ii (1968), 5, 16.

[43] See the appreciation of the Douce Apocalypse in G. Henderson, *Gothic* (Harmondsworth, 1978), 93–5.

[44] See, p. 80.

[45] Brieger 1968, 218, pl. 82b.

[46] For the Windmill Psalter, see A. Bennett, 'The Windmill Psalter: the historiated letter E of Psalm One', *JWCI*, xliii (1981), 52 ff.

[47] See above, p. 21.

[48] Lethaby 1906, 261, fig. 81; W. R. Lethaby, 'Master Walter of Durham, King's Painter c. 1230–1305', *Burlington Magazine*, xxxiii (1918), 3, 7; C. L. Kingsford, 'Sir Otho de Grandison (1238(?)–1328)', *Transactions of the Royal Historical Society*, iii (1909), 125; Lethaby 1927, 123, 140–2; Tristram 1950, 152, supplementary pl. 7. For the drawings of the right-hand part of the painting in the Kerrich collection, see BL Add. MS 6728, fols. 87–8.

[49] Above, p. 20. Also of interest in this context is the painting of a series of standing armed figures holding pennons on the basement of Crouchback's tomb, presumably dating to c.1300. These figures are rather more lively than those of Eleanor's tomb. A framed drawing of this work by Carter, dated 1782, is preserved in the Muniment Room, Westminster Abbey; see also J. Carter, *Specimens of the Ancient Sculpture and Painting now remaining in England*, 2nd edn. (London, 1838), 59 ff.; Lethaby 1906, 269, fig. 89.

[50] L. F. Sandler, *The Psalter of Robert de Lisle* (Oxford, 1983), 14.

[51] I am strongly inclined to accept the identification of the figures on the altar side of the sedilia as (from the left) King Ethelbert, St Peter, King Sebert and St Mellitus, first proposed by Lethaby (1927, 143–6) and Wormald (1949, 175). The dating evidence for the sedilia is more complex than the account of Sandler, *op. cit.* (note 50), 16, tends to suggest, and the material is reviewed in Binski 1983, 113 ff. The translation of the remains of Sebert to this spot in 1307–8 should provide a *terminus post quem* for the erection of the sedilia, and certain considerations suggest that the decorations should have followed this event punctually. The monks of Westminster were presumably raising Sebert to the same sort of status as that of Dagobert at Saint-Denis, and must have been aware of preparations at St Paul's Cathedral to enhance the standing of its similar historical connections, notably by renewing the shrine of St Erkenwald. The iconography, with its reference to Westminster traditions about the establishment of Christianity in London, suggests that Sebert and his relatives were being used by the monks to redress the balance of saintly historical associations with St Paul's at a time when the cult of St Edward was dwindling under Edward II. The paintings would have been done quickly to emphasize the priority of their claims.

[52] The red-blue counterchanging of the colours in the lights is also a feature of the tracery painted on the shafts of Aymer de Valence's tomb (after 1324), but here the architectural details are different. I would qualify Sandler's assertion (*op. cit.* (note 50), 16) that the sculptures on Aymer's tomb are as closely related to the style of the 'Madonna Master' as those on Crouchback, which to me have exactly the rich elaboration and weight of this style. The sedilia architecture also makes much more sense in the context of Crouchback rather

than Aymer. The tracery on the altar in the scene of the Presentation on fol. 124 of De Lisle reproduces that on the sides of the Coronation Chair of *c.* 1300.

53 Sandler, *op. cit.* (note 50), 30, suggests that this illustration was originally not part of the manuscript, but it should be noted that its artist also worked on the Tree of Vices illustration on fol. 128ᵛ.

54 Sandler, *op. cit.* (note 50), 16.

55 The literature on these paintings is extensive, and I am planning a separate study of them; see for example Lethaby 1927, 132 ff.; J. G. Noppen, 'The earlier paintings at Westminster Abbey', *Apollo*, xviii, 108 (1933), 353; *id.*, 'Westminster paintings and Master Peter', *Burlington Magazine*, xci (1949), 305; Wormald 1949, 171; Tristram 1950, 121 ff., 560–2; Brieger 1968, 214–15.

56 Klein, *op. cit.* (note 40), 44–5, accepts at face value Tristram's conclusion that the south transept murals were amongst the images executed in the church *c.* 1270, but the arguments for this identification are extremely weak. A more tempting alternative is to suppose that the *picturae imaginum* paid for in the years 1269–72 were related to the *picturae voltarum ecclesie* under way from 1267, suggesting that Westminster was equipped with vault paintings like those at Salisbury; for the relevant accounts, see Colvin 1971, 426, 428, 430.

57 I am not alone in this opinion, for it was expressed first by Tristram at the time of the discovery of the south transept murals: see E. W. Tristram, 'A recent discovery of wall-paintings in Westminster Abbey', *Burlington Magazine*, lxx (1937), 229 ff.; Margaret Rickert was also of the opinion that these murals 'are all related to the Retable in many respects, but they are of much less fine quality . . . They do not seem to be much earlier than 1300': see *Painting in Britain: the Middle Ages* (Harmondsworth, 1954), 127.

58 cf. The Nuremberg Hours: Turner, *op. cit.* (note 35); Corpus Christi College, Cambridge MS 53: M. R. James, *A Peterborough Psalter and Bestiary of the Fourteenth Century*, Roxburghe Club (Oxford, 1921); the Hours of Alice de Reydon, Cambridge University Library MS Dd. 4.17: P. Lasko and N. Morgan, *Medieval Art in East Anglia 1300–1520* (Norwich, 1973), 12 no. 8.

59 R. Branner, *Manuscript Painting in Paris during the Reign of Saint Louis* (Berkeley, 1977), 138. For the fourteenth-century context of these murals, see the forthcoming study of the Thornham Parva Retable and Musée de Cluny Frontal by E. C. Norton, D. Park and myself.

60 See above, notes 41 and 26.

61 Stone 1972, 141–5.

62 Bony, *op. cit.* (note 10), 9 ff.

63 RCHM, *An Inventory of the Historical Monuments in the City of Oxford* (London, 1939), 76, pls. 145, 148; also H. W. Garrod, *Ancient Painted Glass in Merton College Oxford* (Oxford, 1931), 12 ff. The style of the Merton College canopies relates them to the fine 'Chertsey' tile panels in the British Museum: see E. C. Norton, 'The British Museum Collection of medieval tiles', *JBAA*, cxxxiv (1981), 109–12.

64 For the general decoration of the chapter house, see Tristram 1955, 270, and for the glass, J. R. Knowles, 'An enquiry into the date of the stained glass in the chapter house at York', *Yorkshire Archaeological Journal*, xl (1961), 451; also N. Coldstream, 'York chapter house', *JBAA*, xxxv (1972), 15 ff.; Aylmer and Cant, *op. cit.* (note 14), 139 ff., 139 n. 119. For the Psalter and Hours of Yolande of Soissons, see Gould, *op. cit.* (note 35), and for the illustrated Lancelot, M. A. Stones, 'The Illustration of the French Prose "Lancelot" in Flanders, Belgium and Paris: 1250–1340', unpublished Ph.D. thesis, University of London, 1970, 225 ff., and P. Brieger *et al.*, *Art and the Courts, France and England from 1259 to 1328*, The National Gallery of Canada (Ottawa, 1972), i, 85; ii, pl. 20.

65 D. D. Egbert, *The Tickhill Psalter and Related Manuscripts* (Princeton, 1940), 5–81; for the iconography, see below.

66 Bony, *op. cit.* (note 10), 10–13.

67 Above, p. 21.

68 *KW*, i, 507 n. 5.

69 For the ownership of the Peterborough Psalter, see Sandler, *op. cit.* (note 26), 108–11, and cf. the review by A. Bennett, *Art Bulletin*, lxiv (1982), 502, which raises the possibility that the Psalter might pre-date 1300. For Geoffrey of Crowland, see Walter of Whitlesey, *Historia Coenobii Burgensis*, in J. Sparke, *Historiae Anglicanae scriptores varii, e codicibus manuscriptis* (London, 1723), ii, 153 ff. S. Gunton, *The History of the Church of Peterburgh* (London,

1686), 39–40, associates some works with Geoffrey, including the 'Knight's Chamber' at Peterborough over the abbey gatehouse, containing images of knights holding lands of the abbey, with heraldic displays on the ceiling, the contents of which may perhaps be guessed from the Peterborough Roll of Arms of tenants of the abbey dated after 1321: see A. R. Wagner, *A Catalogue of English Mediaeval Rolls of Arms* (Oxford, 1950), 51; cf. the heraldic decoration in the chamber at Longthorpe Tower: E. Clive Rouse and A. Baker. 'The wall-paintings at Longthorpe Tower near Peterborough, Northants.', *Archaeologia*, xcvi (1955), 1, 25–8, 35 ff.

[70] According to Capon 1835, pl. XLVII, 7, the dado was painted in the manner of a green curtain.

[71] *Gentleman's Magazine* (1819), pt. ii, 390, stating that the texts were 'in some places written small and close, but towards the upper part of the walls large and bold'.

[72] G. Wickham, *Early English Stages 1300 to 1600*, i (London, 1959), 5–103; R. Southern, *The Medieval Theatre in the Round* (London, 1975), 91 ff.

[73] Henderson 1968, 120.

[74] White, *op. cit.* (note 6), 160 ff.

[75] See p. 115.

[76] This total is an estimate based on the band lengths in Crocker's elevation.

[77] Esposito 1960, 30.

[78] See p. 116.

[79] Comte A. de Laborde, *Étude sur la Bible moralisée illustrée* (Paris, 1911–27), i, pls. 111–12: R. Haussherr, *Bible Moralisée* (Graz, 1973), ii, pls. 72–3: Branner, *op. cit.* (note 59), 32 ff.

[80] S. C. Cockerell and J. Plummer, *Old Testament Miniatures* (London, 1969), 76–7 nos. 91–2.

[81] M. Aubert, L. Grodecki *et al.*, *Les Vitraux de Notre-Dame et de la Sainte-Chapelle de Paris*, Corpus Vitrearum Medii Aevi (Paris, 1959), 159 ff., pl. 38. For later German examples, see Munich, Staatsbibliothek Clm. 146 (J. Lutz and P. Perdrizet, *Speculum Humanae Salvationis*, ii (Leipzig, 1909), pl. 76) and Zurich, Zentralbibliothek MS Rheinau XV, fol. 138ᵛ (see K. Escher, 'Die Bilderhandschrift der Weltchronik des Rudolf von Ems in der Zentralbibliothek Zürich', *Mitteilungen der Antiquarischen Gesellschaft in Zürich*, xxxi, 4 (1932–6), 17, pl. VIII, fig 29).

[82] The French instances are more literal in showing the millstone as semicircular in accordance with the Vulgate *fragmen molae*.

[83] Haussherr, *op. cit.* (note 79), pl. 73.

[84] K. Weitzmann, *The Miniatures of the Sacra Parallela* (Princeton, 1979), 66–7; also D. C. Hesseling, *Miniatures de l'Octateuch grec de Smyrne* (Leiden, 1909), pl. 94.

[85] As on the Klosterneuburg ambo: H. Buschhausen, *Der Verduner Altar* (Vienna, 1980), 48, pls. 23–4.

[86] Pierpont Morgan MS M730, which is placed in its context in Harvey Stahl's study 'The Iconographic Sources of the Old Testament Miniatures, Pierpont Morgan Library, M.638', unpublished Ph.D. thesis, New York University, 1974, 37 ff.

[87] Cockerell and Plummer, *op. cit.* (note 80), 170–1 nos. 226–30.

[88] Tudor-Craig 1957, 103 ff.; Brieger 1968, 156; Cockerell and Plummer, *op. cit.* (note 80), 21. There is a measure of disagreement about the Parisian origin of Maciejowski; Branner, *op. cit.* (note 59), 139, was of the opinion that the work is English, and M. A. Stones, 'Sacred and profane art: secular and liturgical book-illumination in the thirteenth century', in *The Epic in Medieval Society*, ed. H. Scholler (Tübingen, 1977), 100 ff., has argued for a north French origin. See also E. Beer, 'Pariser Buchmalerei in der Zeit Ludwigs des Heiligen und im letzten Viertel des 13. Jahrhunderts', *Zeitschrift für Kunstgeschichte*, xliv (1981), 62, 76 ff.

[89] Cockerell and Plummer, *op. cit.* (note 80), 70 no. 81.

[90] *Ibid.*, 60.

[91] H. Buchthal, *Miniature Painting in the Latin Kingdom of Jerusalem* (Oxford, 1957), 54 ff.

[92] *CCR* 1250, 311; *CCR* 1253, 165; Branner, *op. cit.* (note 13), 124–5; *KW*, i, 125.

[93] For Bible picture-books, see R. Fantier, 'The John Rylands Library, Manuscrit French 5, Bible Historiée toute figurée', *Bulletin de la Société Française de Reproductions de Manuscrits à Peintures*, vii (Paris, 1923), 34, 66; the list of picture-Bibles is extended by O. Pächt, 'A Giottesque episode in English mediaeval art', *JWCI*, vi (1943), 51, 61.

[94] See above, p. 17.

[95] Matthew Paris, *Chronica Majora*, ed. H. R. Luard, *RS*, 57, iii (London, 1876), 470–1; *CCR* 1238, 26.

[96] *CLR* 1250, 325; *CCR* 1253, 165.

[97] N. J. Morgan, *Early Gothic Manuscripts*, i: *1190–1250* (London, 1982), 68 ff.

[98] For Winchester, *CLR* 1237, 305; *CLR* 1241, 26; for Windsor, *CCR* 1242, 514.

[99] For the Genesis scenes formerly at Bury, see M. R. James, *On the Abbey of St Edmund at Bury* (Cambridge Antiquarian Society, 1895), 200; for the glass at Canterbury, M. H. Caviness, *The Early Stained Glass of Canterbury Cathedral* (Princeton, 1977), 101 ff.; for Winchester, see D. Park, 'The wall paintings of the Holy Sepulchre Chapel', in *Medieval Art and Architecture at Winchester Cathedral*, BAA Conference Transactions for the year 1980, vi (1983), 38, 43 ff.

[100] The reference is presumably to Henry of Blois's palace at Wolvesey: see T. S. R. Boase, *English Art 1100–1216* (Oxford, 1953), 171–2; Henderson 1967, 127 n. 62; M. Biddle, 'Wolvesey: the *domus quasi palatium* of Henry de Blois at Winchester', in A. J. Taylor (ed.), *Château Gaillard . . . Conference at Battle* (London, 1969), 28; for Henry's minority, see K. Norgate, *The Minority of Henry the Third* (London, 1912).

[101] cf. Borenius 1943, 40–2.

[102] F. Wormald, *The Winchester Psalter* (London, 1973); G. Henderson, 'MS. K.26 in the Library of St John's College Cambridge: a Study of the Style and Iconography of its Thirteenth Century Illustrations', unpublished Ph.D. thesis, Cambridge, 1959; W. Burges, 'The iconography of the chapter-house, Salisbury', *The Ecclesiologist*, xx (1859), 109; P. Z. Blum, 'The Middle English romance "Iacob and Iosep" and the Joseph cycle of the Salisbury chapter house', *Gesta*, viii, 1 (1969), 18.

[103] For Munich and Leiden, Stahl, *op. cit.* (note 86), 39 ff.; Morgan, *op. cit.* (note 97), 60–2; for W. de Brailes, G. Henderson, 'Late-Antique influences in some English mediaeval illustrations of Genesis', *JWCI*, xxv (1962), 172 ff.; Morgan, *op. cit.* (note 97), 117; for the Aelfric Pentateuch, K. Weitzmann, *The Joshua Roll* (Princeton, 1948); G. Henderson, 'The Joshua cycle in B.M. Cotton Claudius B.IV', *JBAA*, xxxi (1968), 38; Stahl, *op. cit.* (note 86), 71 ff.; for the Egerton Genesis, M. R. James, *Illustrations of the Book of Genesis*, Roxburghe Club (Oxford, 1921); also Pächt, *op. cit.* (note 93); Buchthal, *op. cit.* (note 91), 54–6; Stahl, *op. cit.* (note 86), 67 ff.

[104] Sir G. Warner, *Queen Mary's Psalter* (London, 1912). See most recently L. Dennison, 'An illumination of the Queen Mary Psalter Group: the Ancient 6 Master', *Antiquaries Journal*, lxvi (1968) (forthcoming).

[105] Warner, *op. cit.* (note 104), pls. 63–6 (fols. 37ᵛ–39) illustrating Judges, ix, 2–54.

[106] Stahl, *op. cit.* (note 86), 246 ff.; cf. the accounts of Jael and Sisera, and Gideon, Cockerell and Plummer, *op. cit.* (note 80), 72 nos. 83–4, and Warner, *op. cit.* (note 104), pls. 56–7; the slaying of Eli's sons and the capture of the Ark, Cockerell and Plummer, 106 nos, 134–5, and Warner, pl. 83; and Absalom and David, Cockerell and Plummer, 200 no. 271, and Warner, pl. 104.

[107] Warner, *op. cit.* (note 104), 85, pl. 94; Egbert, *op. cit.* (note 65), 47–8, pls. XLII–XLIV.

[108] Stahl, *op. cit.* (note 86), 248; cf. Cockerell and Plummer, *op. cit.* (note 80), 164, and Egbert, *op. cit.* (note 65), pl. xxxv, etc. For the Isabella Psalter, *ibid.*, 82 ff.

[109] Sir G. Warner, *The Guthlac Roll*, Roxburghe Club (Oxford, 1928), pls. XIX–XXV; cf. Cockerell and Plummer, *op. cit.* (note 80), 100–8; Thomas, *op. cit.* (note 35), fols. 67ᵛ–71ᵛ; Warner, *op. cit.* (note 104), pls. 83–4; and fols. 100ᵛ–16ᵛ of the Isabella Psalter.

[110] M. R. James, 'On the paintings formerly in the choir at Peterborough', *Proceedings of the Cambridge Antiquarian Society*, ix (1897), 187; L. F. Sandler, 'Peterborough Abbey and the Peterborough Psalter in Brussels', *JBAA*, xxxiii (1970), 36; Sandler, *op. cit.* (note 26), figs. 17–60; Caviness, *op. cit.* (note 99), 120 ff.; Henderson, 1962, *op. cit.* (note 103), 188 ff.

[111] See J. J. G. Alexander, 'Painting and manuscript illumination for royal patrons in the later Middle Ages', in *English Court Culture in the Later Middle Ages*, ed. V. J. Scattergood and J. W. Sherborne (London, 1983), 141, 144.

[112] De Laborde, *op. cit.* (note 79), i, pls. 173–84.

[113] Ahaziah's fall from the tower was a normal subject for initials to II Kings in Parisian book-painting: see Branner, *op. cit.* (note 59), 178–9, 184–5; for the *Somme le Roi*, see E. G. Millar, *The Parisian Miniaturist Honoré* (London, 1959), pl. 6; R. Tuve, 'Notes on the Virtues and Vices', *JWCI*, xxvii (1964), 42, 49, pl. 8b.

[114] Buchthal, *op. cit.* (note 91), pl. 72; Aubert, Grodecki *et al.*, *op. cit.* (note 81), 275–6, 291–2; see also S. Berger, *La Bible française au moyen âge* (Paris, 1884), 51 ff.

[115] Maciejowski ends at II Sam. xx, 15–22 (fol. 46ᵛ); Morgan MS M730 ends at I Kings, i, 50; Queen Mary ends at I Kings, xi, 43 (fol. 66ᵛ).

[116] St Louis ends incomplete at I Sam. xi, 12–15, Thomas, *op. cit.* (note 35), fol. 78ᵛ. For the Vatican Kings, J. Lassus, 'Les miniatures byzantines du Livre des Rois', *Mélanges d'archéologie et d'histoire*, xlv (1928), v, 38, 69–74; Buchthal, *op. cit.* (note 91), 60; Stahl, *op. cit.* (note 86), 156 ff.

[117] Kauffmann, *op. cit.* (note 32), pl. 229.

[118] H. Swarzenski, 'A chalice and the Book of Kings', in *De Artibus Opuscula*, xl: *Essays in Honour of Erwin Panofsky*, ed. M. Meiss (New York, 1961), 437, 441 n. 118; P. Lasko, *Ars Sacra 800–1200* (Harmondsworth, 1972), pl. 204; N. Stratford, 'The "Henry of Blois plaques" in the British Museum', in *Medieval Art and Architecture at Winchester Cathedral*, *op. cit.* (note 99), 28, 32, pl. xiiia; cf. also the murals of *c.* 1360 in the cloister of the Emmaus monastery in Prague: V. Dvořáková, J. Krása *et al.*, *Gothic Mural Painting in Bohemia and Moravia 1300–1378* (London, 1964), 71 ff., 140 ff.

[119] Formerly in the Burckhardt–Wildt collection: see H. Buchthal, 'Some Sicilian miniatures of the thirteenth century', in *Miscellanea Pro Arte*, Essays for H. Schnitzler, ed. P. Bloch and J. Hoster (Düsseldorf, 1965), 185, and Sotheby's *Catalogue of Single Leaves and Miniatures from Western Illuminated Manuscripts* (25th April, 1983), Lot 73, 126–7.

[120] Buchthal, *op. cit.* (note 119), 189, and *The 'Painter's Manual' of Dionysius of Fourna*, trans. P. Hetherington (London, 1981), 24.

[121] Buchthal, *op. cit.* (note 119), 188–90, fig. 6.

[122] G. Swarzenski, *Die Salzburger Malerei* (Stuttgart, 1969), i, 129, 132–3; ii, figs. 122, 128 (fols. 117ᵛ, 171ᵛ); Buchthal, *op. cit.* (note 119), 188.

[123] F. Bucher, *The Pamplona Bibles* (Yale, 1970).

[124] Divided between the manuscripts thus: Harburg, fols. 139–139ᵛ; Amiens, fols. 120ᵛ–132ᵛ (II Kings); Amiens, fols. 152–152ᵛ; Harburg, fols. 165–166, 154ᵛ (Isaiah): Bucher, *op. cit.* (note 123), pls. 284–310, 352–6.

[125] Harburg fol. 139ᵛ; Amiens fol. 120ᵛ.

[126] At this point the two-tier picture layout in Amiens may also be relevant. On fol. 127ᵛ Naaman is seen mounted before Elisha's house and then in the frame below is depicted in the Jordan; the Painted Chamber replaces the top scene with Naaman bearing the money and the letter to the king of Israel, who rends his clothes, II Kings, v, 5–7, but portrays the bathing Naaman beneath. Similarly, the next scene in the Painted Chamber shows Naaman above, with Elisha as in II Kings, v, 15–19, and then Gehazi with Naaman and the chariot below, a sequence reproduced in Amiens fol. 128, with the exception that Naaman is seen with the mules.

[127] Amiens fols. 129–132ᵛ. Further observations on the Spanish iconography of the blinding of Zedekiah, in the context of the Bayeux Tapestry, are to be found in D. Bernstein, 'The blinding of Harold and the meaning of the Bayeux Tapestry', in *Anglo-Norman Studies*, v, Proceedings of the Battle Conference 1982, ed. R. Allen Brown (Woodbridge, 1983), 40, 60–4, which postulates access in England to a Spanish picture-Bible after the Conquest.

[128] Amiens fol. 152ᵛ, Harburg fols. 165–165ᵛ. The Harburg version of the destruction of the Assyrian camp and death of Sennacherib, fols. 166, 154ᵛ, is less close, however.

[129] J. W. Williams, 'A Castilian tradition of Bible illustration; the Romanesque Bible from San Millán', *JWCI*, xxviii (1965), 66, 83–4.

[130] W. Neuss, *Die katalanische Bibelillustration* (Bonn and Leipzig, 1922), 79–80, pls. 26–7, figs. 85–8, fols. 159ᵛ–161.

[131] H. Swarzenski, *Die lateinischen illuminierten Handschriften des XIII. Jahrhunderts* (Berlin, 1936), i, 25 ff., 101; ii, pl. 39 fig. 223, for fol. 18ᵛ of the Mainz Evangeliary, which depicts the bound captives of Jerusalem being led off in a manner similar to the Painted Chamber; for the *Concordantia*, see H. Rost, *Die Bibel im Mittelalter* (Augsburg, 1939), 237 ff.

[132] The *Sacra Parallela* goes no further than II Kings, viii: see Weitzmann, *op. cit.* (note 84), 92–101, figs. 170–80.

[133] F. M. Powicke, *The Thirteenth Century, 1216–1307*, 2nd edn. (Oxford, 1970), 226.

[134] Bucher, *op. cit.* (note 123), 69 ff.

[135] *Ibid.*, 25, 63 ff.

[136] R. McGrath, 'The Romance of the Maccabees in Mediaeval Art and Literature', unpublished Ph.D. thesis, Princeton, 1963, 160–3.

137 De Laborde, *op. cit.* (note 79), iii, pls. 447–68; iv, pls. 701–8; Buchthal, *op. cit.* (note 91), pl. 80; McGrath. *op. cit.* (note 136), 149 ff.

138 J. E. Gaehde, 'The pictorial sources of the illustrations to the Books of Kings, Proverbs, Judith and Maccabees in the Carolingian Bible of San Paolo fuori le Mura in Rome', *Frühmittelalterliche Studien*, ix (1975), 359, 384 ff.

139 Neuss, *op. cit.* (note 130), 106–7, pls. 45 (figs. 131–2); 46–7 (figs. 133–5).

140 A. Merton, *Die Buchmalerei in St Gallen* (Leipzig, 1923), 64, pls. LV–LVII; A. Goldschmidt, *Die Deutsche Buchmalerei*, i (Munich, 1928), 22, 58–9, pls. 72–3.

141 Swarzenski, *op. cit.* (note 122), i, 129, 134–5; ii, pls. XLIV, XLV fig. 140.

142 C. Oursel, *La Miniature du XIIe siècle à l'abbaye de Cîteaux, d'après les manuscrits de la Bibliothèque de Dijon* (Dijon, 1926), 68, pls. XIV, XV (after MS 14, fol. 191).

143 W. Oakeshott, *The Two Winchester Bibles* (Oxford, 1981), pl. IV.

144 Thus the campaign of Antiochus against Ptolemy is illustrated in the St Paul's Bible, the story of Nicanor is included in the Ripoll Bible and the fate of Judas Maccabeus is included in the St Paul's and Gumpert Bibles.

145 M. R. James, 'On two series of paintings formerly at Worcester Priory', *Proceedings of the Cambridge Antiquarian Society*, x (1900–1), 99, 110 ff.

146 Swarzenski, *op. cit.* (note 122), pl. XLIV.

147 McGrath, *op. cit.* (note 136), 10 ff.; G. A. Bertin and A. Foulet, 'The Book of Judges in Old French prose: the Gardner A. Sage Library fragment', *Romania*, xc (1969), 121; most recently, M. Keen, *Chivalry* (Yale, 1984), 119–21.

148 J. Bonnard, *Les Traductions de la Bible en vers français au moyen âge* (Paris, 1884); Stahl, *op. cit.* (note 86), 249 ff.

149 P. Meyer, 'Notice du MS Bibl. Nat. Fr. 6447', *Notices et extraits des manuscrits de la Bibliothèque Nationale*, xxxv, 2 (1897), 435; McGrath, *op. cit.* (note 136), 166 ff.; J. Folda, *Crusader Manuscript Illumination at Saint-Jean d'Acre, 1275–1291* (Princeton, 1976), 73 n. 148.

150 Morgan, *op. cit.* (note 97), 69–71, this feature of the manuscript perhaps being explicable by a female patron.

151 Bonnard, *op. cit.* (note 148), 167 ff.; H. Everlien, *Über Judas Machabée von Gautier de Belleperche* (Halle, 1897); McGrath, *op. cit.* (note 136), 15 ff., 179 ff.

152 J. R. Smeets, *La Chevalerie de Judas Macabé* (Assen, 1955); McGrath, *op. cit.* (note 136), 22, 103 ff.

153 Smeets, *op. cit.* (note 152), xxxvii, vv. 7798–7846; McGrath, *op. cit.* (note 136), 26.

154 *Ibid.*, 45 ff., 330 ff.; for the Nine Worthies, see H. Schroeder, *Der Topos der Nine Worthies in Literatur und bildender Kunst* (Göttingen, 1971); Vale, *op. cit.* (note 30), 42 ff.; Keen, *op. cit.* (note 147), 121–4.

155 McGrath, *op. cit.* (note 136), 330 ff.

156 See, for example, J. J. Rorimer and M. B. Freeman, 'The Nine Heroes tapestries at The Cloisters', *Metropolitan Museum of Art Bulletin*, vii (1948), 243; P. Deschamps and M. Thibout, *La Peinture murale en France au début de l'époque gothique* (Paris, 1963), 229; Vale, *op. cit.* (note 30), 45; Keen, *op. cit.* (note 147), 121.

157 J. von Schlosser, 'Ein veronesisches Bilderbuch und die höfische Kunst des XIV. Jahrhunderts', *Jahrbuch der kunsthistorischen Sammlungen des Allerhöchsten Kaiserhauses*, xvi (1895), 215, 218, 219, 224.

158 i.e. *gules, a fess between six martlets or*; compare the use of a raven or golden blackbird in the arms of Judas in the later Anglo-French iconography of the Nine Worthies: Schroeder, *op. cit.* (note 154), 234–5, pls. 5, 7, 14, 21.

159 McGrath, *op. cit.* (note 136), 216–7, 260 ff.

160 cf. the intrusion into Marian iconography of war scenes such as that on fol. 45^v of the Lambeth Apocalypse, where St Mercurius kills Julian the Apostate with the aid of the Virgin, and the representations of the battle of Stamford Bridge on fol. 60 of *La Estoire de Seint Aedward le Rei*, and the defeat of Shobach by David in the Maciejowski Bible, which all employ essentially the same iconography; see Henderson 1968, pls. 46a, b; Cockerell and Plummer, *op. cit.* (note 80), 186; see also H. Buchthal, *Historia Troiana* (London, 1971), 10–12, 16 n. 4. An instance of greater literalism occurs on fol. 64 of *La Estoire*, depicting the Battle of Hastings. This includes not only the episode where William removed his helm to identify himself in the course of the battle (at the top of the scene), but also Harold's death,

for a crowned figure is hit in the eye by an arrow in the bottom right of the scene. Both events are of course illustrated *in extenso* in the Bayeux Tapestry: Stenton, *op. cit.* (note 31), pls. 68, 71. Folda, *op. cit.* (note 149), 73 n. 148, however, confuses a literal biblical cycle with the more conventional imagery of the romances in writing of 'the problem of precise identification often met elsewhere with Maccabees, as in the "Painted Chamber" of Henry III'.

[161] Esposito 1960, 26.

[162] The literature is very extensive, but see especially R. S. Loomis, 'Edward I, Arthurian enthusiast', *Speculum*, xxviii (1953), 114; A. Gransden, *Historical Writing in England c. 550 to c. 1307* (London, 1974), 453, 459, 478, 480; Vale, *op. cit.* (note 30), 4–24; Klein, *op. cit.* (note 40), 171–84.

[163] Loomis, *op. cit.* (note 162), 126; Vale, *op. cit.* (note 30), 20–2.

[164] Vale, *op. cit.* (note 30), 23.

[165] J. C. Parsons, *The Court and Household of Eleanor of Castile in 1290* (Toronto, 1977), 13, 90; J. D. Bruce, *The Evolution of the Arthurian Romance from the Beginning down to the Year 1300*, ii (Göttingen and Baltimore, 1923), 275–6, 283–5.

[166] Loomis, *op. cit.* (note 162), 117–25; McGrath, *op. cit.* (note 136), 179 ff.; Stones, *op. cit.* (note 64); Vale, *op. cit.* (note 30), 4 ff.

[167] Loomis, *op. cit.* (note 162), 116 n. 12; McGrath *op. cit.* (note 136), 179, 196, 199; Gould, *op. cit.* (note 35), 53.

[168] Edward of course reversed his father's policy of prohibiting tourneys, Vale, *op. cit.* (note 30), 16 ff. At King's Langley in 1292 Edward ordered to be painted a series of shields forming a *salle aux écus*, together with the images of four knights seeking a tourney: *KW*, ii, 972.

[169] The reference in Esposito 1960, 26, to Maccabean ideals arises in the context of Edward's crusade of 1270; see also Powicke, *op. cit.* (note 133), 264–7; Vale, *op. cit.* (note 30), 21; Klein *op. cit.* (note 40), 183. As the sudden popularity of Antioch imagery in the 1250s under Henry III suggests, crusading ideals tended to be more than usually topical: see p. 111.

[170] Lethaby 1927, 140–2.

[171] Powicke, *op. cit.* (note 133), 515–16; *KW*, i, 370; Gransden, *op. cit.* (note 162), 439–86. See also *Anglo-Scottish Relations 1174–1328*, ed. E. L. G. Stones (Oxford, 1970), 96–109; M. T. Clanchy, *From Memory to Written Record, England 1066–1307* (London, 1979), 256, 260–1; Vale, *op. cit.* (note 30), 18–20.

[172] Gransden, *op. cit.* (note 162), 453–63.

[173] *Flores Historiarum*, ed. H. R. Luard, *RS*, 95, iii (London, 1890), 283, 317–18.

[174] See *Chronicles of the Reigns of Edward I. and Edward II.*, ed. W. Stubbs, *RS*, 76, ii (London, 1883), 3 ff.; Gransden, *op. cit.* (note 30), 459 ff. Vale, *op. cit.* (note 30), 20. It may also be noted that the interest shown in the texts from I Maccabees in the number of soldiers, horses, etc., used in the biblical armies reflects a similar concern in some contemporary historical writing about military campaigns; see the account of Edward's activity in Scotland in the Hagnaby Chronicle: L. Stones, 'English chroniclers and the affairs of Scotland, 1286–1296', in *The Writing of History in the Middle Ages*, essays presented to R. W. Southern, ed. R. H. C. Davis and J. M. Wallace-Hadrill (Oxford, 1981), 323, 345–8.

[175] See E. H. Pearce, *The Monks of Westminster* (Cambridge, 1916), 69.

[176] Topical use of Maccabean imagery occurs more frequently in the fourteenth century. John Barbour compared Robert the Bruce to Judas Maccabeus as a liberator of his people in *The Bruce*, while the 'Lanercost' chronicle compares William Zouche, Archbishop of York, to Mathathias; again, the story of Joab and Abner is taken as a type for treachery in the *Vita Edwardi Secundi*, much as it was at Klosterneuburg in the twelfth century: see A. Gransden, *Historical Writing in England*, ii: *c. 1307 to the Early Sixteenth Century* (London, 1982), 83, 117, 34.

[177] A. Katzenellenbogen, *Allegories of the Virtues and Vices in Mediaeval Art* (Nendeln/Liechtenstein, 1977), 15–17, figs. 14, 15, 54, 55; for the *Somme le Roi*, see Tuve, *op. cit.* (note 113), and E. Kosmer, 'A Study of the Style and Iconography of a Thirteenth-Century *Somme le Roi* (British Museum Ms. Add. 54180)', unpublished Ph.D. thesis, Yale, 1973, 23 ff.

[178] Contrast the coherent relationship between the Virtues and Vices and the narratives in the Arena Chapel in Padua: see, for example, R. Smith, 'Giotto: artistic realism, political realism', *Journal of Medieval History*, iv (1978), 267, 280 ff.

[179] Caviness, *op. cit.* (note 99), 128–30; for John of Salisbury and the Bible, see A. Saltman, 'John of Salisbury and the world of the Old Testament', in *The World of John of Salisbury*, ed. M. Wilks, Studies in Church History Subsidia 3 (Oxford, 1984), 343.

[180] A. Linder, 'John of Salisbury's *Policraticus* in thirteenth-century England: the evidence of MS Cambridge Corpus Christi College 469', *JWCI*, xl (1977), 276.

[181] *Ibid.*, 278.

[182] *Ibid.*, 280.

[183] Klein, *op. cit.* (note 40), 171 ff.

[184] *PL*, cviii, cols. 1171–5; see also Bede, 'De Abimelech', in *Quaestiones super librum Judicum, PL*, xciii, cols. 427–8; R. K. Emmerson, *Antichrist in the Middle Ages* (Manchester, 1981), 26, 30, 41.

[185] De Laborde, *op. cit.* (note 79), i, pls. 106, 111–12.

[186] Haussherr, *op. cit.* (note 79), pls. 72–3; Emmerson, *op. cit.* (note 184), 120–1.

[187] Caviness, *op. cit.* (note 99), 128; the text reads 'ISTI SPINOSI LOCUPLETES DELICIOSI. NIL FRUCTUS REFERUNT QUONIAM TERRESTRIA QUERUNT', translated by Rackham: 'These thorny ones are the rich and luxurious; they bear nought of fruit since they seek earthly things.' Such sentiments explain the obviously uncomplimentary token of the goat's head semée on Abimelech's surcoat. Rokewode (1885, 30) took this to refer either to Gideon's ephod or Abimelech's birth of a concubine. Goats were associated with *Luxuria* (Katzenellenbogen, *op. cit.* (note 177), 61), and were regarded as being concupiscent in medieval writing; see Rhabanus Maurus, *Allegoriae, PL*, cxii, cols. 952–3; Hugh of St Victor, *De bestiis*, iii, xvi, *PL*, clxxvii, col. 89; and for Antichrist, Rupert of Deutz, *De Trinitate*, ii, xxxi, *PL*, clxvii, col. 819. Such heraldry is typical of the illustrated Apocalypses; thus frogs are found on the shields of the armies of Satan on pp. 87–8 of the Douce Apocalypse.

[188] Emmerson, *op. cit.* (note 184), 95–101, 136–40.

[189] *PL*, cix, cols. 1126, 1134 ff.; Emmerson, *op. cit.* (note 184), 28.

[190] G. Cary, *The Medieval Alexander* (Cambridge, 1967), 118 ff.

[191] See Daniel, xi. Antiochus is seen in the Painted Chamber going down before the abomination of desolation prophesied in Daniel, xi, 32, in illustration of ii Macc. vi, 2. See also M. Reeves, *The Influence of Prophecy in the Later Middle Ages* (Oxford, 1969), 305; Emmerson, *op. cit.* (note 184), 44–5, 60.

[192] De Laborde, *op. cit.* (note 79), iii, pl. 473; Emmerson, *op. cit.* (note 184), 121. The scene showing Antiochus' fall from the chariot is also highly unusual; a later example of the chariot-ride occurs in a copy of the *Miroir Historial*, Leiden, Bibliotheek der Rijksuniversiteit, Cod. Vossianus Gallicus 3A., fols. 210ᵛ–12ᵛ, see L. DeLisle, 'Exemplaires royaux et princiers du Miroir historial (XIVe siècle)', *Gazette archéologique*, xi (1886), 7, 95.

[193] cf. fols. 21, 31ᵛ, of the Lisbon Apocalypse.

[194] L. DeLisle and P. Meyer, *L'Apocalypse en français au XIIIe siècle* (Paris, 1900–1). The Maccabean Martyrdom also occurs in martyrologies, and its iconography is reminiscent of that genre; compare the same scene in the Stuttgart Passional, Landesbibliothek MS Bibl. Fol. 56, fol. 40ᵛ: see A. Boeckler, *Das Stuttgarter Passionale* (Augsburg, 1923), 5, 48–9, pl. 71, and cf. also pls. 32, 73, for the bellows-blowing motif. For other Romanesque examples of the Maccabean Martyrdom, see the Ripoll Bible, fol. 352, Neuss, *op. cit.* (note 130), 107, pl. 47, fig. 135, and Gumpert's Bible, Swarzenski, *op. cit.* (note 122), i, 134–5; ii, pl. xlv, fig. 140 (fol. 310).

[195] V. H. Galbraith, 'The literacy of the medieval English kings', *Proceedings of the British Academy*, xxi (1935), 201, 215–16.

[196] C. Roth, *A History of the Jews in England* (Oxford, 1964), 68, 85.

[197] Roth (*ibid.*, 85) notes that the decision was taken on the ninth of Ab, the anniversary of disasters of the Jewish people from the destruction of Jerusalem onwards. My thanks to Mary Minty for drawing these considerations to my attention.

[198] For example, see A. Martindale, 'Painting for pleasure—some lost fifteenth-century secular decorations of northern Italy', in *The Vanishing Past*, ed. A. Borg and A. Martindale, BAR International Series 111 (Oxford, 1981), 109, 111.

[199] Keen, *op. cit.* (note 147), 14, 53, 120.

[200] cf. those episodes thought fit by the poet Baudri de Bourgueil to adorn the bed chamber of Adela of Blois in the years *c.* 1100: see P. Abrahams, *Les Oeuvres poétiques de Baudri de Bourgueil* (Paris, 1926), 196 ff.; see also the narrative cycles recorded under Carolingian

patronage: J. von Schlosser, *Schriftquellen zur Geschichte der karolingischen Kunst* (Vienna, 1892), 321 no. 925, 364 no. 1007; Stenton, *op. cit.* (note 31), 45 ff.; C. R. Dodwell, *Painting in Europe 800 to 1200* (Harmondsworth, 1971), 17–23.
[201] Rouse and Baker, *op. cit.* (note 69), 35–7.

Conclusion

[1] H. M. Colvin, 'The "Court Style" in medieval English architecture: a review', in *English Court Culture in the Later Middle Ages*, ed. V. J. Scattergood and J. W. Sherborne (London, 1983), 129–31.

[2] P. Brieger *et al.*, *Art and the Courts, France and England from 1259 to 1328*, The National Gallery of Canada (Ottawa, 1972).

[3] R. Branner, *Manuscript Painting in Paris during the Reign of Saint Louis* (Berkeley, 1977), 140.

[4] *Ibid.*, 63, 139–41.

[5] Colvin, *op. cit.* (note 1), 135–6.

[6] *Ibid.*, 138–9.

[7] *KW*, i, 94.

[8] See above, p. 44.

[9] *KW*, i, 93–6, 162–3.

[10] *Ibid.*, 506.

[11] *CCR* 1259, 366; Tristram 1950, 94, 100, 445–50, 574–5, 622–3; *CCR* 1239, 158, 185.

[12] For the 'beloved painter' (*dilecto nostro . . . pictori*), Tristram 1950, 449; *CCR* 1256, 326; for the keeper of the works, *KW*, i, 101 ff.

[13] *CPR* 1270, 462.

[14] Colvin 1971, 422.

[15] See A. Martindale, *The Rise of the Artist* (London, 1972), 35 ff.

[16] Tristram 1950, 443–58; *KW*, i, 226–7.

[17] Tristram 1955, 282–7; *KW*, i, 510 ff., 518–19.

[18] *Ibid.*, 518.

[19] PRO E101/468/6, rolls 25, 36.

[20] PRO E101/468/21, fol. 58ᵛ.

[21] Evrard is recorded in Parisian *taille* documents in the 1290s: see F. Baron, 'Enlumineurs, peintres et sculpteurs parisiens des XIIIe et XIVe siècles d'après les rôles de la taille', *Bulletin archéologique*, iv (1968), 37, 70, working in the parish of Saint-Eustache; he is also recorded as king's painter: see B. Prost, 'Quelques documents sur l'histoire des arts en France', *Gazette des beaux-arts*, xxxv (1887), 322, 325–6, and also B. Prost, 'Recherches sur 'les peintres du roi' antérieurs au règne de Charles VI', *Études d'histoire du moyen âge dédiées à Gabriel Monod* (Paris, 1896), 389, 393. F. Baron, 'Enlumineurs peintres et sculpteurs parisiens des XIVe et XVe siècles', *Bulletin archéologique*, vi (1970), 77, 108, notes that Evrard lived by the Rue de Mauconseil in Paris; he was employed at the nearby Hotel d'Artois by Mahaut, countess of Artois in 1313, and from there went to her château at Conflans; see P. Deschamps and M. Thibout, *La Peinture murale en France au début de l'époque gothique* (Paris, 1963), 207–8, for Conflans especially.

[22] *KW*, i, 175.

[23] *Ibid.*, 227.

[24] *Ibid.*, 507 n. 5, 510–13.

[25] Colvin, *op. cit.* (note 1), 136.

[26] By its nature, the presence of either Kentish masons or East Anglian painters at Westminster would seem to argue for pre-existing traditions in those regions capable of producing work to court standards: cf. Wormald 1949, 175–6, and L. F. Sandler, *The Peterborough Psalter in Brussels and other Fenland Manuscripts* (London, 1974), 135. Doubtless Thomas was re-employed at Westminster because he had a particular understanding of the working methods employed there under his father.

[27] P. Klein, *Endzeiterwartung und Ritterideologie* (Graz, 1983), 35–6, 68; Sandler, *op. cit.* (note 26), 127; for the last two manuscripts see A. Bennett, review of *id.*, in *Art Bulletin*, lxiv (1982), 502, 504.

[28] See most recently R. K. Lancaster, 'Henry III, Westminster Abbey, and the Court School of

illumination', in *Seven Studies in Medieval English History and other Historical Essays, presented to H. S. Snellgrove,* ed. R. H. Bowers (Jackson, Mississippi, 1983), 85 ff.

29 For the Westminster Psalter, noted as the second of two 'psalteria quorum unus fuit domini *Regis Henrici tertii* cum Apocalipsi in fine alterum vero cum diversis ymaginibus depictis post kalendare', in J. Wickham Legg, 'On an inventory of the vestry of Westminster Abbey, taken in 1388', *Archaeologia,* lii (1890), i, 195, 234, see Sir G. F. Warner and J. P. Gilson, *British Museum Catalogue of Western Manuscripts in the Old Royal and King's Collections,* i (London, 1921), 36–8. The extent of the competence of the scriptorium provided for in Abbot Ware's Customary is unknown: see J. A. Robinson and M. R. James, *The Manuscripts of Westminster Abbey* (Cambridge, 1908), 2–3.

30 Henry had a 'great book of romances' fitted with clasps in 1237: *CCR* 1237, 288. In 1250 a copy of the *Gestes* of Antioch 'gallico ydiomate scriptum' was sent from the Temple for the use of the queen (see below, note 57): *CCR* 1250, 283. For the Temple, see A. Sandys, 'The financial and administrative importance of the London Temple in the thirteenth century', in *Essays in Medieval History presented to Thomas Frederick Tout,* ed. A. G. Little and F. M. Powicke (Manchester, 1925), 147 ff.; see also M. T. Clanchy, *From Memory to Written Record, England 1066–1307* (London, 1979), 131–2. For the purchase of liturgical manuscripts, see, for example, *CLR* 1251, 11 (provisions for the royal chapel at Nottingham).

31 For the artists in Eleanor's household, see J. C. Parsons, *The Court and Household of Eleanor of Castile in 1290* (Toronto, 1977), 13, 86, 107–8. For other romances, see above, p. 97. Rusticiano da Pisa refers to the 'book of the Lord Edward, the English King', which he used in compiling his romance *Meliadus,* see J. Vale, *Edward III and Chivalry* (Woodbridge, 1982), 19–22. For Edward's patronage of Vegetius' *De Re Militari,* see J. Folda, *Crusader Manuscript Illumination at Saint-Jean d'Acre, 1275–1291* (Princeton, 1976), 129–30, 199 no. 18.

32 Branner, *op. cit.* (note 3), 4–7.

33 E. Kosmer, 'Master Honoré: a reconsideration of the documents', *Gesta,* xiv, 1 (1975), 63 ff.

34 Colvin, *op. cit.* (note 1), 135–6. A connection with London manuscript painters is implied by the entry 'Primarium empt' pro filio Regis, Willielmo Bokbindre de London', pro uno Primario de eodem empto ad opus Domini Edwardi filii Regis . . .' in the *Liber Quotidianus Contrarotulatoris Garderobae* (Society of Antiquaries of London, 1787), 55 (1299–1300).

35 E. Hutton, *The Cosmati* (London, 1950), 24; J. G. O'Neilly and L. E. Tanner, 'The shrine of St Edward the Confessor', *Archaeologia,* c (1966), 129; J. Gardner, 'Arnolfo di Cambio and Roman tomb design', *Burlington Magazine,* cxv (1973), 420; S. H. Wander, 'The Westminster Abbey Sanctuary Pavement', *Traditio,* xxxiv (1978), 137.

36 See J. Blair, 'English monumental brasses before the Black Death', in *Collectanea Historica: Essays in Memory of Stuart Rigold,* ed. A. Detsicas (Kent Archaeological Society, 1981), 256–7.

37 See S. Badham, 'A lost bronze effigy of 1279 from York Minster', *Antiquaries Journal,* lx (1980), 59.

38 Stone 1972, 135, pl. 105.

39 For the effigies of Edward II at Gloucester, John of Eltham at Westminster and Queen Isabella at the Friars Minor, Newgate, *c.* 1327, *c.* 1340 and 1359 respectively, Stone 1972, 160–4, pls. 119, 123, 124a, and F. D. Blackley, 'The tomb of Isabella of France, wife of Edward II of England', *Bulletin of the International Society for the Study of Church Monuments,* viii (1983), 161.

40 *KW,* i, 491–3.

41 *Ibid.,* 97, 135–6.

42 Including Peter of Spain and Walter of Durham: Colvin 1971, 210, 230, 238, 252–8, 262–84; *CPR* 1258, 613; above, p. 57.

43 Abbot Richard donated tapestries of the Lives of Christ and St Edward to the abbey in 1246: see J. Flete, *The History of Westminster Abbey,* ed. J. A. Robinson (Cambridge, 1909), 24 ff.; for Abbot Ware, see Wander, *op. cit.* (note 35), 141–2, 154.

44 Thus Colvin calculates that under Edward, some £80,000 were spent on the Welsh castles in the years 1277–1304, £20,000 on the Tower of London between 1275 and 1285, £10,000 on the Palace of Westminster, of which £4,000 went on the new chapel in the years 1292–7, and £2,000 on the Eleanor memorials; a significant drop in outlay on the Palace of Westminster occurred under Edward II: *KW,* i, 161, 522. See also J. G. Edwards, 'Edward I's castle-building in Wales', *Proceedings of the British Academy,* xxxii (1946), 15.

[45] *KW*, i, 370.

[46] M. Prestwich, *War, Politics and Finance under Edward I* (London, 1972), 247 ff.; *KW*, i, 499, 512; for the end of work on the Coronation Chair, see the account in G. G. Scott, *Gleanings from Westminster Abbey*, 2nd edn. (Oxford and London, 1863), 122 n.

[47] See above p. 74.

[48] *KW*, i, 150; work restarted in 1376. There remains the possibility that Edward had a hand in completing both the shrine of St Edward and the tomb of Henry III after 1272; it is well known that Henry's effigy was made in the 1290s, but generally accepted that the shrine base was finished by 1269: see *KW*, i, 148–50. The earliest source for the inscription on the shrine base in fact gives 1279 rather than 1269, the date of the translation of St Edward. It is not inconceivable that Edward continued his father's project of equipping the shrine area with cosmatesque memorials at some point in the 1270s: see Gardner, *op. cit.* (note 35), 424. Donations for glazing in the abbey are noted in the 1280s and 1290s (*KW*, i, 150), and Edward paid for three marble columns for the shrine in 1290–1: Scott, *op. cit.* (note 46), 136 n. (after unpublished Liberate Roll PRO E403/1256).

[49] For Vale Royal, *KW*, i, 248 ff.

[50] *Ibid.*, 252.

[51] Thus Florence of Worcester, 'Dominus rex regem, patrem suum, apud Westmonasterium intumulatum, nocte Dominicae Ascensionis (10 Maii), subito et inopinate amoveri fecit, et in loco excelsiore, juxta S. Eadwardum collocari', *Florentii Wigorniensis monachi, Chronicon ex Chronicis*, ed. B. Thorpe, ii (London, 1849), 242–3.

[52] *KW*, i, 514.

[53] Sandler, *op. cit.* (note 26), 135.

[54] Edward's patronage of shrines continued throughout the 1280s; however, see A. J. Taylor, 'Edward I and the shrine of St Thomas of Canterbury', *JBAA*, cxxxii (1979), 22.

[55] R. S. Loomis, 'Edward I, Arthurian enthusiast', *Speculum*, xxviii (1953), 114, 117; F. M. Powicke, *The Thirteenth Century, 1216–1307*, 2nd edn. (Oxford, 1970), 515–16; the *Itinerarium* (Esposito 1960, 26) makes no reference to the cult of St Edward at all in its account of Westminster Abbey, noting Edward I's tomb instead.

[56] Loomis, *op. cit.* (note 55), 115, 122

[57] An Alexander Chamber existed at Clarendon under Henry III (*KW*, ii, 914); an Alexander cycle was painted in the queen's chamber at Nottingham (*CLR* 1252, 17–18). The image of Richard I was ordered in 1251 for the king's chamber under the chapel at Clarendon (Tristram 1950, 528–9); Richard and Saladin were depicted on tiles at Clarendon, not in the Antioch Chamber as stated in *KW*, ii, 914, but in the queen's chapel, see E. A. Eames, 'A tile pavement from the queen's chamber, Clarendon Palace, dated 1250–2', *JBAA*, xx–xxi (1957–8), 95, 104 ff. In 1250 the queen recalled a copy of the 'gesta Antiochie et regum etc. aliorum' from the London Temple (see above, note 30), evidently a large illustrated volume; it cannot be coincidental that the next two years saw the execution of Antioch stories at Clarendon, the Tower of London and Westminster (Tristram 1950, 89, 528–9, 578, 575); in 1251 an Antioch story was also painted in Rosamund's chamber at Winchester Castle (*KW*, i, 129). The fact that this 'liber magnus' was in French may align the imagery of these Antioch cycles with either the Chanson d'Antioche or the chronicles of the crusades of the sort associated with William of Tyre and the *Gesta Francorum*; the court evidently favoured imagery from the first as well as the third crusade. Conceivably the queen took a considerable initiative in the choice of these decorations at the time when Henry elected to take up the Cross.

[58] Clanchy, *op. cit.* (note 30), 256.

[59] *Ibid.*, 260–1.

[60] F. Saxl and H. Meier, *Verzeichnis astrologischer und mythologischer illustrierter Handschriften des lateinischen Mittelalters* (London, 1953), iii, pt. 1, 319–20; pt.2, pl. XVII, 42–3; W. H. Monroe, 'Two medieval genealogical roll-chronicles in the Bodleian Library', *The Bodleian Library Record*, x (1981), 215. For Brutus imagery in this context, see *The Chronicle of Pierre de Langtoft*, ed. T. Wright, *RS*, 47, i (London, 1866), xiii, 3–5; *Foedera*, ed. T. Rymer, ii (London, 1816), 932; *The Anonimalle Chronicle, 1333 to 1381*, ed. V. H. Galbraith (Manchester, 1970), xx–xxi; M. D. Legge, *Anglo-Norman Literature and its Background* (Oxford, 1963), 278 ff.; A. Gransden, *Historical Writing in England c. 550 to c. 1307* (London, 1974), 476 ff.; for York, see Powicke, *op. cit.* (note 55), 688.

61 *Ibid.*, 511 ff.

62 *KW*, i, 504–5.

63 *Ibid.*, 505; Powicke, *op. cit.* (note 55), 653.

64 For the most important survey, see J. Guerout, 'Le Palais de la Cité à Paris des origines à 1417', *Mémoires, Fédération des Sociétés Historiques et Archéologiques de Paris et de l'Île-de-France*, i (1949), 57; ii (1950), 23.

65 *Ibid.*, 1950, 64 ff.

66 *Ibid.*, 23 ff.

67 *Ibid.*, 24, 42–4; E. A. R. Brown, 'Philippe le Bel and the remains of St Louis', *Gazette des beaux-arts*, xcv (1980), 175; for the *Grand' Salle*, Guerout 1950, *op. cit.* (note 64), 128 ff. The theory that the Cité had a cycle of Old Testament paintings which stimulated the choice of scenes in the Painted Chamber proposed by Tudor-Craig 1957, 103 ff., is not supported by what is known of the palace as Henry may have known it. Of the two royal palaces in Paris, the Cité and the Louvre, only the Cité seems to have been visited by Henry in 1254; Matthew Paris states that his entourage was based at the Old Temple, and that Henry saw the other palace 'in medio civitatis', a description suited only to the Cité: see *Chronica Majora*, ed. H. R. Luard, *RS*, 57, v (London, 1880), 478 ff. Henry's retinue was far too big for the Cité, which had earlier also proved limited when Henry II visited Paris in 1158: Guerout 1949, *op. cit.* (note 64), 151. As Guerout shows, there is no evidence that the Cité possessed lavish secular decorations in the mid-thirteenth century: *ibid.*, 147 ff., 158 ff.

68 R. Branner, 'The Montjoies of Saint Louis', in *Essays in the History of Architecture presented to Rudolf Wittkower*, ed. D. Fraser, H. Hibbard and M. Lewine (London, 1967), 13.

69 Colvin, *KW*, i, 508 n. 7. The two rooms were by this stage used as a functional unit; thus see the memorandum printed in *KW*, ii, 1042 no. 10: 'pro festis quando Rex comesturus est in parva aula vel in camera depicta'.

70 S. Erdeswick, *A Survey of Staffordshire* (London, 1820), 211: in the palace was 'a goodly hall, wherein hath been excellently well painted, but now much decayed, the coronation, marriage, wars, and funeral of Edw. I; and some writing, which there is also yet remaining, which expresseth the meaning of the history: where is especially mentioned the behaviour of sir Roger Pewlisdon, of Emerault, in Flintshire, and others, against the Scots, where the said earls and lords are very lively portrayed, with their banners of arms bravely before them . . .'

71 See A. Martindale, 'Painting for pleasure—some lost fifteenth-century secular decorations of northern Italy', in *The Vanishing Past*, ed. A. Borg and A. Martindale, BAR International Series 111 (Oxford, 1981), 109, 111.

Index

PLATE I

The Painted Chamber: Coronation of St Edward (Cat. no. 1), incomplete copy by Crocker

PLATE II

Photograph: Ashmolean Museum, Oxford

The Painted Chamber: Coronation of St Edward (Cat. no. 1), finished copy by Crocker

PLATE III

Photograph: Ashmolean Museum, Oxford

The Painted Chamber: Guardian of Solomon's Bed
(Cat. no. 2), copy by Crocker

PLATE IV

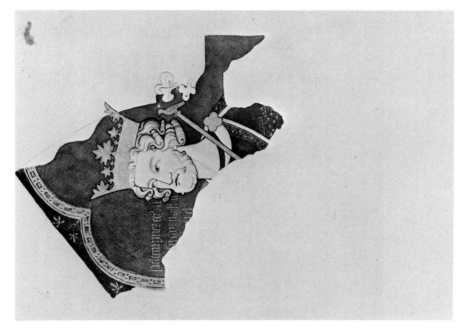

b. St Edward with the Ring (Cat. no. 4)

a. St John the Pilgrim (Cat. no. 3)

The Painted Chamber, copies by Stothard
Photographs: Society of Antiquaries

PLATE V

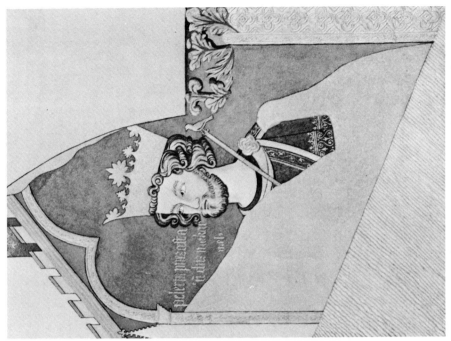

a. St John the Pilgrim (Cat. no. 3)

b. St Edward with the Ring (Cat. no. 4)

The Painted Chamber, copies by Crocker

Photographs: Ashmolean Museum, Oxford

PLATE VI

a. Largesce-Covoitise (Cat. no. 5)   *b. Debonereté-Ira* (Cat. no. 6)

The Painted Chamber, copies by Crocker

Photographs: Ashmolean Museum, Oxford

PLATE VII

Photograph: Ashmolean Museum, Oxford

The Painted Chamber: *Vérité* (Cat. no. 8), copy by Crocker

PLATE VIII

a. Copy by Stothard

b. Copy by Crocker

The Painted Chamber: a Virtue (?Fortitude) (Cat. no. 9)

Photographs: a, Society of Antiquaries; b, Ashmolean Museum, Oxford

PLATE IX

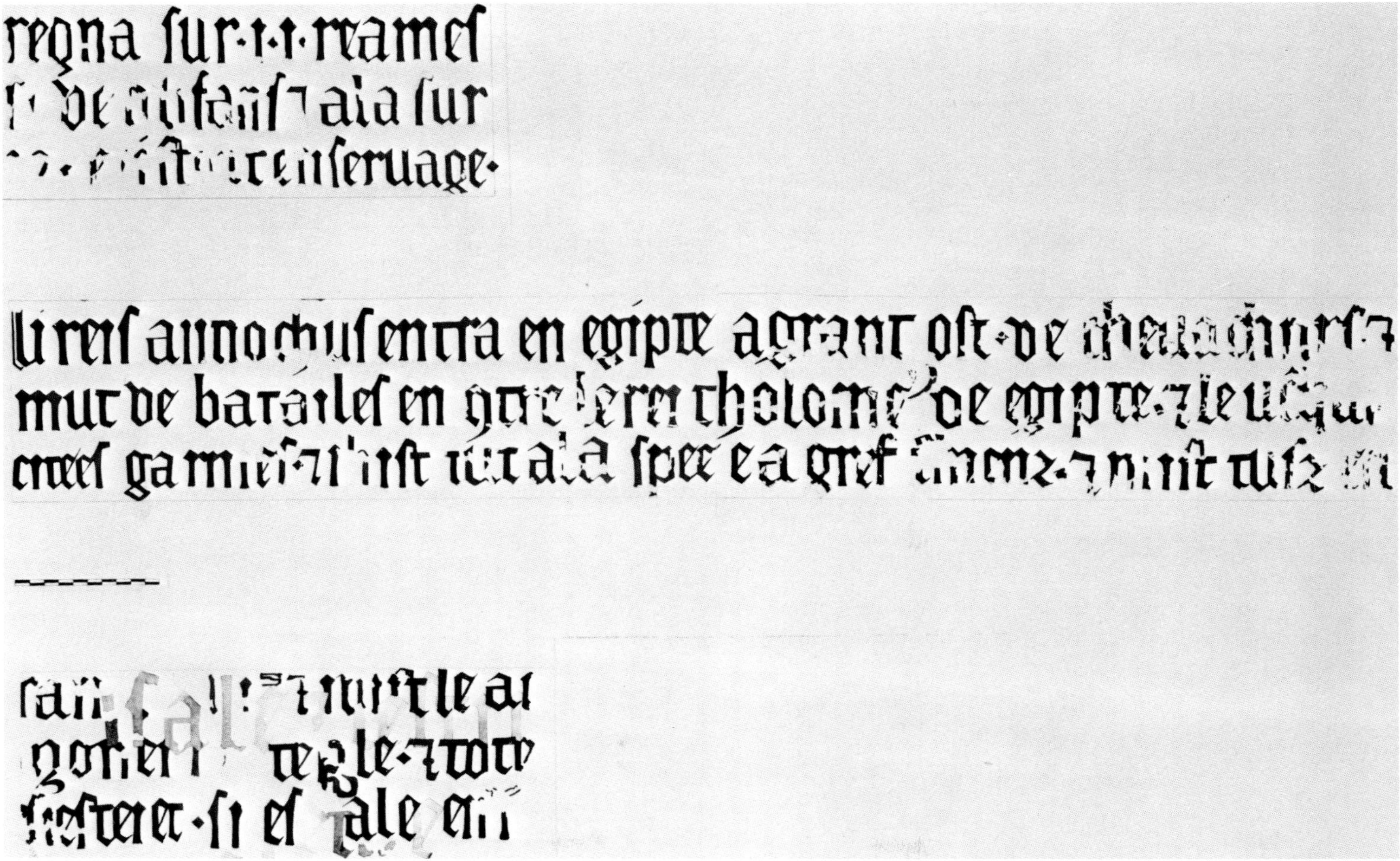

Photograph: Ashmolean Museum, Oxford

The Painted Chamber: inscriptions from First Book of Maccabees, i (Cat. no. 10), copies by Crocker. The third line shows evidence of being palimpsest

PLATE X

a. Copy by Stothard

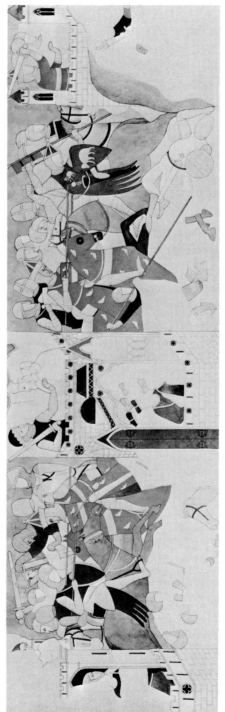

b. Copy by Crocker

The Painted Chamber: Warfare of Judas Maccabeus and Nicanor (Cat. no. 14)
Photographs: a, Society of Antiquaries; b, Ashmolean Museum, Oxford

PLATE XI

b. Copy by Crocker

a. Copy by Stothard

The Painted Chamber: the Ambush of the Jambrites' Wedding (Cat. no. 15)

Photographs: a, Society of Antiquaries; b, Ashmolean Museum, Oxford

PLATE XII

a. Copy by Stothard

b. Copy by Crocker

The Painted Chamber: Elijah and Ahaziah (Cat. no. 16)

Photographs: a, Society of Antiquaries; b, Ashmolean Museum, Oxford

PLATE XIII

The Painted Chamber: Miracles of Elisha (Cat. no. 17), copy by Crocker

PLATE XIV

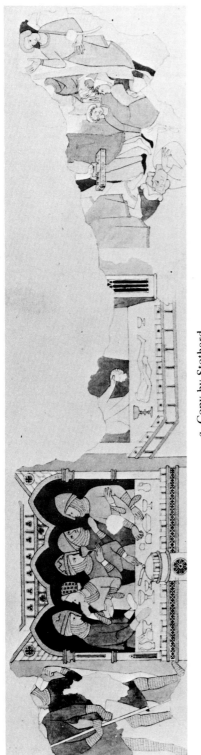

a. Copy by Stothard

b. Copy by Crocker

The Painted Chamber: Famine in Samaria (Cat. no. 18)

Photographs: a, Society of Antiquaries; b, Ashmolean Museum, Oxford

PLATE XV

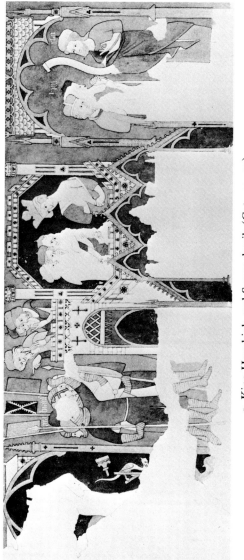

a. King Hezekiah and Sennacherib (Cat. no. 19)

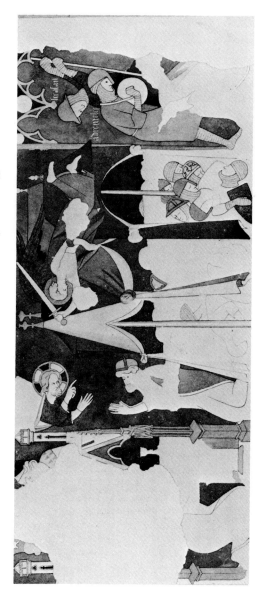

b. Destruction of Sennacherib (Cat. no. 20)

The Painted Chamber, copies by Stothard

Photographs: Society of Antiquaries

PLATE XVI

a. King Hezekiah and the Destruction of Sennacherib (Cat. nos. 19, 20)

b. Nebuchadnezzar and Jehoiachin (Cat. no. 21)

The Painted Chamber, copies by Crocker

Photographs: Ashmolean Museum, Oxford

PLATE XVII

Photograph: Society of Antiquaries

The Painted Chamber: Nebuchadnezzar and Jehoiachin (Cat. no. 21), copy by Stothard

PLATE XVIII

Photograph: Society of Antiquaries

The Painted Chamber: Zedekiah and the Fall of Jerusalem (Cat. no. 22), copy by Stothard

PLATE XIX

The Painted Chamber: Zedekiah and the Fall of Jerusalem (Cat. no. 22), copy by Crocker

Photograph: Ashmolean Museum, Oxford

PLATE XX

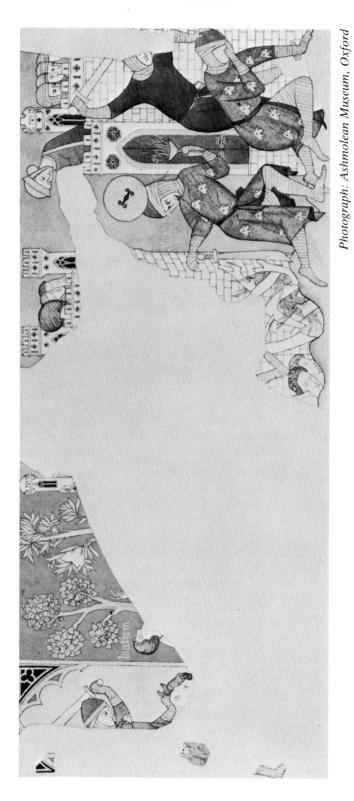

Photograph: Ashmolean Museum, Oxford

The Painted Chamber: Story of King Abimelech (Cat. no. 23), copy by Crocker

PLATE XXI

The Painted Chamber: Story of King Abimelech (Cat. no. 23), with other details, sketch by J. Buckler, 1819

PLATE XXII

a. Copy by Stothard

b. Copy by Crocker

The Painted Chamber: Antiochus and the Maccabean Martyrs (Cat. no. 24)
Photographs: a, Society of Antiquaries; b, Ashmolean Museum, Oxford

PLATE XXIII

Photograph: Society of Antiquaries

The Painted Chamber: Fall of Antiochus (Cat. no. 25), copy by Stothard

PLATE XXIV

Photograph: Society of Antiquaries

The Painted Chamber: Murder of Abner (Cat. no. 26), copy by Stothard

PLATE XXV

b. Fragment of Decorative Painting from blocked window (Cat. no. 28)

a. Warriors in Flight (Cat. no. 27)

The Painted Chamber, copies by Stothard

Photographs: Society of Antiquaries

PLATE XXVI

Photograph: Society of Antiquaries

Interior of Painted Chamber, looking east, before the discovery of its murals: view by
W. Capon, 1799

PLATE XXVII

East end of Painted Chamber.

North side of Painted Chamber.

Drawn & Etched by J.T.Smith

London. Published as the Act directs October 20.1805 by John Thomas Smith, N.516, Lisson Street, Bedford Street.

Photograph: by permission of the Syndics of Cambridge University Library

Exterior of the Painted Chamber from east and north: view by J. T. Smith, 1805

PLATE XXVIII

Photograph: Westminster City Libraries, Archives Department

Interior of Painted Chamber, looking east, acting as Court of Claims: view by Stephanoff, 1820

PLATE XXIX

The Painted Chamber in the aftermath of the 1834 fire, looking east

PLATE XXX

Photograph: by permission of the Syndics of Cambridge University Library
The Painted Chamber: details by J. Carter, 1799

PLATE XXXI

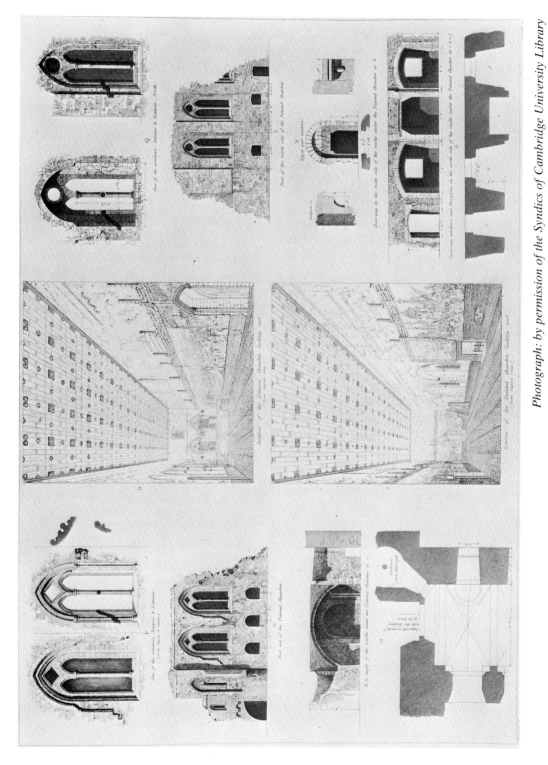

The Painted Chamber: details by F. Mackenzie and W. Capon, 1842

PLATE XXXII

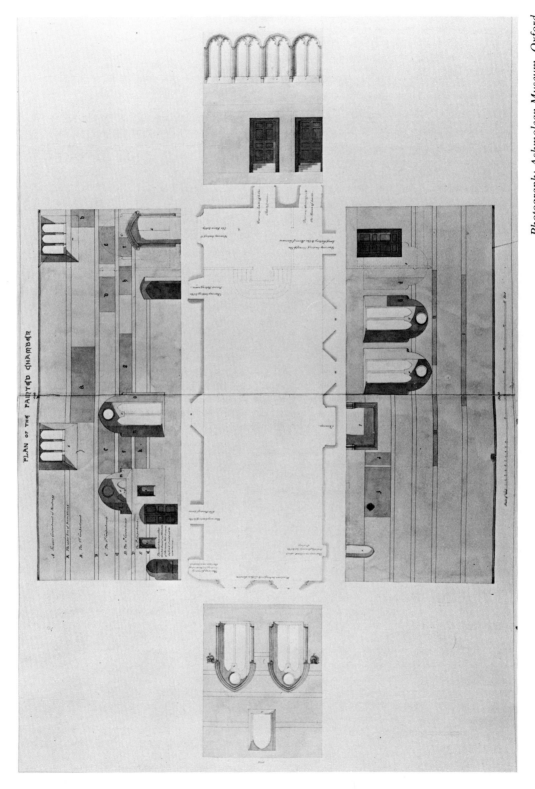

Plan and internal elevation of the Painted Chamber, by Crocker

PLATE XXXIII

Photograph: by courtesy of the Trustees of Sir John Soane's Museum

Wooden *patera* from ceiling of the Painted Chamber, in Sir John Soane's collection

PLATE XXXIV

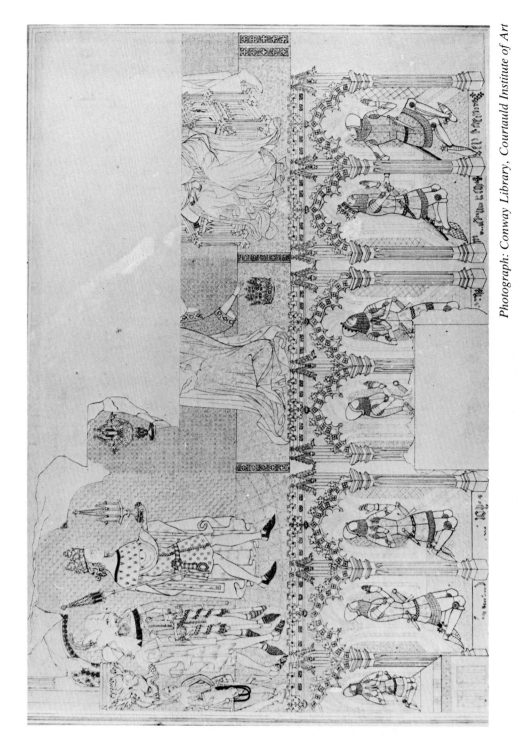

St Stephen's Chapel, Westminster: murals on east wall, copy by R. Smirke

PLATE XXXV

EDMUND CROUCHBACK EARL OF LANCASTER 2nd SON OF HENRY 3rd Died 1296.
from his Monument in Westminster Abby.

Photograph: by permission of the Syndics of Cambridge University Library

Effigy of Edmund Crouchback, Earl of Lancaster, in Westminster Abbey: copy by Stothard, 1814

PLATE XXXVI

Photograph: by permission of the Provost and Fellows of Eton College

Coronation of Edward I: 'Merton' *Flores Historiarum*

PLATE XXXVII

Photograph: by permission of the Governors of Chetham's Library

a. Coronation of St Edward: Chetham *Flores Historiarum*

Photograph: by permission of the Syndics of Cambridge University Library

b. St Edward welcomed by the barons and crowned: *La Estoire de Seint Aedward le Rei*

PLATE XXXVIII

Photograph: by permission of the Syndics of Cambridge University Library

a. St Edward gives a ring to the pilgrim St John: *La Estoire de Seint Aedward le Rei*

Photograph: Calouste Gulbenkian Foundation and Conway Library, Courtauld Institute of Art

b. Virtues and Vices, illustration of Berengaudus' Commentary on Revelation, xiii, 1: Lisbon Apocalypse

PLATE XXXIX

Photograph: RCHM (England)

Salisbury Cathedral, chapter-house entrance, Virtues and Vices

PLATE XL

The Merchants and the Whore of Babylon: Douce Apocalypse

PLATE XLI

b. Angel bearing a crown over *Debonereté* (Cat. no. 7), sketch by J. Buckler

Photographs: a, Bodleian Library, Oxford; b, British Library

a. Angel, detail, Douce
Apocalypse

PLATE XLII

a. Westminster Retable, Virgin, detail

b. Largesce, detail, after Stothard

c. Westminster Retable, St John

Photographs: a, c, Warburg Institute; b, Society of Antiquaries

PLATE XLIII

b. Coronation of St Edward (detail), after Stothard

Photographs: a, Warburg Institute; b, Society of Antiquaries

a. Westminster Retable: Feeding of the Five Thousand (detail)

PLATE XLIV

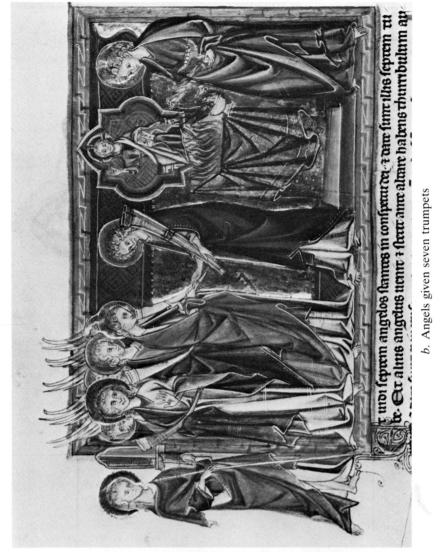
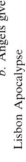

a. Moses

b. Angels given seven trumpets

Lisbon Apocalypse

Photographs: Calouste Gulbenkian Foundation and Conway Library, Courtauld Institute of Art

PLATE XLV

a. God of Creation (detail)

b. Abraham adoring the three angels

St John's College, psalter

Photographs: The Master and Fellows of St John's College, Cambridge, and Conway Library, Courtauld Institute of Art

PLATE XLVI

b. Westminster Retable: shaft bases from central section

c. Douce Apocalypse: Measuring of the Temple (detail)

a. Westminster Retable: Raising of Jairus' Daughter (detail)

Photographs: a, Malcolm Crowthers; c, Bodleian Library, Oxford

PLATE XLVII

St John adores the Son of Man: Douce Apocalypse

PLATE XLVIII

Photograph: Conway Library, Courtauld Institute of Art

Moses scenes: London *Somme le Roi*

PLATE XLIX

Photograph: Caisse Nationale des Monuments Historiques et des Sites

a. Paris, Sainte-Chapelle: niche on north side

Photograph: Society of Antiquaries

b. Coronation of St Edward (detail of canopy), after Stothard

PLATE L

a. Westminster Retable: patterned shafts from central section

b. Westminster Abbey, tomb of Aveline: patterned shafts

Photographs: a, Warburg Institute; b, RCHM (England)

PLATE LI

Photograph: Conway Library, Courtauld Institute of Art

Westminster Abbey, tomb of Edmund Crouchback: detail of internal face of canopy cusp

PLATE LII

a. Lateral gables from south
b. Embattled cornice from shaft
c. Painted tracery on shafts

Westminster Abbey, tomb of Edmund Crouchback

Photographs: a, c, RCHM (England); b, Conway Library, Courtauld Institute of Art

PLATE LIII

b. Westminster Abbey: Coronation Chair

a. Canterbury Cathedral, chapter house: throne and wall arcade at east end

Photographs: a, C. Wilson; b, RCHM (England)

PLATE LIV

Photograph: British Museum

Castle of Love: lid of an ivory casket, French, early fourteenth century

PLATE LV

Photograph: RCHM (England)

Horsham St Faith Priory, Norfolk: detail of refectory mural

PLATE LVI

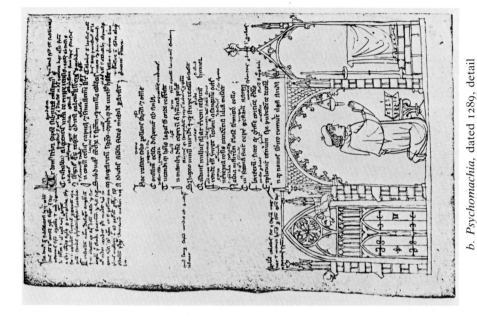

b. Psychomachia, dated 1289, detail

a. Virtues: London *Somme le Roi*

Photographs: a, Conway Library, Courtauld Institute of Art; b, by permission of the Syndics of Cambridge University Library

PLATE LVII

Photograph: Bodleian Library, Oxford

St John writes to the angel in the church at Pergamum: Douce Apocalypse

PLATE LVIII

Photograph: RCHM (England)

Westminster Abbey, tomb of Eleanor of Castile: left half of painting on ambulatory side

PLATE LIX

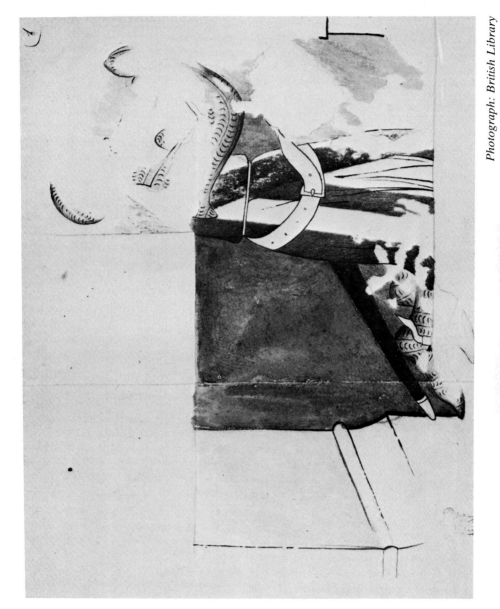

Westminster Abbey, tomb of Eleanor of Castile: right half of painting on ambulatory side, copy c. 1800

PLATE LX

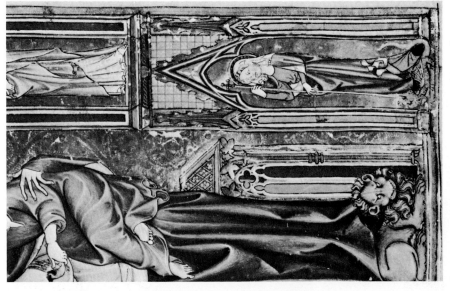

a. Westminster Abbey, tomb of Edmund Crouchback: detail of
weeper arcade

b. De Lisle Psalter: detail from fol. 131ᵛ

Photographs: a, Conway Library, Courtauld Institute of Art; b, British Library

PLATE LXI

Photograph: Conway Library, Courtauld Institute of Art
Gospel scenes: De Lisle Psalter

PLATE LXII

Photograph: RCHM (England)
Westminster Abbey: mural of St Faith

PLATE LXIII

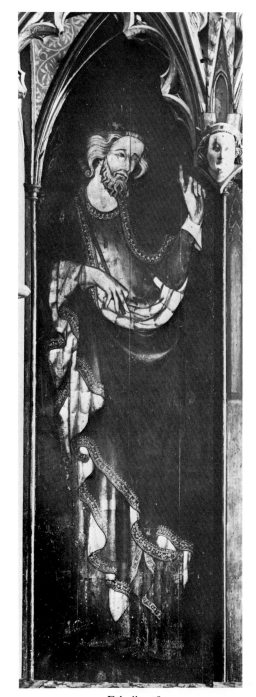 

a. Ethelbert?　　　　　　　　　　　　　*b.* Sebert?

Westminster Abbey, sedilia: kings on sanctuary side

Photographs: Conway Library, Courtauld Institute of Art

PLATE LXIV

Photograph: RCHM (England)

Westminster Abbey, south transept: St Thomas

PLATE LXV

Photograph: RCHM (England)

York Minster: figure of St Edmund from former vault web of chapter house

PLATE LXVI

Photograph: Bodleian Library, Oxford

King Abimelech signifying Antichrist: Moralized Bible

PLATE LXVII

Photograph: Bodleian Library, Oxford

King Abimelech signifying Antichrist: Moralized Bible

PLATE LXVIII

a–b. The story of King Abimelech: Maciejowski Bible

Photographs: by permission of the Syndics of Cambridge University Library

b

a

PLATE LXIX

Photograph: by permission of the Syndics of Cambridge University Library

King David, Joab and Abner: Maciejowski Bible

PLATE LXX

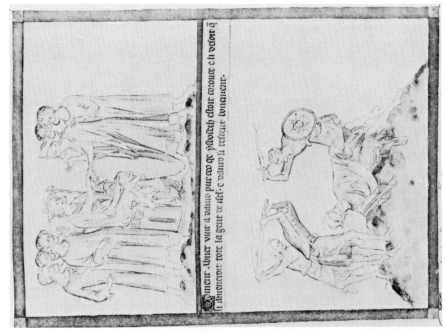

a. The death of Abimelech

b. The murder of Abner

Queen Mary's Psalter

Photographs: by permission of the Syndics of Cambridge University Library

PLATE LXXI

Photograph: Collection of H. P. Kraus

Story of Sennacherib: Sicilian miniature, late thirteenth century

PLATE LXXII

b. Isaiah addresses Eliakim and Shebna; Hezekiah in the temple

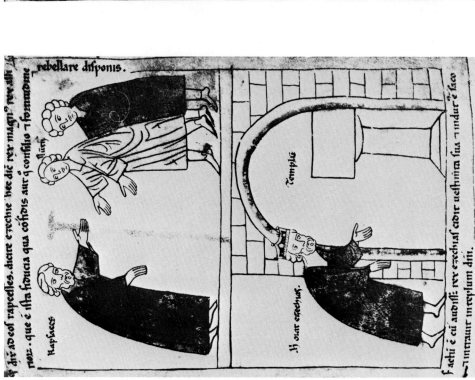

a. Rabshakeh and Hezekiah's servants; Hezekiah goes into the temple

Pamplona Bible

Photographs: Universitätsbibliothek, Augsburg

PLATE LXXIII

b

a. Pamplona Bible: Isaiah and the destruction of Sennacherib's army

b. Illustration from Maccabees romance

Photographs: a, Universitätsbibliothek, Augsburg; b, Bibliothèque Nationale, Paris

a

PLATE LXXIV

Judas Maccabeus as member of the Nine Worthies: mural at Dronninglund (Denmark), sixteenth century

Photograph: National Museum, Copenhagen